The HORSE RIDING & CARE HANDBOOK

THE LYONS PRESS
Guilford, Connecticut
An Imprint of the Globe Pequot Press

The HORSE RIDING & CARE HANDBOOK

Bernadette Faurie

Foreword by HRH The Infanta Doña Pilar de Borbón

The Lyons Press is an imprint of The Globe Pequot Press

ISBN 1 58574-517-0 (soft cover)

Publishing Manager: Mariëlle Renssen
Editor: Gill Gordon
Designer: Daniel Jansen van Vuuren
Illustrator: Anton Krugel
Picture Researcher: Carmen Watts
International Consultants: Sylvia Sullivan (UK and Europe),
Judy Harvey FBHS (UK), Moira Harris (USA),
Dr David Mullins, B.Vet Science (South Africa)

Reproduction by Unifoto (Pty) Ltd
Printed and bound in Singapore

The Library of Congress Cataloging-in-Publication Data is available on file.

Author's Dedication

Cocoa, the first pony I ever rode, made me feel safe and gave me the thrill of my first canter. George, my friend throughout my teens, taught me that if a horse really trusts you he'll let you into secrets, and try harder for you than for anyone. I've been lucky to know a lot of horses in my life, and learn something from all of them. Then there was Massey. Beautiful, talented, and as complex a character as you could ever imagine. I wish I'd known then what I know now. Buying her – damaged goods going cheap and all I could afford – was the catalyst for making so many friends, meeting so many people in so many countries with so much knowledge. Together we went through triumph, and far, far too much tragedy, but that's another story. I loved that horse and without her I would not be where I am today. I'm not saying that horses will always change your life, but looking at Massey's portrait as I write this, I will tell you that they can if you let them, and if you do, you'll never regret it. Thanks to all my early teachers, and to Marjorie and Richard in particular. To Miranda who made me write about horses in the first place, Carl who pulls me up when I ever doubt, and the 'Tosh Club' who got going when the going got tough. On this project, thanks to Christoph for the encouragement and Judy for checking the whole thing out.

FOREWORD

Not many other sports are as exciting and as attractive as the equestrian disciplines. I see several reasons for this: horse riding involves developing and nurturing a relationship with a beautiful animal, which requires our respect and admiration; it allows participants to set their own level of activity, from the occasional rider trotting through fields and country lanes to the breathless exhilaration of a world-class cross-country course; our sport is also one of the very few where men and women compete on equal terms, from novice classes right up to Olympic level.

The horse has been closely tied to the development of mankind for centuries. It is difficult to parallel the trusted relationship and intimate bond which grows from mutual confidence, understanding and respect between the animal and man.

Bernadette Faurie's *The Horse Riding and Care Handbook* presents many diverse aspects of life with horses, from owning and caring for a horse through to general riding and competition. It offers advice, information and insight for both novices and established horse owners. Most of all, it shows the passion, commitment and dedication of those people, famous or not, who devote their life to horses.

On behalf of the FEI (International Equestrian Federation), I would like to wish great success to *The Horse Riding and Care Handbook*.

HRH The Infanta Doña Pilar de Borbón

President : Fédération Equestre Internationale

Lausanne, Switzerland

October 1999

CONTENTS

CHAPTER ONE

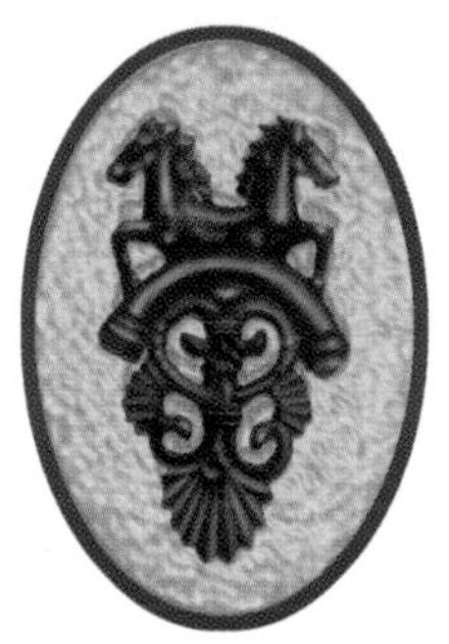

HISTORY AND DEVELOPMENT

Eohippus

Mesohippus

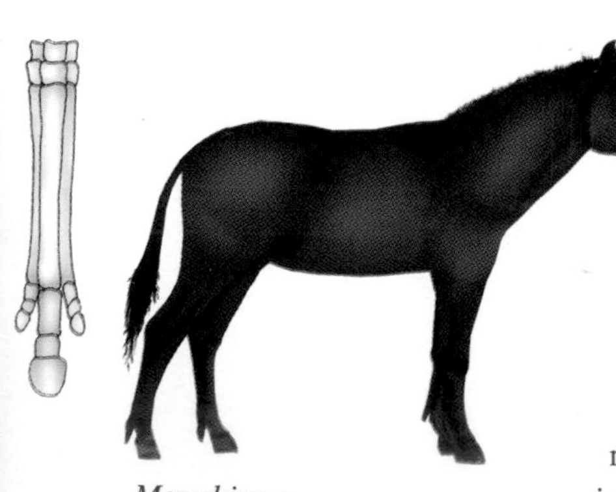

Merychippus

The evolution of the horse is one of the best documented of all mammals due to an exceptionally complete fossil record, which suggests that the forerunners of the modern horse were forest browsers on the American continent.

Fifty million years ago, the prototype of the horse was only about the size of a fox. Unlike today's horse, it had toes instead of hooves (three on the back feet and four on the front), and its skull and teeth were adapted for browsing on leaves in the swampy forests and woodlands of its prehistoric home.

This was *Hyracotherium*, also called *Eohippus*, or the 'dawn horse' (from the Greek *eos* – dawn), the forerunner of the present-day horse.

Over millions of years, as the climate and vegetation gradually changed, *Eohippus* evolved into *Mesohippus*, a sheep-sized, browsing animal with longer legs and neck, and, again, toes instead of hooves.

Between 25 and 10 million years ago, *Merychippus* appeared. Pony-sized, but still retaining a three-toed foot, *Merychippus* marked the transition from a browsing to a grazing animal. It lived on the great plains and grasslands that proliferated across what is now northern Europe and America while the ice caps melted and the forests thinned.

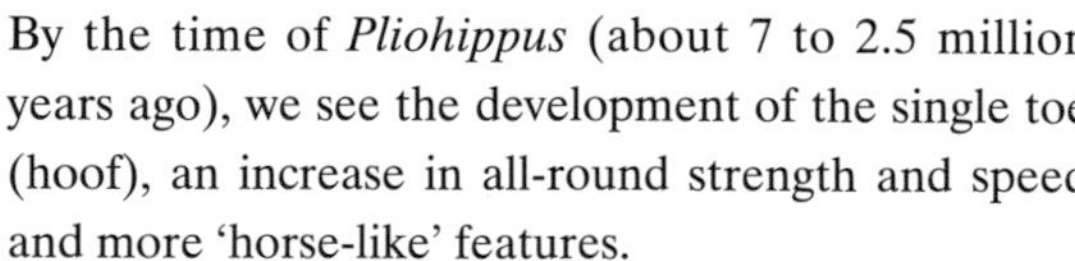

By the time of *Pliohippus* (about 7 to 2.5 million years ago), we see the development of the single toe (hoof), an increase in all-round strength and speed and more 'horse-like' features.

The final stage in the evolutionary chain was *Equus,* which appeared less than two million years ago, and is the forerunner of today's modern horses and other related species such as asses and zebras. During the Pleistocene era, which lasted from 2.5 million to 10,000 years ago, *Equus* slowly migrated from the forests and plains of the Americas to the

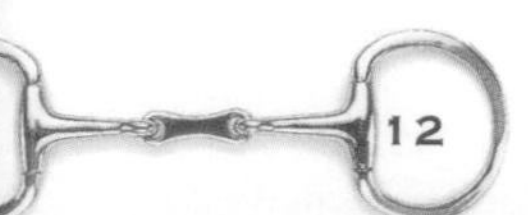

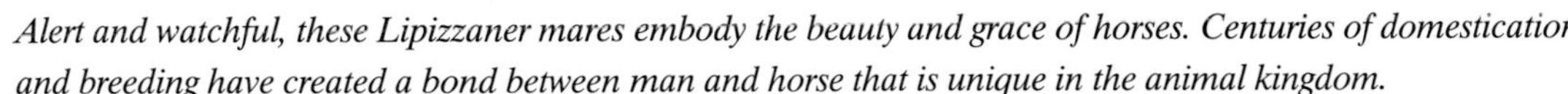

Alert and watchful, these Lipizzaner mares embody the beauty and grace of horses. Centuries of domestication and breeding have created a bond between man and horse that is unique in the animal kingdom.

Pliohippus

Equus

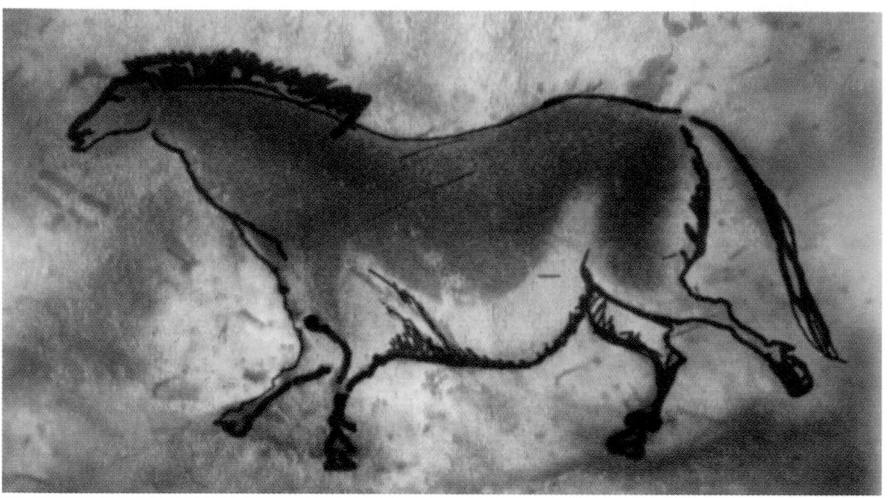

Horses are represented in cave art, such as that found in Lascaux, France, which dates from c15,000BC.

open Eurasian steppes, via the land-bridge that emerged across what is now the Bering Strait, between Asia and America. Between 10,000 and 8000 years ago, the horse vanished completely from both North and South America, not to appear again on its native continent until reintroduced by the Spanish explorers and conquistadors of the 16th century.

Despite its disappearance in the Americas, *Equus* continued to flourish in the 'old world', with the modern horse *Equus caballus* becoming widespread throughout central Asia and most of Europe.

By the Mesolithic era (Middle Stone Age), from about 12,000–3,000BC, the ice sheets were once again retreating northward. In southern Europe, this was followed by the Neolithic (New Stone Age) period (9000–2400BC), which marks the transition from the nomadic life of the hunter-gatherer to the beginnings of settlement, cultivation and the domestication of animals. Horses were probably first domesticated during the Neolithic era by the tribes that inhabited the steppes around the Black and Caspian seas. Although the first domesticated horses were most likely used as draught animals, pulling crude wagons with solid wheels, it could not have been long before man realized the advantages of riding and began to breed and maintain horses for his own use.

The development of civilization is linked intrinsically to man's relationship with the horse. Being mounted gave early man a different perspective on his world and a new understanding of his role in shaping the environment around him. He was able to cover greater distances in search of food, and the ability to get closer to his prey was a significant survival factor in those harsh times. As a means of transport and conveyance, horses enabled man to expand his boundaries, bringing him into contact, and often conflict, with other tribes and clans. From the earliest times, the horse has played a vital role in war and conquest, exploration and colonization.

As early man migrated southward, seeking ever warmer climates, he settled in the 'fertile crescent' valley formed by the Tigris and Euphrates rivers of ancient Mesopotamia (modern-day Iran and Iraq). This pastoral way of life was disrupted by the great floods of c3000BC, which swept away many of the ancient civilizations and paved the way for the great cultures upon which modern history is based.

Records dating from the Middle Kingdom of Egypt (c2000–1500BC) document the use of horse-drawn chariots by the Hyksos, or Shepherd Kings, who dominated Upper Egypt and the delta area. Horse-drawn chariots were also used in the conquest of Phoenicia and Palestine during the New Kingdom (1570–715BC). Horses were used for hunting, riding and warfare during the powerful Mycenaean empire of Crete (c1900–1200BC), and probably brought to Greece between 800–700BC by the Scythians, who were instrumental in developing the art of horsemanship and the concept of riding for pleasure.

The origins of the tack and equipment we use today are rooted equally far back in time. The use of saddles, stirrups and nailed-on shoes can be traced to the Chinese in pre-Christian times. Evidence of the first bits, made of bronze and dating to 1500BC, suggest they were used by the nomadic tribes of the Ukraine, although the earliest examples were probably used for driving rather than riding. Even much later, when the Arabs started to ride, they used a type of adapted bitless halter, the *haqma*, a term which became anglicized into the present word for a bitless bridle, the hackamore.

It was in Greece that the horse first began to appear more frequently as a subject in literature, art, pottery and relief sculpture, such as the friezes on the Parthenon in Athens. The Greek lyrical poet Sappho (c610–580BC) wrote 'On the black earth, say some, the thing most lovely is a host of horsemen ...' Around 400BC, Athenian soldier, historian and horseman, Xenophon, wrote a treatise entitled *Peri hippikes* (On the Art of Horsemanship). Xenophon's feeling for the horse is apparent throughout his work

Equine art dating from the earliest times has been found throughout Europe and the Middle East.

and many of his principles, particularly training by kindness rather than force, hold true to this day.

It is the stuff of legend that Alexander the Great (336–323BC) rode at the head of his conquering armies on Bucephalus, a horse no-one but the young Alexander was able to break. Having carried his master through the successful Asian campaigns, the horse died three years before Alexander and was buried on the banks of the Jhelum River in India.

Through war and peace, invasions and migrations, the horse propelled man on his journey through history, but the development of riding as an art was frozen with the demise of the Greek empire.

The horse facilitated the expansion of the Roman empire from Hannibal to Hadrian; enabled mounted tribes from the eastern steppes, such as the Vandals, Franks and Goths, to invade central Europe in the 4th and 5th centuries; and took the Crusaders from Europe into the Holy Land, where they came into contact with skilled Arab horsemen and their desert-bred mounts.

It was the discovery of these fleet-footed Arabian horses, with their legendary stamina, intelligence and character, that was to have a profound influence on the later development of the horse.

The dominant image of the Middle Ages is of chainmail-clad knights on large, heavily armoured horses. Jousting for their lady's favour in the pageantry of the tournament demanded gallantry of the knights rather than speed or manoevrability in their horses. However, on the battleground, the sheer weight of the knights' armour and weaponry, often as much as 400kg (900 lb), made fighting from horseback cumbersome and inefficient. This eventually gave rise to one of England's great tactical victories when, in 1415, Henry V's lightly-equipped and highly mobile archers and foot soldiers defeated the heavily armoured French cavalry on the soggy ground of Agincourt.

Ultimately, the discovery of gunpowder and the development of firearms in the 15th century made it possible for mounted warriors to discard some of their heavy armour. Speed, mobility and manoevrability were paramount for the type of warfare that guns delivered.

Riding his legendary horse Bucephalus, Alexander the Great led his armies to victory in the Asian campaigns.

It was largely the possession of firearms and horses that enabled the Spanish conquistadors Hernán Cortés to defeat the Aztecs in Mexico, and Francisco Pizarro to overthrow the Inca kingdom in Peru, thereby reintroducing the horse to its original birthplace, the Americas.

Meanwhile, in Renaissance Europe, the ancient methods of training and riding horses were being rediscovered and explored, as riding academies allied to the royal courts were founded to provide equestrian education to young noblemen.

One of the pathfinders in this discovery was Frederico Grisone. His *Gli Ordini di Cavalcare* (The Orders of Riding) was published in 1552. Similar in many respects to the teachings of Xenophon, Grisone's methods lacked one significant aspect, that of harmony and understanding with the horse. It was a pupil of the Naples school, Frenchman Antoine de Pluvinel (1601–1643), a teacher of Louis XIII and author of *Manège Royal*, who promoted the enhancement of the horse's natural movements through training rather than the often brutal subjugation used by many during these times.

In 1733 François Robichon de la Guérinière published the first edition of his work *École de Cavalerie* (School of Cavalry), the fundamentals of which still form the basis, if not the 'bible', of the training system of the Spanish Riding School of Vienna, founded in the late 16th century and still today regarded as the protectorate of classical riding.

Guérinière's greatest achievements include the development of the *selle à la français* (French saddle), still used today at the French cavalry centre, Cadre Noir, at Saumur, which enabled the development of the modern seat and leg position, as well as his composition of the first real riding instructions.

As riding styles evolved, new horse breeds were developed for specific functions, such as hunting and carriage driving. For centuries, horses provided the chief means of transport; from the smallest Shetland pony working on island crofts to teams of matched pairs drawing elegant coaches through the cities and countryside of Europe, they were a central factor in the daily lives of many of the world's peoples.

Through war and peace, exploration and exploitation, the horse's influence on man's development remained unparalleled until the advent of the steam engine in 1769. The dawning of the Industrial Revolution changed the nature of man's dependence on the horse. As engines took over many of the horse's former functions, the relationship between horse and man subtly altered from one primarily linked to work to one where the love of horses, and riding for pleasure, have become the main focus.

Developing the Bond Between Man and Horse

The relationship between man and horse is an enduring one. But dealing with animals is always easier and more enjoyable when you have empathy and understanding. To be able to relate to horses, you need to understand their psychology; in order to anticipate horses' reactions you have to understand how they think and why they behave in certain ways.

The bond between man and horse is best established at an early age. Here two mothers introduce their offspring, initiating a pattern of trust and companionship that will last a lifetime.

A good understanding also builds confidence on both sides – human and equine.

When faced with a threatening situation, the horse's natural instinct is one of flight, and therefore its perspective on life is one of vulnerability rather than attack. As humans, how we react and feel in certain situations depends on our upbringing and experience. It is the same with horses, which is why careful early handling and training are so important.

We can never expect a horse to go against its natural instinct, that is, never to be frightened or wary – but with good training we can control these instincts and show the horse, in a positive way, that a particular situation or object need not be feared.

Horses are gregarious herd animals, welcoming the company of other horses, as well as other creature companions and humans. Even domesticated stabled horses establish their own 'pecking order'.

Either the stallion at the end of the row calls loudest when feed time is due or, as many top riders report, their retired star kicks the stable door demanding attention first when what it considers as 'its' rider walks into the stableyard in the morning.

It is widely acknowledged that the horse responds best to praise and encouragement from its trainer or rider in order to overcome its natural flight instinct and not be dominated. 'Breaking-in', the term formerly associated with a young horse's first conditioning to carry a rider, has now commonly been replaced with terms such as 'starting', which infer much less the idea of domination.

From the disabled child fearlessly enjoying the company of ponies as part of therapy to the most successful of international competitive combinations, a common bond – that of trust and empathy between rider and horse – is being developed.

MEMORY AND LEARNING

One moment of fear can be imprinted on the horse's memory for years, if not for its lifetime. Places and circumstances are remembered, which is why a normally phlegmatic horse may suddenly shy or run away from what appears to be nothing. A reaction can be triggered by the horse finding itself in the same place or situation as a previous unsettling incident. Horses don't forget things that upset them, however early in their life they occurred.

This aspect of horse psychology should not deter anyone from getting to know horses. Instead, it can be turned to the advantage rather than to the detriment of the relationship between horse and rider. Pleasant experiences are reacted to in just the same way as unpleasant ones, which is why it is important to be clear and careful when training horses. International riders can often be heard remarking, 'My horse loves this show' or 'I don't go there, the horse hates it'. Horses recall situations clearly and a good or bad experience is a memory that has been imprinted forever.

The horse looks on its human contacts as part of its 'herd'. In the herd hierarchy, the human rider and trainer's intellectual capacities give him or her the 'upper hand'. This is why the man/horse relationship has worked so well for several thousand years, and humans can control an animal with many times their own strength and power.

To a domesticated horse, the freedom of the open plains may be part of a distant collective memory, but it is never quite forgotten. This stallion celebrates his independence with a display of high spirits.

Riders in their early lessons will often be told, 'Don't be nervous'. Although at this stage the rider should be learning from an experienced horse (often referred to as a 'schoolmaster'), and therefore should be able to relax, the fact that horses need reassurance and security is something to bear in mind and cultivate from the start of a riding career.

Learning by example

A new-born foal is on its feet and bonding with its mother soon after birth, as the instinct of the wild makes the foal prepared to follow her in case of danger. Even in a secure environment, foals automatically follow and learn from the reactions of their mothers and other 'herd members'.

Young horses respond to the good influence of an older horse, and an experienced horse, a 'schoolmaster', is very useful in teaching young horses. Horses mimic the behaviour of others and the reliable, older horse that accompanies a younger horse on its first rides outside the school can demonstrate that there is no need to be worried by water, cars or baby buggies! The same applies to the young horse's first show or cross-country fences. Once initial confidence has been established, the young horse can go on to accomplish things on its own. This is why the schoolmaster needs to set a good example. A young horse stabled next to an older horse with a vice such as crib-biting (chewing the stable door) will learn to mimic this undesirable behaviour very quickly.

The average horse is fully grown by the age of four. From three onwards, depending on physical maturity, a horse can be backed to carry a rider, then turned away in the field for several months to continue maturing, before training begins in earnest.

Throughout the horse's life, praise is an important aspect of training. A pat or a stroke, combined with vocal encouragement, becomes associated with a movement or exercise that has been performed well. If a horse is taught something new in a way it can understand, it will generally grasp it straightaway. Positive new experiences are imprinted on the horse's mind, which is why it is so important to teach a horse in a calm, gentle environment.

While a whip or loud voice can force a horse to do things it fears, this creates a situation where the threatening object (the whip), becomes the only thing that will make the horse repeat the lesson.

In the wild, horses establish a natural 'pecking order' in the herd hierarchy, with each animal knowing its place in relation to its elders and peers.

Left *Positioned on each side of the head, the horse's eyes give it a wide field of vision.*
Centre *Mutual grooming is a pleasurable occupation.*
Right *The configuration of the ears can indicate a range of emotions, from fear to a willingness to work.*

UNDERSTANDING THE HORSE'S SENSES

A major help in understanding how a horse reacts to things is if you can understand what the horse hears, sees and feels from its own perspective.

SIGHT

One often hears remarks on a particular horse's beautiful or expressive eyes. Horses have the largest eyes of any land mammal, and their eyes convey states of mind such as trust, uncertainty or fear. In common with most animals that are preyed upon, the horse's eyes are positioned on each side of its head, not the front, affording it a very wide field of vision. With a huge field of peripheral vision available to it, the horse has only two 'blind spots'; one directly behind it and the other around six feet directly in front of or beneath its nose, where vision is out of focus, at the least. If you walk towards a horse, there comes a point where it can't focus on you, so it will turn its head away or back up until it can see you again. For example, when going to catch a horse from the field, the reaction described above could be interpreted as the horse not wanting to be caught when, in fact, if you approach from the side and the horse can keep you in sight, it will stand happily for you to reach it. If you stand behind a horse it will generally turn its whole body or head and neck to get a constant view, but a young or nervous horse can easily react with a warning kick to an intrusion it can't see.

Because of the particular position of its eyes, the horse needs to use its head and neck when reacting to visual stimuli. With the head held high, a horse can't see the ground in front of it. If you watch a horse pick its way across rough ground, it will lower its head almost to the surface it is traversing. A strange or unfamiliar object on the ground or in a hedge to its side, for example, will have the horse tilting its head to the side for a closer examination. If it is 'alien', the horse will pass the object with this sideways tilt of the head and a sideways step of the body. This forms the basis of 'shying' and in training it is important that the rider understands this impulse, and gives the young horse a chance to look at the object. If the reaction is punished, either by

design or by mistake when the rider becomes unbalanced and pulls on the reins, the horse rapidly learns to avoid such hazards in future, which can be the foundation of a very real problem.

It was once thought that horses were colour blind, but evidence suggests the opposite – although horses seem to recognize yellows, greens and blues more easily than reds, purples and shades of grey.

Horses also have excellent long-range vision (picture a horse in the field gazing at something the human eye can't see), and good night vision.

Touch

Horses are highly sensitive to touch. A horse can even feel a fly on its back (watch it twitch until it goes away), which is indicative of this acute sensitivity. When being ridden, a horse unwilling to go forward from the pressure exerted by the rider's leg will, nine times out of ten, have become 'desensitized' by the misuse or over-use of the rider's leg signal. At all times, when riding or handling horses, a gentle but firm touch will yield the best results. The daily ritual of grooming helps to establish a positive sense of touch, and is a soothing experience for the horse. This can be observed when a group of horses are together in the field, as mutual 'grooming' is part of bonding and friendship among the herd.

Hearing

A horse's ears are very expressive. Apart from providing sensitive hearing, they are highly mobile, 'swivelling' in the direction of the sound or stimulus that has their attention. A dressage horse that is concentrating on its work will have its ears swivelled back softly in the direction of its rider, signalling that its attention is focused on the rider.

A horse attuned to some distant sound on the horizon will have its ears pointed forwards in the direction of the sound.

An angry or upset horse can lay its ears flat back, as if to block out the offending situation or noise.

Smell

A horse's sense of smell is an important part of its behaviour pattern. Mares identify their foals by smell, as a stallion does an in-season mare.

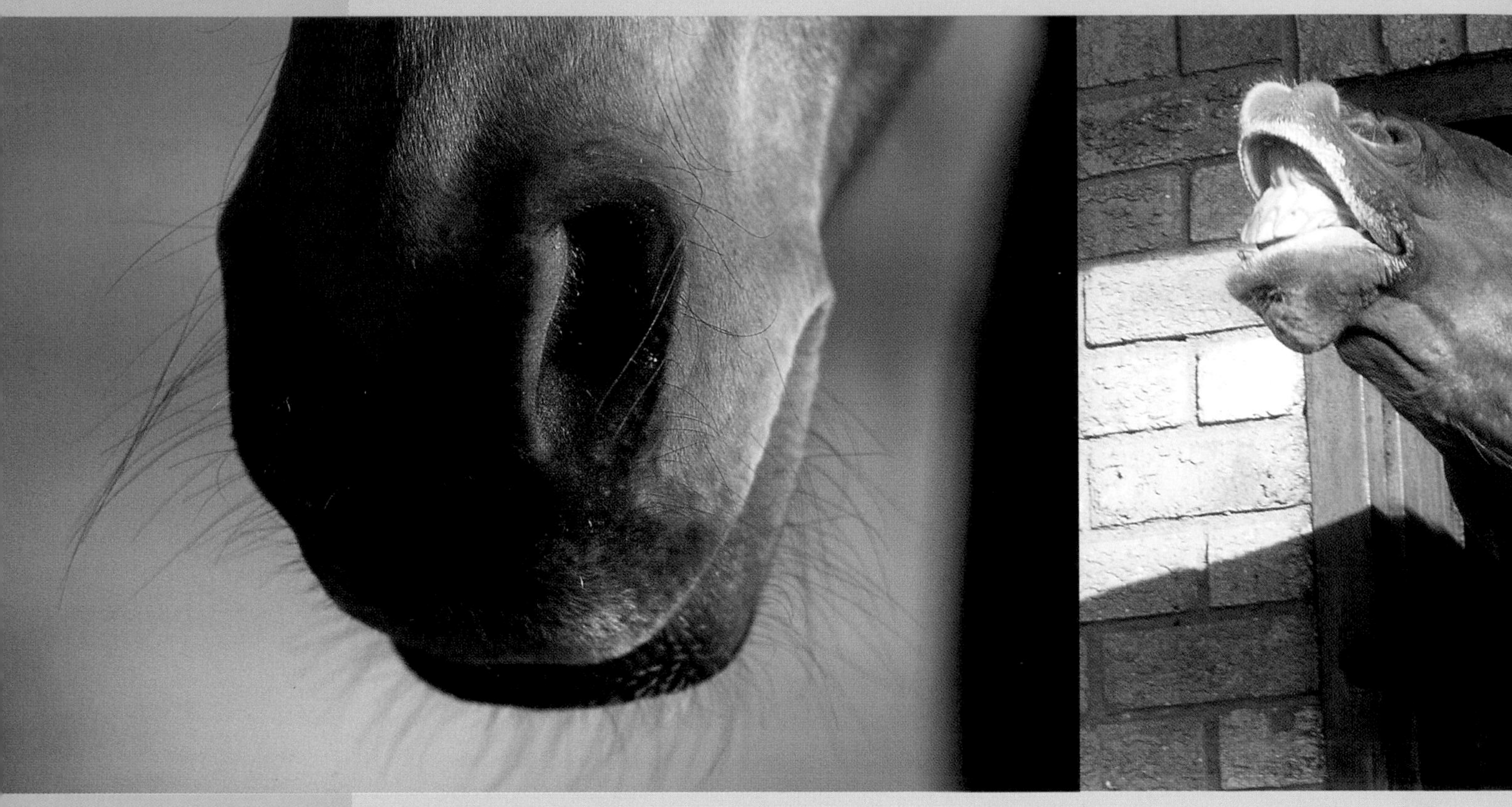

Left *Horses have a well developed sense of smell and taste.*
Centre *This expression, known as flehmen, is used when assessing interesting or unusual smells.*
Right *Whinnying is a means of communicating with stable mates.*

Far right *A well-schooled, experienced horse can help a young or inexperienced rider to gain confidence.*

Wild horses will find water by smell from some distance away and mountain ponies instinctively know how to use their sense of smell to avoid hazards such as marshy or boggy ground.

TASTE

Horses generally like sweet-tasting food. Their natural sense of smell and taste will lead them to turn away from poisonous plants, which are generally bitter. A horse will quickly spit out an alien taste in the manger, or after discovering a plant it doesn't like in a mouthful of sweet grass or hay. It can also easily develop a taste for 'tidbits', and soon learns to search pockets for carrots, polo mints or sugar cubes.

SOUND

The sounds a horse makes convey expression, from the soft nicker of a mare to her foal and the shrill call of a stallion defending his territory to the whinny that greets the rider when he or she comes into the stable. In a horse being ridden, snorting or sneezing is mostly an expression of willingness, concentration and response to a command.

EXPRESSIONS

Horses display many visual forms of expression through both their bodies and faces. A softly swinging tail, for instance, is a sign of relaxation, whereas a clamped, tensed-down tail indicates tension or anticipation of flight. Sweating is not just an indication of exertion but can also be a product of tension or excitement, such as before a big class at a show.

MATCHING HORSE AND RIDER

Just as with humans, horses have very different temperaments and characteristics depending on their breeding, talents, and how quickly or slowly they grow up. There is really no such thing as a 'bad-tempered' horse, merely one that has reacted antagonistically to some bad experience. 'Bad horses' are made, not born.

Apart from training the horse properly, to ensure these bad experiences do not occur and leave a negative imprint, it is as important to match the right horse to the right job as it is to match horse to rider. A highly nervous, quick-reacting thoroughbred will lose confidence with an inexperienced handler just as quickly as the handler will. Similarly, a laid-back, big-framed cob forced to go fast in a jump-off every week is going to be just as unhappy as its frustrated rider who fails yet again to win a prize. In these situations, it is less an admission of failure than one of common sense to acknowledge that both horse and rider would be happier with a partner better suited in temperament, objectives and riding skill.

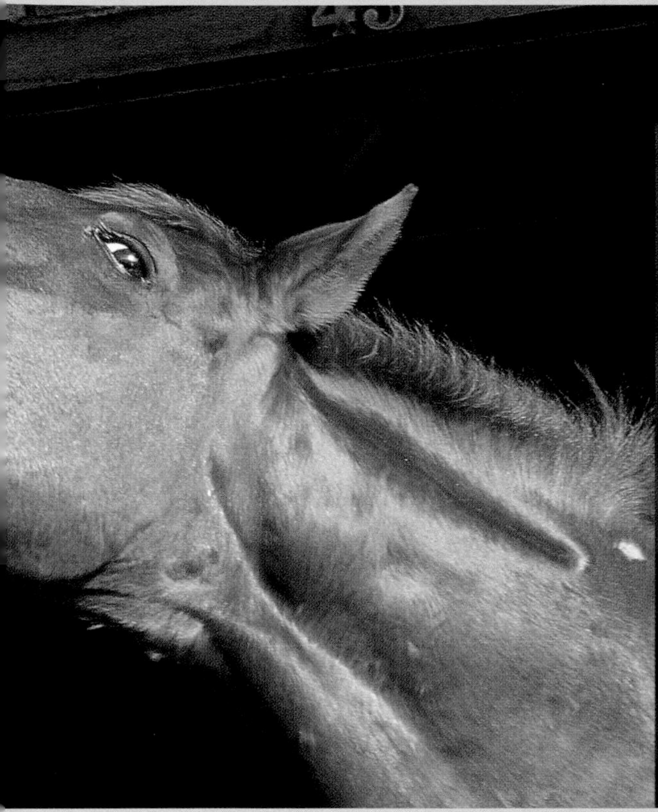

As a general principle, a young horse needs an experienced rider and a novice rider is better off on a steady, experienced horse. While we should not attribute human emotions to animals, it is correct to surmise that horses can feel emotion, that they can pick up 'vibes' and react to a negative or positive environment. Trust and harmony form the basis of any relationship, and it is the same with horses. When these qualities are present, the relationship between horse and rider is capable of bringing much reward and pleasure.

CHAPTER TWO

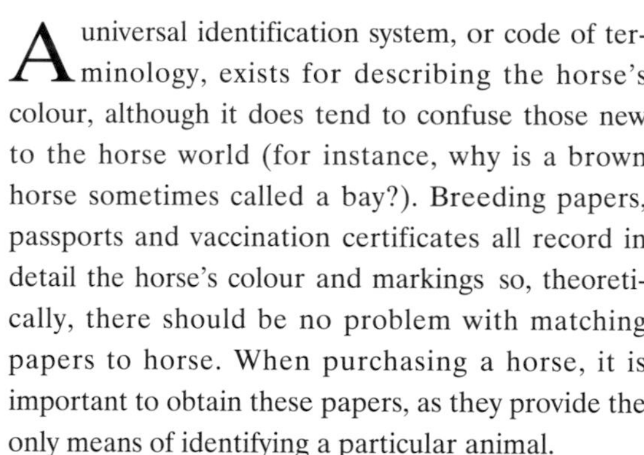

IDENTIFICATION AND BREEDS

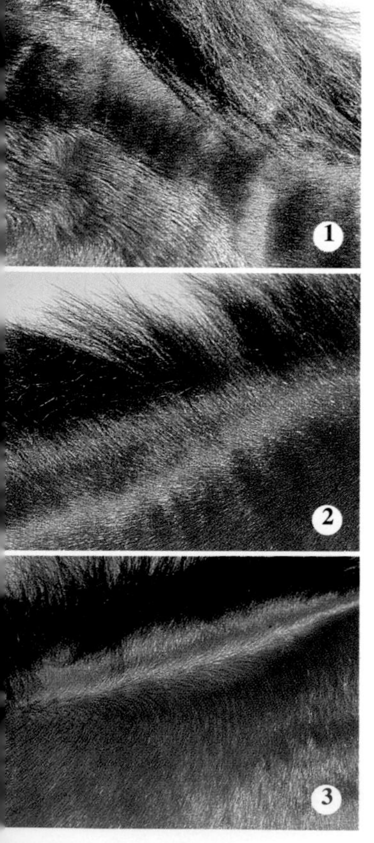

A universal identification system, or code of terminology, exists for describing the horse's colour, although it does tend to confuse those new to the horse world (for instance, why is a brown horse sometimes called a bay?). Breeding papers, passports and vaccination certificates all record in detail the horse's colour and markings so, theoretically, there should be no problem with matching papers to horse. When purchasing a horse, it is important to obtain these papers, as they provide the only means of identifying a particular animal.

A full description of a horse on its pedigree, passport or other documentation will contain details of its name, parentage, sex, breed or type, age, height, colour, markings on head, body and limbs, any distinguishing marks and acquired marks such as scars or brands.

Colour classification largely depends on colour density, as not all horses have a coat of only one hair colour. Colours are defined as follows:

Black (1): The horse's coat, mane and tail must be black. No hairs of any other colour are allowed, except for white markings.

Brown (2): The coat contains a mixture of black and brown hairs, forming generally a dark brown overall colour. The mane, tail and often the lower limbs will be of predominantly black hairs.

Bay (3): Body hair varies from mahogany to light brown in colour with black mane, tail and lower limbs. In lighter bay horses, the coat around the flanks is almost toffee-coloured. A dark bay often has a lighter muzzle, with black mane, tail and lower limbs.

Chestnut (4): Shades range from lightish brown (liver chestnut) to gold. The mane, tail and legs are the same colour as the coat, or a shade darker, with no black hairs. The Palomino is a chestnut horse with a golden shine to the coat and a mane and tail of flaxen colour, but ideally as white as possible.

Roan (5): Any of the above colours, mixed with grey. Chestnut and grey combined is called strawberry

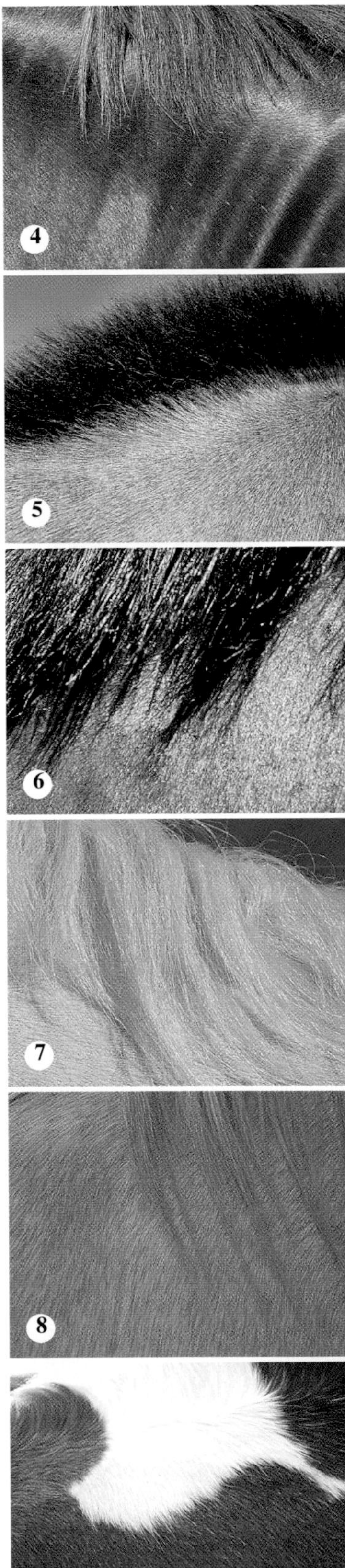

The Arabian horse is renowned throughout the world for its purity of breed, elegant lines and exceptional grace.

roan; bay and grey result in a red roan; while a blue or grey roan has a mixture of black and grey hair.

Dun (6): The Dun is a form of bay, with black points and generally a black stripe, known as an 'eel stripe', running the length of the back. To be termed Dun, the coat colour would be yellowish- to mousey-grey.

Grey (7): As they age, grey horses generally lighten in colour to almost white or cream. A dappled grey has a mottled grey coat with darker patches.

Cream or Albino (8): White or cream hair on pink or unpigmented skin, often with pink or blue eyes.

Painted and spotted horses (9): Also called coloured or pinto horses, these have a variegated coat, combining white with another colour in an irregular patchwork. They include the Piebald, which has distinctive large patches of black and white; and the Skewbald, which combines white with any colour other than solely black; and the spotted horse, such as the American-bred Appaloosa, which is characterized by spotted markings of different sizes and all colours. The coat patterns are known as blanket, marble, leopard, snowflake and frost.

MARKINGS

For the purpose of identification documents, descriptions of head and leg markings are very detailed and follow an internationally accepted format. For example, a blaze may be defined as: 'Wide blaze, irregular at top, extending to left at base'. There are a number of generally used terms that make it easy to identify any horse, anywhere in the world.

Blaze *Snip* *Star*

Stripe *White face*

HEAD MARKINGS

Blaze: A white marking down the length of the face, often wider over the forehead and tapering towards the nose.

Snip: A white patch in the lip or nostril area.

Star: Any patch of white hair on the forehead, often star or diamond-shaped.

Stripe: A white marking down the length of the face, generally narrower in width than the nasal bone.

White face: A broad covering of white extending over the width of the face, more extensive than a blaze.

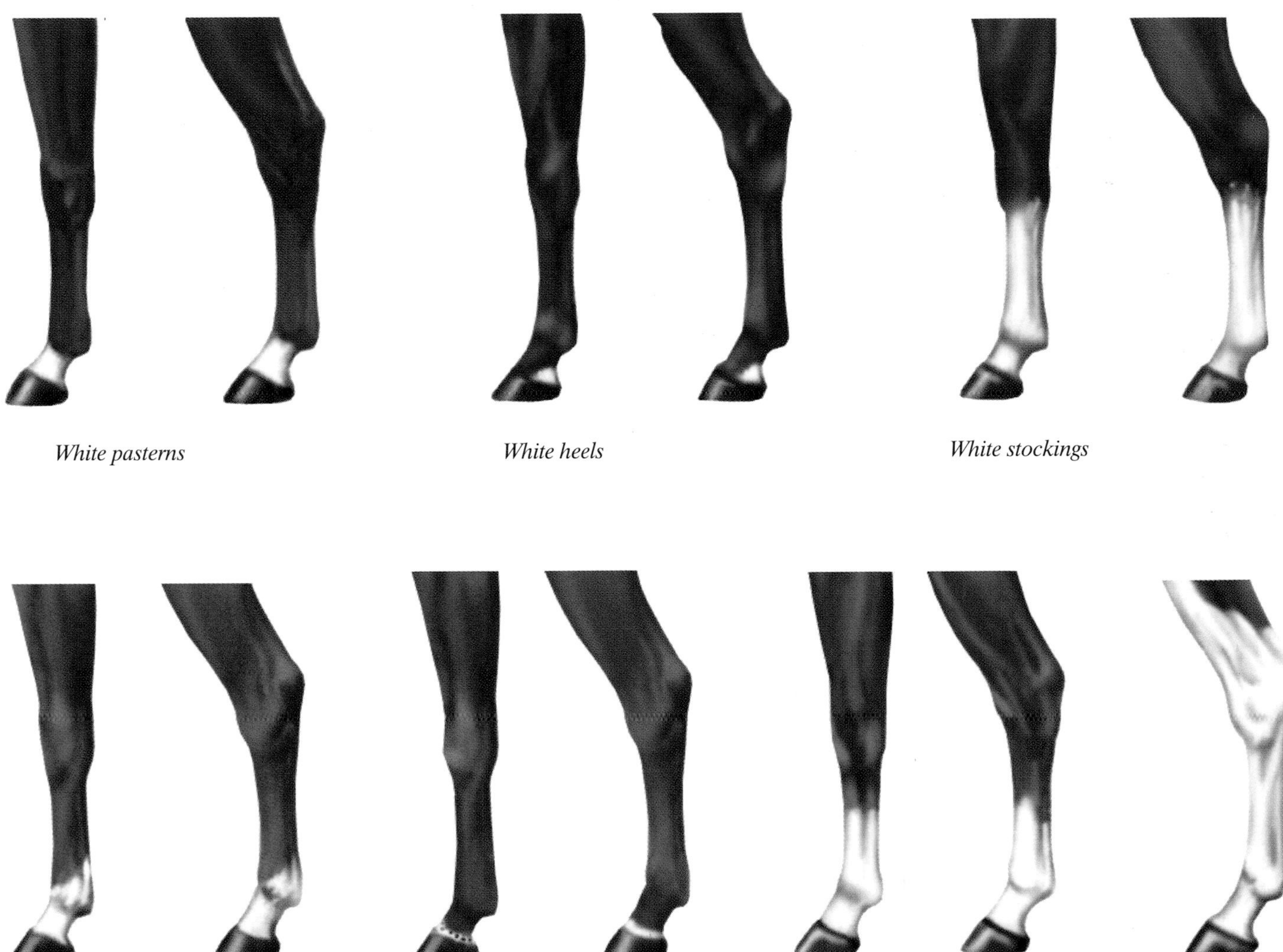

White pasterns *White heels* *White stockings*

White fetlocks *Ermine* *White coronet* *White socks* *Full stocking*

Leg Markings

Leg markings, which are usually white, normally describe the area they cover. Some horses have markings on only one leg, while others may be marked on two or more legs.

Sock: White hair extending up the leg to below knee or hock level, but not encompassing the joint, is called a sock.

Stocking: White hair extending up the leg, past the knee or hock level is known as a stocking.

Ermine marks are spots of black on white around the coronet area at the top of the hoof.

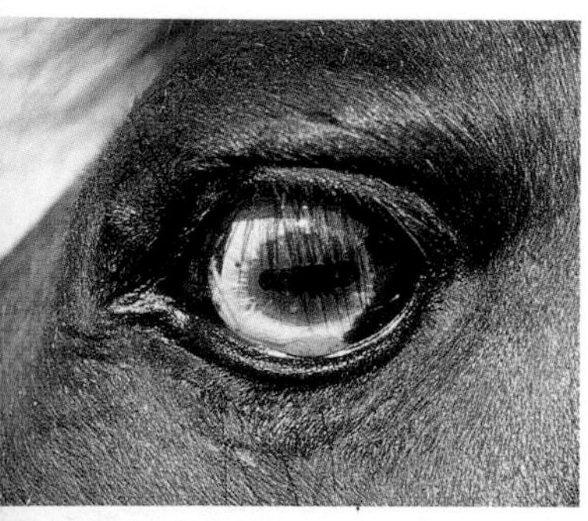

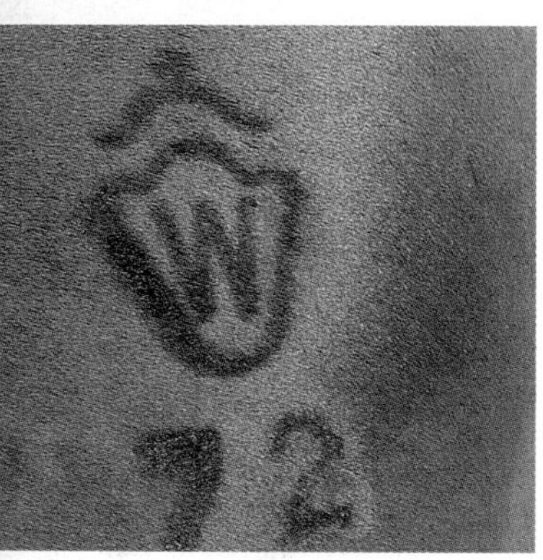

Top *A wall-eye lacks pigment in the iris.*
Above *The brand mark of a Westphalian horse.*

Other distinguishing coat marks are the eel stripe (also called a ray or dorsal stripe), a dark line extending down the back; the flesh mark, which is a patch of uncoloured skin; and the whorl, an often circular-shaped patch of hair that lies against the normal line of the coat.

A 'wall-eye' describes an eye that is blueish-white in appearance, due to lack of colour in the iris. It is often found as one 'wall-eye' on a white-faced horse.

Brand marks

These clearly defined symbols show the breeding district, or country of origin, of horses where such an identification system is used. In Germany, for example, horses are branded on the left thigh to show the breeding district they come from (such as Hanoverian, Westphalian, Bavarian). Mares registered to a studbook will also be branded with a registration brand on the left-hand side of the neck. Denmark, Sweden, Holland and other countries employ their own unique branding systems.

Although Thoroughbreds are not branded, they often have an identification number tattooed on the inside top lip, and those that are registered to Weatherbys, the international studbook control organization, usually have passports from birth.

Telling age

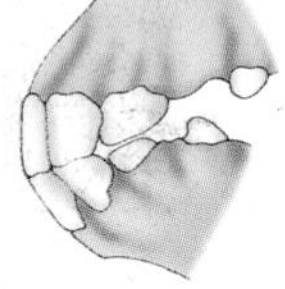
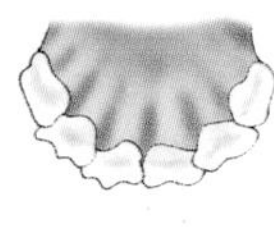

At five years, the horse will have all its permanent teeth.

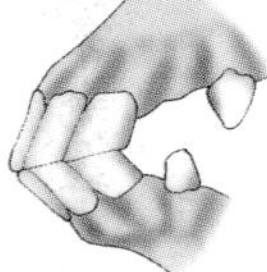
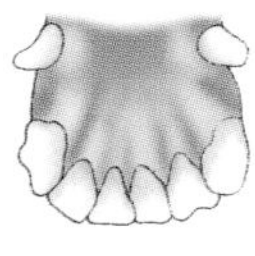

By 12 years the tables have become more oval.

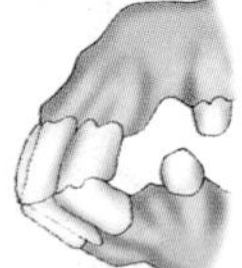
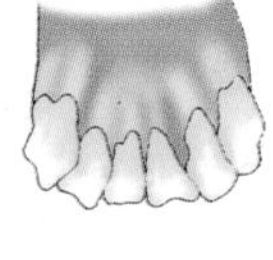

With advancing age, the teeth slope further forward.

Age and the horse's teeth

Every Thoroughbred horse has an 'official birthday' (1 January in the northern and 1 September in the southern hemisphere). The horse's age increases every time it passes that date. This system of ageing horses is followed by most countries. In Germany, however, any non-thoroughbred horse born between 1 November and 31 December is also aged from January of the following year.

Although it is not an exact science, the age of the horse on its papers should correspond to evidence from the wear and pattern of its teeth, generally accepted as the most reliable way of determining the age of an unknown horse.

Horses' teeth are divided into incisors (cutting teeth) at the front, and molars (grinding teeth) at the back. As with humans, horses have milk teeth, which are later replaced by permanent teeth. By the age of three and a half, the permanent lateral incisors have appeared, and one year later the horse will have all its permanent teeth. The emerging teeth normally push out the temporary, or milk, teeth. In the earlier years, gauging a horse's age by its permanent teeth is best done by judging the infundibula. These are the dark grooves or cavities in the wearing surface of the incisors, three layers deep in the lower teeth and six deep in the upper jaw.

By the age of six, the infundibula in the central incisors of the lower jaw will have disappeared, at seven in the lateral incisors and at eight in the corners. In the upper jaw these marks will have disappeared from the centre at nine, the lateral incisors at 10 and the corners at 11. From around age nine, one can find a hook on the corner top teeth which will disappear by 10 or 11 years old.

From the age of 12, when these infundibula have generally disappeared, depending on wear, ageing can be approximated by the shape of the tables (tops) of the teeth, which gradually change shape through a horse's teens from round to oval, often becoming triangular in very old horses. With advancing age, the side view of the teeth takes on more of a forward-sloping angle. It should be noted that hardier native ponies often wear their teeth less quickly, so the age of ponies can easily be underestimated.

Conformation

Conformation is the term applied to the shape of the individual horse, how it is 'put together'. No horse is perfect, and horses with what may be termed less-than-perfect conformation should not be written off at first glance. Conformation has to be assessed as part of the bigger picture, as it applies to the intended purpose of the horse. Certain conformation faults may render a horse unsuitable for a particular job, such as three-day eventing, but won't impair it from giving a rider great pleasure as an all-rounder. In reality, there have been in the past, and will be in the future, superstar horses with less than perfect figures. A general rule when assessing conformation is that everything should be in proportion.

The **head** should be in proportion and representative of the type of horse. For instance, an Arabian will have a slightly dished face, while a cob type will have a rounder nose and heavier, less defined outline to the shape of the head.

The **upper and lower jaws** should meet evenly in front, as horses with ill-matched jaws can have feeding problems.

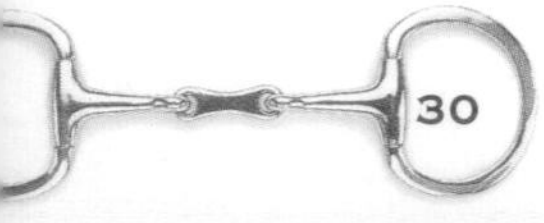

Previous page *The Arabian's dished face is a distinctive characteristic of the breed.*

A kind, bright, interested **eye**, well set on the side of the head, is generally accepted as a representation of a similar temperament. An eye with too much white surrounding it is frequently considered to denote a cheeky, if not bad-tempered, horse.

Head and neck: The way the head is set onto the neck is important. A horse with a very thick jowl (the area under the jaw) will find it less easy to flex through the jaw and poll (the top of the neck, behind the ears) and will therefore find it more difficult to round and soften into a good shape in response to the rider's contact. It will also find it difficult to flex softly into a bend in circles and turns. In a good riding horse the neck should be well set on, coming up and out of the wither and tapering to the head, with good muscle above and no obvious bowed muscle underneath, which is representative of a horse with a tendency to hollow its back, or of bad training. A good 'length of rein' describes a sufficiently long neck; a short neck can be difficult to round, as can a low-set neck. Stallions will have a thicker, more muscular neck than geldings or mares.

Body: The horse should stand at an equal height, or higher, at the wither than at the croup. A horse said to be 'croup high' will find it more difficult to carry weight on the hindquarters. The withers should be well formed and, together with a good sloping shoulder, will provide a naturally comfortable place for a saddle to sit. A short, upright shoulder may indicate a short, choppy stride.

The **chest** should be deep and broad, providing good room for the internal organs, including the heart and lungs.

Back and loins: When the horse is looked at from the side, the back should form a rectangle with the legs, and it should look as if a saddle would fit neatly into place in the middle of the back. Mares tend to have longer backs than male horses. A hollow back is considered a weakness or fault, as is a roach back (one with a convex rather than concave slope to the loins). The loins should be well muscled and strong. Anything less is usually a sign of undernourishment or weakness.

The **croup** should slope gently downward towards the dock and be strong and well muscled. At rest, the tail should extend in a natural curve from the croup, but it should be carried proudly when the horse is moving. A clamped tail is often a sign of nerves and tension, whereas a very highly carried tail is a sign of temporary excitement. A tail carried to one side may indicate a back problem.

The **hind limbs** and hindquarters are the horse's 'engine', and their action propels it forward. The whole of the upper hind leg, incorporating the thigh and stifle, should appear strong and powerfully muscled and the thigh should be long and broad.

The **hock** is a crucial joint in the horse and takes a lot of strain, particularly in collected work, such as advanced dressage, and fast work, such as racing. The hock should be well defined but not fleshy. It should point rearward, not inward (known as cow-hocked), nor should it bow out. When the horse is standing squarely, from the point of the hock down the back of the leg should appear as a vertical line and, ideally, should line up plumb with the outer point of the hindquarters. The hind limbs should appear angled through the hock joint and horses with straight hocks will normally find it more difficult to engage the hind legs under the body.

The **cannon bones,** which make up the leg from knee and hock downward, should appear short to the ground for strength and balance. The term 'clean legs' means that the tendons stand out as clean lines without lumps, bumps or swelling.

The **front limbs** should appear parallel when viewed from the front. From the side, they should form a vertical line to the ground, which ideally should line up plumb from midway along the top of the shoulder blade, down the middle of the leg and reach the ground at the back of the heels.

The ideal **elbow** is large, well formed and stands free from the chest wall. Horses that appear 'tied in' in this area will not move freely out of the shoulder on the flat or over fences.

The **knee** should be broad and large when viewed from the front. A small, narrow knee appearing 'tied-in' above or below is an indication of weakness. A horse with a natural knee position slightly in advance of the lower limb is known as 'over at the knee' and tends to have a more elastic knee joint than horses with very straight legs. The opposite, known as 'back at the knee' or 'calf-kneed', will put more strain on tendons.

The **fetlock** should be well shaped and strong, neither puffy nor too rounded. The angle from fetlock to hoof, the pastern, ideally forms a smooth line.

POINTS OF THE HORSE

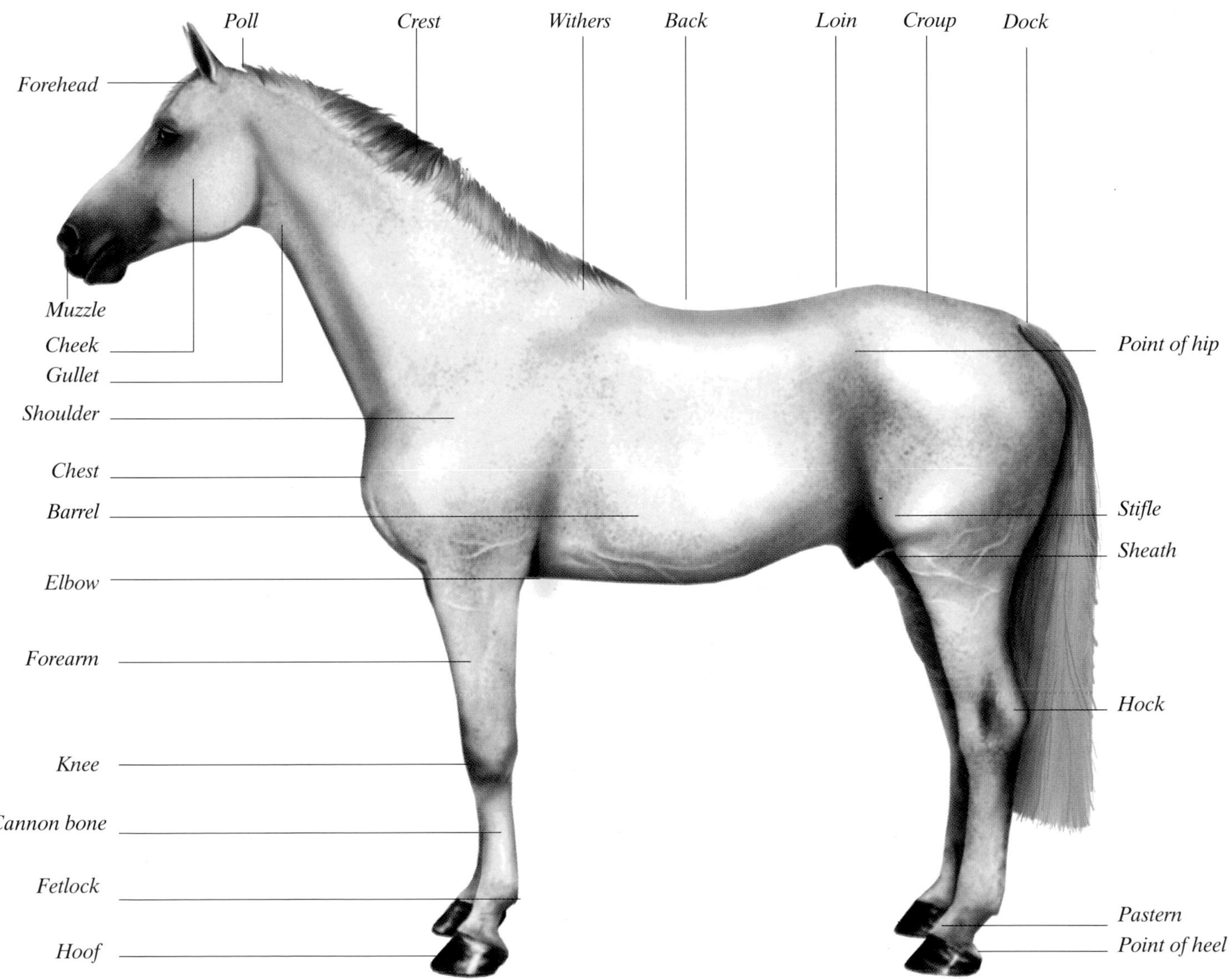

Upright pasterns can lead to more concussion in movement, while long pasterns impede steadiness in movement and put extra strain on the tendons. The hind pastern tends to be more flexible than the front pastern. The angle from the pastern through the hoof should be harmonious.

The **hoof** should be constructed of healthy, strong horn and not be brittle or show evidence of cracks or ridges. When the foot is picked up the frog (the soft, leathery pad on the underside of the foot) should be healthy, well formed and surrounded by a defined area of sole. The bars of the hoof and heel should be well defined, as flat feet tend to be weak.

Overall, the **feet** must be right for the size and type of the horse and the work it is expected to perform. Heavier horses will have larger, broader feet than lighter riding horses, while a fine-boned Arabian or Thoroughbred should have feet to match. From the front, the feet should appear straight, not pigeon-toed (pin-toed) or splayed out. Boxy, small, upright feet will be more vulnerable to problems, as will feet with an exaggerated slope.

THE HORSE IN ACTION

After assessing the way a horse is put together while standing square (its conformation), the next stage of assessment is based on the way the horse moves, both naturally and with a rider on its back (see also pp 84–85 and 131).

From the point of view of the riding horse, the most important aspect is that it moves with clean, true gaits (the natural way of moving) at all times. While a show jumper will be expected to have a good quality canter, and an event horse should be able to stretch at a steady gallop, these traits can be developed through good training. Provided the natural gaits are sound in the first place, most horses can be trained to meet special requirements.

The way a horse moves is an indication of its willingness to go forward, and is an essential ingredient for both competition and riding horses. Generally, in all gaits the horse should move with energy, rhythm, regularity and elasticity. Transitions between gaits should be smooth, and a well-trained horse should respond instantly to its rider's commands to increase or decrease speed.

Opposite *The trot is a clear two-time rhythm, where the footfalls are made in diagonal pairs, as this horse shows.*

THE GAITS

The walk: A four-time gait made up of a diagonal series of footfalls: left fore, right hind, right fore, left hind. The walk steps should be equally spaced and cover the same amount of ground. At free walk, the hind feet should land beyond the imprint of the fore feet (known as over tracking).

The trot: A two-time gait where the footfalls are made in diagonal pairs and two definite, regular beats are heard. The horse should move straight when observed from the front, and the leg action should be even, that is both fore and hind legs should be used equally. The amount of knee action depends on the breed or type, but the horse should move freely from the shoulder, with a supple back and active hindquarters and hocks.

WALK

TROT

The canter: A three-time gait where the sequence includes a moment of suspension, as the horse moves from the leading foreleg to the opposite diagonal fore and hind leg, followed by the remaining hind leg. A good canter should look and feel 'uphill', as the hind legs come well under the horse. A young horse needs time to develop the balance to canter in a school or restricted area.

The gallop: A fast, flowing four-time gait, including a moment of suspension, when all four feet may leave the ground. In a good gallop, the horse moves with speed and lightness, covering a great deal of ground with each stride. It is essential for riders to have a secure seat before attempting to gallop.

Assessing the gaits: When assessing a horse it is always useful to ask the horse to move backwards (rein back), to ensure it moves in a straight line. Getting the horse to walk and trot in a small circle to each side is also advisable, as reluctance to do this can indicate stiffness in the back.

CANTER

GALLOP

BREEDS AND TYPES

There are many breeds and types of horses throughout the world. Breeds have developed their characteristics over generations, according to the climate, terrain and conditions of their native land and through their customary use.

Although the horse has served man through the ages as a means of transport in war and peace, in agriculture and industry, nowadays, for much of the world, the horse has become part of the leisure industry, ridden only for pleasure and sport, and breeds have had to adapt to the change.

New crosses between breeds, and the introduction of new blood to improve and refine breeds, tell the story of the development of the modern horse.

A breed is technically a strain without the introduction of blood from any other strain. While this criterion may cloud the definition of a 'breed' as opposed to a type (which is determined by the type of work a horse does, such as a hunter, for example), the horse world refers constantly to horse breeding, breeding championships, breed societies and so on, so the newcomer should not feel intimidated by such technicalities. Indeed, if we look back over the centuries, most 'breeds' have been influenced, improved and refined by the injection of 'foreign' bloodlines.

Arabian

Each breed has its own history, but there are two real breeds whose influence surpasses all others, the Arabian and the Thoroughbred.

ARABIAN

The Arabian horse is probably the purest breed, and is certainly one of the world's oldest and most intelligent, with a romantic history that has influenced the development of the horse in the modern world.

It was developed as a distinct breed by the desert tribes of the Arabian Peninsula. Legend has it that Allah spoke to the south wind, saying, 'I will cause a creature to come forth from you, and take substance' and so the Arabian horse was created. It is also said that the prophet Mohammed decreed that special care be given to the animal, ensuring the status of the Arabian horse within the faith of Islam.

It was the fast, agile and hardy Arabian horse that carried the troops of Islam out of Arabia to conquer Egypt in the 7th century, later advancing further into north Africa, France and Spain, where Arabian bloodlines were introduced to improve native stock, the start of the vast influence of the breed that has persisted through centuries. Latterly Arabian blood has improved and refined Warmblood and pony lines, and of course founded both the part-bred Arabian, and Anglo-Arab types that are especially prolific in French performance horse breeding.

Characteristically, the purebred Arabian should have a small, elegant tapering head with the classical 'dished' face, a broad forehead with prominent large eyes, small ears and a small muzzle with flaring nostrils. The back is shorter, as the Arabian has one vertebra less than other breeds. The full tail is normally carried high. Its limbs may look more delicate than those of other breeds but are deceptively tough. Traditionally, the Arabian was a small horse, rarely exceeding 14 hands high, but newer trends in breeding have succeeded in increasing the height without diminishing the characteristics of the breed.

Flat racing with Arabian horses is becoming increasingly popular around the world and the Arabian also comes into its own in the sport of endurance riding, where its intrinsic stamina, intelligence and agility are highly valued.

The popular and enduring Arabian horse is now widely bred around the world, with extensive followings in both the USA and Australia.

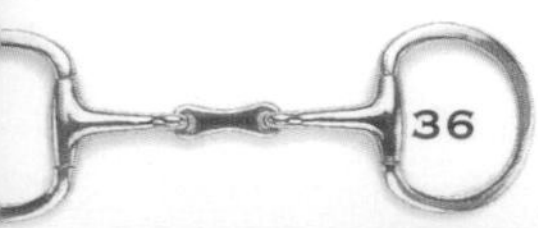

Thoroughbred

THOROUGHBRED

Fast, beautiful and valuable, the Thoroughbred is the noblest of breeds. Prolifically successful in racing, eventing and, to a lesser extent as a purebred, in show jumping, the Thoroughbred pervades the entire horse world through its influence on other breeds. But where did it come from?

Racing began in England as early as the late 14th century and successive monarchs, following the example of King Henry VIII, imported Spanish, Arabian and other 'oriental' animals to improve the speed of native racing stock. However, it is easiest to look at the origins of the Thoroughbred from the end of the 17th to the beginning of the 18th centuries when three eastern-bred stallions, regarded as the founders of the modern Thoroughbred breed, were brought into England.

The Byerley Turk was the first, captured from the Turks at the Battle of Buda, and imported in 1689 by Captain Robert Byerley. Richard Darley of Yorkshire imported the Darley Arabian in 1704. The Godolphin Arabian was imported from Paris in 1730 and later acquired by the second Earl of Godolphin. From these three Arabians were bred the four famous racehorses, Herod, Eclipse, Matchem and Matchem's son Highflyer, who founded the male lines of the modern Thoroughbred. Today, all registered Thoroughbreds can trace their ancestry to one of these stallions.

To be eligible to race and be registered as a pedigree Thoroughbred, a horse must fulfil the criteria for entry into the General Stud Book, which was founded in 1793 and is currently administered by Weatherby's in England and Ireland. Forty-seven other countries have associated studbooks and champion Thoroughbreds have been bred not only in England and elsewhere in Europe, but also in Canada, the USA and New Zealand. The Thoroughbred horse can be any size over 142cm (14.2hh) and any solid colour. Alert, sensitive horses with refined, quality looks, they are strong and have great stamina. As a breed, Thoroughbreds generally have excellent freedom of movement, enhanced speed, and great powers of recovery from exertion – all qualities which have proved important for refining many other breeds.

ANGLO-ARAB

The Anglo-Arab is a popular riding horse that traditionally combines the best of both Arabian and Thoroughbred blood, with at least 25 per cent of each. Part-bred Arabians, such as the Anglo-Arab, may be associated with another studbook or breed area, even though they contain only a minimum percentage of Arab blood. The qualifying amount varies in different countries.

Anglo-Arab

RIDING AND SPORT HORSES

The original use of the term 'warmblood' denoted a lighter, riding type of horse as opposed to a heavy draught animal known as a 'coldblood'. However, warmblood is now accepted as the collective term for the modern-day riding, or sport, horses produced under continental lines and accepted for registration into the relevant breed society.

Dutch Warmblood

The Netherlands has a thriving horse breeding industry, organized along similar lines to Germany, but falling under one main administration, the KWPN, the Royal Studbook of the Netherlands.

Over time, the original heavy working and carriage-horse breeds typical of the Netherlands (such as the Groningen and Gelderlander), were combined with English Thoroughbred, and German and French bloodlines to establish the Dutch Warmblood, a fine riding type and a highly successful sport horse.

Dutch Warmblood

Irish Sport Horse

With surefootedness, athletic ability and an intelligent but sensible temperament, the Irish Sport Horse, which combines Thoroughbred blood with the indigenous Irish Draught Horse type, has enjoyed considerable success in eventing and show jumping.

German Sport Horse

Germany has a long tradition of horse breeding, which it maintains to this day. Originally, four main types of horse were required to meet the varying needs of the army, industry, agriculture and sport. At the beginning of the 20th century the first three categories made the most demand, but with the advance of mechanization, a surplus followed by a dramatic fall in the country's horse population occurred until the mid-1950s, when the breeding industry underwent a dramatic change.

At this time, the growing demand for horses for pleasure and sport riding was recognized and breeding policies were adapted to produce the characteristics of the modern German Sport Horse. Farsighted policies implemented throughout Germany's different breeding regions have put the nation at the forefront of world breeding and the warmblooded German Sport Horse excels in all disciplines.

The selection process for stallions and the system of grading mares is rigorous and promotes the best. In the past, exports of breeding stock from Germany were not always the best quality (understandably the nation did not want to let its best horses go abroad), but modern technology enables frozen semen to be transported anywhere, provided each country's import regulations are complied with, resulting in worldwide access to the best stallions.

The German Sport Horse is deemed to be Hanoverian, Westphalian and so on, according to the area in which it was born. However, as many top stallions are approved for use by more than one breeding region, it is not accurate to call them breeds as such. For example, a horse of Holstein bloodlines born in the south of Germany can be branded Zweibrucken rather than Holstein; while a horse born in the Hanoverian region by a Trakehner stallion out of a Hanoverian mare will be branded Hanoverian. A horse by an Oldenburg stallion, bred by artificial insemination to an Oldenburg mare but born in the UK, will be branded a British Warmblood.

In many instances certain characteristics of a particular region are also linked with interesting backgrounds and histories.

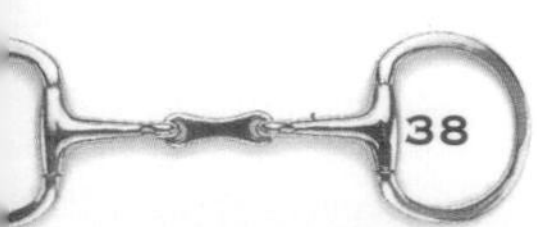

Hanoverian

Hanoverian
In 1736 the first 12 Hanoverian stallions stood at the State Stud at Celle. The Stud, founded the previous year by King George II of England and the Duke of Brunswick, is still the heart of Hanoverian breeding. For the first 40 years or so, most of the stallions came from the Holstein area, along with some East Prussian, Neapolitan, Andalusian and some English Thoroughbred stock.

The original product of the stud was good, hardy horses, easily adaptable for work on the land or for general riding, but with the emphasis on the former, and during the 19th century a considerable amount of heavy stock was introduced from Britain, including Cleveland Bay and Yorkshire coach horses.

The fortunes of the Hanoverian horse varied during the early 20th century until the implementation of a revised leisure and sport horse breeding programme introduced the Thoroughbred, Arabian and Trakehner stock that has refined and lightened the Hanoverian type into the top quality riding and competition horse of today.

Holstein
The district of Schleswig-Holstein, in northern Germany, is believed to have been a horse breeding area since the early Middle Ages. Its influence extended to areas such as Hanover and neighbouring Denmark.

At one time Holstein was renowned for breeding fast, big-framed, strong coach horses. To develop the lighter-bodied modern riding type, English Thoroughbreds were used extensively.

This influence, particularly that of Ladykiller and his sons Lord and Landgraf, as well as the Selle Français stallion Cor de la Bryère, has produced many top show jumpers in the past, and continues to do so, as well as some exceptional dressage horses.

Although not one of the largest breeding areas in Germany, the Holstein district can lay claim to a number of top performance horses, up to Olympic level.

Westphalian
Westphalia, in northwest Germany, is the heart of German horse country, producing successful and influential horses for show jumping, eventing, dressage and general riding. The Westphalian State Stud at Warendorf, founded in 1826, is the home of the German National Riding Centre. The Westphalian is Germany's second most popular breed, after the Hanoverian.

Holstein

Trakehner

The Trakehner has a long history which, despite the influence of war, can be traced back to East Prussia in the 13th century. Modern Trakehner breeding was founded at the Royal Stud set up in 1732 by Friedrich Wilhelm I and expanded over the years via regional satellite studs. After World War II, fewer than 1000 breeding horses reached West Germany after a gruelling 1300km (800-mile) trek from East Prussia. Although by the mid-1950s the Trakehner Verband, the successor to the East Prussia Studbook, registered fewer than 700 animals, it is now the third largest breed association in Germany, and has been influential in refining the stock of other breeding districts.

Trakehner

There is a great deal of Thoroughbred blood in the Trakehner breed, which is typically refined, elegant, free-moving and tending towards the blood horse in temperament.

Oldenburg

The original Oldenburg was a heavy coach horse. Count Johann von Oldenburg imported oriental, Spanish and Neapolitan horses in 1580 as foundation stock. His son, Count Anton Günther von Oldenburg, was known as the 'Stable Master of the Holy Roman Empire' for his promotion of horse breeding, which included the establishment of schools where farmers could learn about horse management. The Oldenburg preserved its original characteristics and bloodlines for far longer than any other German regions until, after World War II, the demand for lighter riding horses resulted in an injection of Thoroughbred blood. The original type can still be found in some Polish studs, for example, but the modern competition type established itself as a success in a very short time. Apart from the ridden sports, horses from Oldenburg are still used for coaching and four-in-hand driving.

OTHER INFLUENTIAL BREEDS

The prevalence of certain breeds and types is often a matter of geography, with some countries and continents showing a trend towards horses developed for their unique climatic and riding conditions. Some popular riding breeds are listed below.

Andalusian

While the origin of the Andalusian as a breed is not entirely certain, this Spanish horse has had a great influence on other breeds in Europe, but most particularly in the USA, through its introduction to that continent by the Conquistadors. The Andalusian has a strong association with bull fighting in Spain, but in recent years has begun to enjoy renewed popularity among dressage enthusiasts, especially those interested in the classical high school movements.

Usually grey, black or bay, the Andalusian is a horse of great presence, with a strong front and proud neck. The temperament is excellent and the natural movement ideally suited to dressage. The emergence of a competitive Spanish dressage team in 1995, with two members mounted on Andalusians, has done much to further the breed's popularity.

Lusitano

This agile, showy Portuguese horse probably originated from Andalusian blood, and like its Spanish counterpart has been associated with mounted bull fighting. It is favoured by European and American classical dressage enthusiasts.

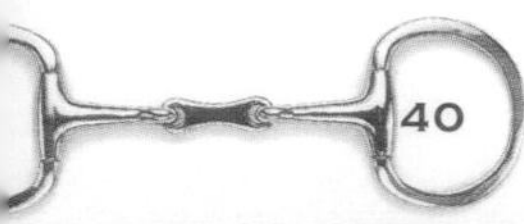

Quarter Horse

The first all-American breed, the Quarter Horse originated in Virginia, USA, where early settlers used to run horses over quarter-mile races, hence the name. The breed was developed from original stock brought to the Americas by the Spanish, together with the addition of Thoroughbred blood imported by the English settlers.

Quarter Horse

The modern Quarter Horse, which is claimed to be the most popular horse in the world, enjoys widespread popularity, particularly in the USA, where it is used for Western riding, showing, flat racing and general riding. More than three million horses are currently registered with the American Quarter Horse Association.

Lipizzaner

The breed is named after the Lipica Stud near Trieste, which was founded in 1580 by the Hapsburg Archduke Charles II, son of Emperor Ferdinand I of Austria. The stud, which still exists today as a breeding, riding and tourist centre, hosted the 1993 European Dressage Championships.

The Lipizzaner is believed to have descended from the Andalusian breed originally, with the later introduction of Arabian blood. The breed lines of the founding stallions (Maestoso, Siglavy, Pluto, Conversano, Favory and Neopolitano) have been maintained, and are found today in all purebred Lipizzaners, including the horses at the internationally renowned Spanish Riding School of Vienna, where the traditions of classical dressage are upheld.

Cleveland Bay

Originating from Yorkshire in England, the history of the Cleveland Bay can be traced to the Middle Ages. Always bay in colour, and known for substance and power, the breed also enjoys something of a unique position as a 'purebred' warmblood, that is, a horse free of crossing with other bloodlines for around 100 years. Popular as a carriage horse, the Cleveland Bay also shows talent in dressage and jumping and has a developed following in Australia, the USA and the UK as a competition horse (either as a purebred or, latterly, crossed with Thoroughbred bloodlines to improve performance).

Selle Français

The French saddle horse, as the name translates, is a product of the breeding system instigated in 1958, which brought together all the French provincial studbooks under one banner. The Selle Français type developed originally from the use of Thoroughbred stallions on native mares, later with a significant infusion of Arabian and Anglo-Arab bloodlines. The Selle Français has demonstrated remarkable success in show jumping.

Appaloosa

Although spotted horses have been known throughout the ages, in the 18th century the Nez Percé Indians developed a distinctive breed, which the first white settlers called 'a Palouse horse' after the

Palouse Valley of Idaho and Oregon, USA. The term eventually became known as the Appaloosa.

The Indians applied a skillful breeding policy to original Spanish stock, from which evolved a hardy horse of good temperament and endurance, which has become popular worldwide as a riding horse, both for pleasure and for competition.

Not all painted or spotted horses are Appaloosas, however, and there are five recognized, distinctive Appaloosa coat patterns: Blanket – white rump or back spotted with any colour; Marble – mottled all over the body; Leopard – spots of any colour or mixed colour on light background; Snowflake – white on any colour except grey; and Frost – white on a dark background. In general, the skin is a mottled black and pink and the eye is surrounded by a white sclera. The hooves may be striped and the mane and tail are frequently short and sparse.

Appaloosa

American Saddlebred

Developed during the 19th century to provide a comfortable, well-mannered ride for plantation owners in the southern states of the USA, the American Saddlebred is the best known of the so-called gaited breeds. In addition to a highly elevated walk, trot and canter, these horses are schooled to produce two artificial four-beat gaits, the high stepping 'slow gait', and the extremely fast 'rack'.

Originally evolved from the Narragansett Pacer and Canadian Pacer, an infusion of Thoroughbred, Arabian and Morgan blood gave this horse its eye-catching, proud looks. Popular with enthusiasts as a show horse, the Saddlebred's artificial carriage and gaits are produced by leaving the feet long and shoeing with heavy shoes.

Australian Stock Horse

The first horses imported into Australia are believed to have come from South Africa in the late 1780s. Of mixed blood, they were bred to later imports from Europe (mainly Arabian and Thoroughbred), producing a hardy, agile, quality horse suitable for long hours of work on the vast sheep and cattle stations. During World War I the Waler, as the horse bred in New South Wales was known, came to be regarded as an exceptional cavalry horse.

The modern Australian Stock Horse combines the Waler's characteristic courage, strength, stamina and good nature with a more refined appearance. As well as excelling in the ranching and farming duties for which they were originally bred, Australian Stock Horses make good all-round riding and competition horses. They are popular with both experienced and novice riders in their home country and have been successfully exported around the world.

Australian Stock Horse

NATIVE HORSES AND PONIES

The native ponies of the British Isles, also known as Mountain and Moorland breeds, still roam wild in their own areas. Although the herds are smaller in number than they used to be, under the protection of their breed societies survival in their native habitat has enabled these wild ponies to retain their distinctive characteristics. It is these inherent characteristics, such as robustness and good temperament, which have made the domesticated versions popular as riding horses and ponies throughout the world.

In common with other native breeds, such as the Icelandic and Norwegian Fjord, the often harsh conditions of the natives' habitat has produced strong, agile and hardy characteristics.

WELSH PONY

This breed has a reputation for producing excellent all-round animals for riding and competition. Originally bred for work in the coal mines, the Welsh Pony has exerted an important influence on the breeding of riding ponies throughout the world. From as early as the 12th century, the breed is believed to have been influenced by Arabian blood, derived from eastern stallions brought to Europe and Britain by knights returning from the Crusades.

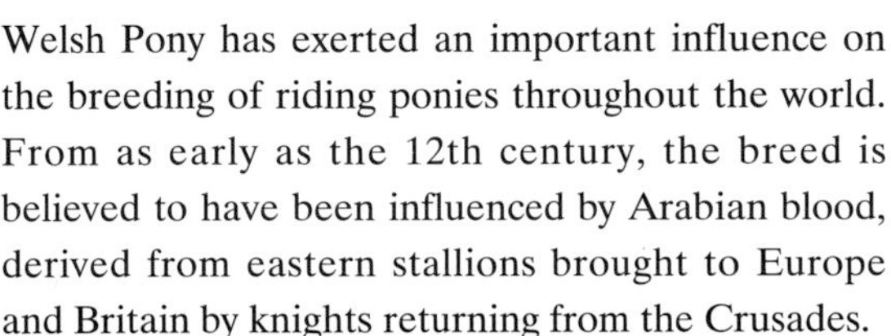

Welsh Mountain Pony

At a later stage, Thoroughbred and carriage-horse bloodlines influenced the development of the largest variety of Welsh Pony, the Welsh Cob.

The categories registered in the Welsh Cob and Pony Society Studbook all share some general characteristics, including hardiness, robustness and inherent soundness. As Welsh Ponies are able to live out in all weather, they are economical to keep.

Welsh Section A: Known as the Welsh Mountain Pony, with a maximum height of 122cm (12hh). This type has a defined, pretty head and tough but slender legs and is often grey in colour. Mountain Ponies have lived in the Welsh hills since before the Roman invasion of Britain.

Welsh Section B: With a maximum height of 137cm (13.2hh), this type was originally a larger version of the Section A, but the introduction of outside blood has clouded these characteristics. This type has proved very successful as a competition pony.

Welsh Section C: Also called a Welsh Pony of Cob Type, this is a cross of a Section A or B pony with the Welsh Cob. Similar to the Cob, but not exceeding 137cm (13.2hh), Section C ponies are good jumpers and are popular for trail riding.

Welsh Cob (Section D): The distinctive high trotting action has made the Welsh Cob popular for general riding and as a driving horse. It is hardy, robust, and economical to keep. Strictly speaking a horse rather than a pony, the Welsh Cob can be any height above 142cm (14.2hh).

Welsh Cob

CONNEMARA

Originating from the region of the same name on the west coast of Ireland, the Connemara pony is hardy, compact and strongly built, having evolved in the mountains and bogs common in this area. Merchant travellers probably introduced some Arabian blood several hundred years ago, which may well have produced the attractive head that is characteristic of the breed.

Connemaras are usually well put together with well set-on necks and good sloping shoulders. They also tend to be good movers. Traditionally the Connemara is grey or dun, but any colour other than mixed colour is permitted. They are very popular as riding ponies, and for dressage and jumping.

Crossing native Connemaras with Thoroughbred blood has proved highly successful, producing larger riding and competition horses.

NEW FOREST

Herds of New Forest Ponies still run and breed free in their native habitat, the New Forest in Hampshire in the south of England, where they have lived since the 11th century, but they also flourish in domesticated conditions. The New Forest Pony can range in size from 130–148cm (13–14.8hh) and can be any solid colour apart from mixed colour or cream. It typically has rather a large, although intelligent, head.

A good-natured all-rounder, the New Forest is a popular pony for pleasure riding and competition by both children and adults. The breed has been exported to many parts of the world.

New Forest Pony

DARTMOOR

A small, hardy pony from Dartmoor in the south-west of England, this breed has proved an ideal first riding pony for children as it is both gentle and small, reaching only 116–122cm (12.2hh). Dartmoor Ponies are usually black, brown or bay.

EXMOOR

One of the most distinctive native pony breeds, from the moor of the same name in Somerset, England, the Exmoor has a 'mealy' (lighter coloured) muzzle and the same colouring around the eyes. Like its southern counterpart, the Dartmoor, the Exmoor makes an excellent riding pony.

SHETLAND

One of the smallest breeds in the world, the Shetland has found popularity as a child's pony or driving pony in many parts of the world, far from its native habitat in the Shetland Isles of Scotland.

The Shetland Studbook Society rules that a true Shetland should not stand more than 106.5cm high (this is one breed whose height is measured only in centimetres, not in hands). They can be of any colour, including mixed colour, although the traditional colours are black and white-grey. The Shetland Pony has a small expressive head, sturdy legs and a solid body. It develops a very woolly coat in winter.

HAFLINGER

A Tyrolean breed, the Haflinger Pony's original purpose was as a surefooted mountain pack horse. Sturdy, with a neat head, Haflingers are always palomino- or chestnut-coloured witha flaxen mane and tail.

Good temperament and an excellent weight-carrying ability have made the Haflinger Pony a popular leisure pony in many countries of the world for general riding as well as carriage driving.

WESTPHALIAN MOORLAND PONY

Germany's two native pony breeds, the Dülman and Nordkirchen, were originally used for light agricultural work. Since the injection of Arabian blood into the breeds, there has been some successful evolution to the children's riding pony type.

ICELANDIC

The native Icelandic horse is distinguishable by its special gait. In addition to the normal walk, trot and canter, the Icelandic has a gait called the 'tölt', a sort of four-beat, smooth, running walk that is used to cover large distances over rough ground. Usually chestnut in colour, the Icelandic is popular throughout Europe as a riding horse, and special competitions, such as tölting races, are held for enthusiasts.

FRIESIAN

This is a small, thickset horse bred in the Friesland district of the Netherlands. Always black, these horses traditionally have long flowing manes, feathered (hairy) heels and a high stepping gait. Friesian horses were introduced to Britain by the Romans, where they formed the basis of the Dales and Fell native breeds.

In recent years, the good-natured Friesian, whose ancestors were initially war horses, and later farm horses, has enjoyed popularity as a specialist dressage and display horse.

CAMARGUE

The wild white horses of the Rhône delta in the south of France have been the subject of mystery and legend for hundreds of years. Somewhat shaggy and wild looking, they nevertheless make excellent mounts once they have been caught and trained.

NORWEGIAN FJORD

An ancient breed dating back to Viking times, this native of western Norway was originally used for agricultural purposes. It is now used throughout Scandinavia and elsewhere in Europe as a leisure horse for general riding, in harness and for the acrobatic sport of vaulting. An eye-catching horse, the Norwegian Fjord *(right)* is usually dun or cream coloured, with a curved, upright mane and a dorsal stripe (a dark line running along the length of the back from the mane to the tail).

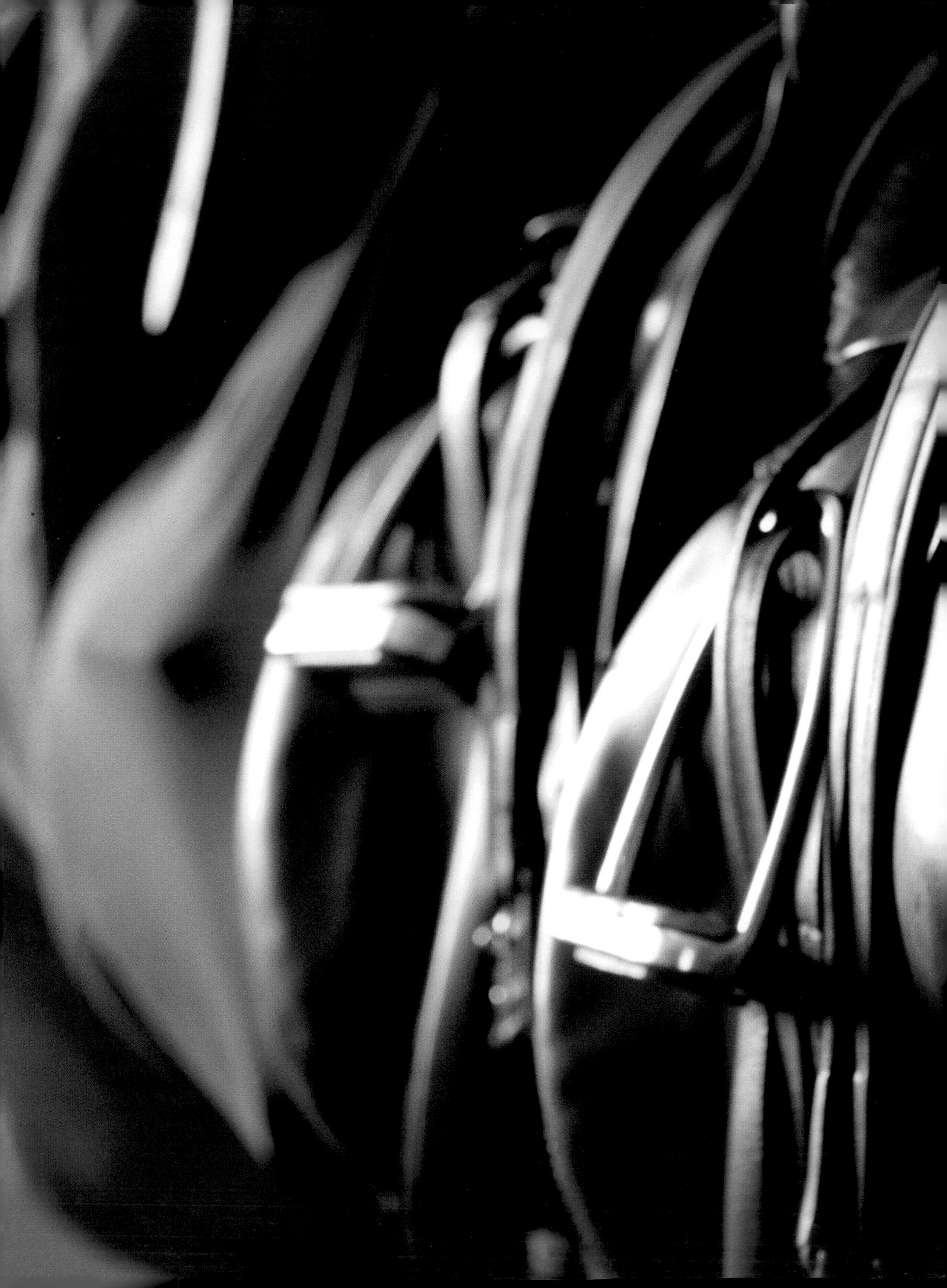

CHAPTER THREE

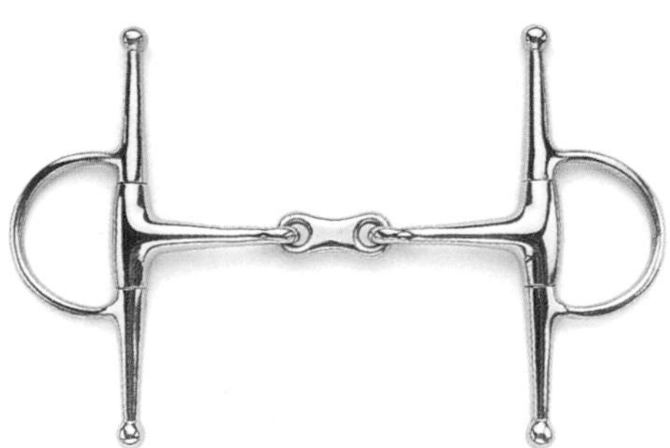

TACK AND EQUIPMENT

Any equipment used for riding horses can be embraced by the general term of 'saddlery' or 'tack'. The most basic items of riding equipment are the saddle and bridle, both of which are selected according to the type of horse, the required purpose (hacking or show jumping, for example) and the level of experience of the rider. Then there are the many additional articles, from rugs (blankets) to bandages, which fall under the heading of horse clothing, and are used for keeping horses warm and comfortable.

BRIDLES

Bridles come in various styles, colours and trims. The differences are not merely aesthetic – thinner leather work on a horse with a delicate, pretty head will also prove more comfortable for the animal. Whatever the style, good quality leather; sound stitching, buckles and fastenings; and regular checks on their state of repair are vital for safety reasons.

The reins (there are two reins, buckled together) are made in many different styles and materials: from plain leather through webbing and leather to rubber-covered. The latter ensures a better grip for the rider, especially in wet conditions.

THE SNAFFLE BRIDLE

The simple, general purpose snaffle bridle is widely used for everyday riding, for training in jumping, as well as for competitions.

The primary difference between the types of snaffle bridle is in the choice of noseband. The purpose of the noseband is to keep the horse's top and bottom jaws aligned. If it is fitted too loosely it has no purpose, but it should not be fitted too tightly either, as it is not supposed to clamp the jaws together.

The plain **cavesson noseband** should fit comfortably just below the bottom of the horse's cheekbone. This is the only noseband suitable for use with a double bridle.

The **flash noseband** is similar to a cavesson, but has a narrower, secondary strap which fits from the centre of the cavesson down under the bit rings.

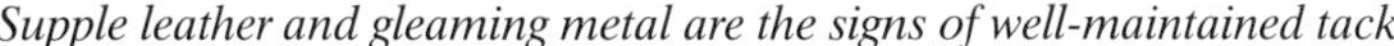

Supple leather and gleaming metal are the signs of well-maintained tack.

Top *A cheek snaffle with a correctly fitting flash noseband.*
Above *A grakle, or figure-eight, noseband is used mainly for horses in fast work.*

The secondary strap should be fitted so it does not pull the cavesson part downward. This is a useful noseband for horses with mobile mouths and is a popular choice for use in basic training.

The **grakle, or crossover, noseband** (also called a figure-eight noseband) has a similar purpose to the flash noseband. It is used mainly on horses in fast work, such as the cross-country phase of eventing.

The **drop noseband** is hinged via two small rings. The nosepiece rests clearly above the nostrils and the chin strap is fitted below the bit. It is a useful noseband for stronger horses, but care should be taken that it does not interfere with the horse's breathing.

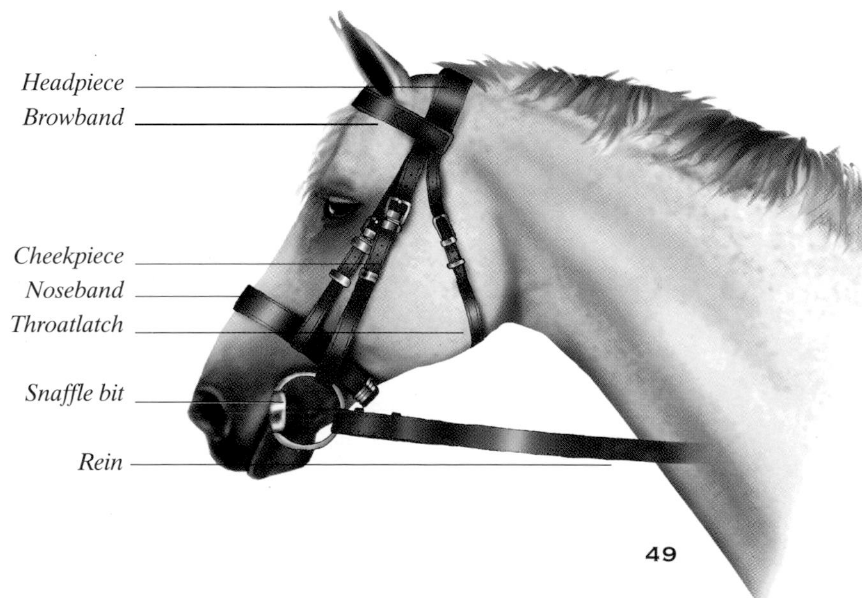

Experienced riders use the double bridle to allow the application of light, almost invisible, aids.

The hackamore bridle, widely used in Western riding, controls the horse by means of pressure on its neck.

THE DOUBLE BRIDLE

This is used mainly by experienced riders in advanced dressage competitions, as its purpose is to provide a refinement of the aids and a more definitive action on the jaw, not more stopping power!

The two bits used are the bridoon, a smaller version of the snaffle, and the curb, or 'weymouth'. The curb, which comes in various forms, has cheekpieces and is fastened with a curb chain. The longer the cheekpieces the stronger the action of the bit. The curb chain should lie flat along the horse's chin groove. If it is too tight it will cause painful pinching, but if it is too loose it will be ineffective.

THE HACKAMORE BRIDLE

The hackamore, or bitless, bridle acts on the poll, nose and chin groove. Although it is used primarily in Western riding, it can be used on horses with mouth problems or injuries that prevent the use of a conventional bit. Some show jumpers have performed successfully at high levels in the hackamore, but it is not allowed for dressage. It is a fallacy, however, to assume that no bit means more kindness, as this equipment can be very severe if used less than sensitively or by an inexperienced rider.

BITS

The **snaffle bit,** which comes in several forms, acts on the tongue and bars (the space in the jaw where there are no teeth) of the horse's mouth. There is a choice of varying sized rings; and the mouthpiece, which comes in various materials and thicknesses, can be made up of either a single or double joint in the middle, or a straight bar. Generally, the thinner the mouthpiece, the more severe the action, but a comfortable and effective bit is one that best fits the

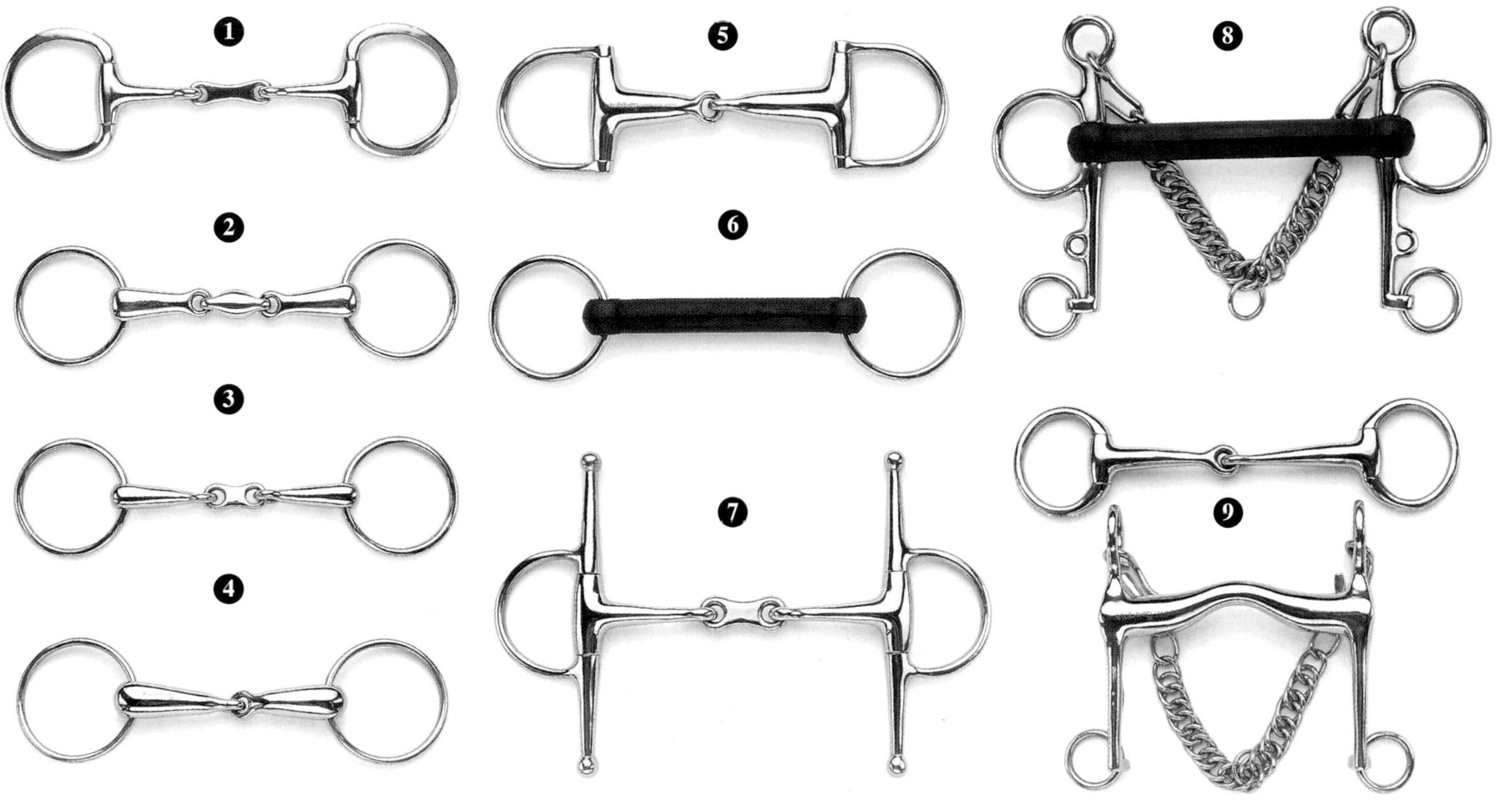

shape of the horse's mouth. A mouthpiece that is too thick can be just as uncomfortable for a horse with a small mouth as a thin bit on a horse with a highly sensitive mouth. The correct bit size is also imperative – too wide and it will slide around in the horse's mouth, too narrow and it will pinch the corners of the mouth.

The **loose-ring snaffle** is a favourite 'starter' bit. Its action is mild yet effective, and trainers find it a subtle bit for establishing a good mouth contact.

The **eggbutt snaffle** has rings that are finished in a rounded, 'D' shape and hinge to the mouthpiece. This is a popular bit for beginner riders, as well as for horses that tend to fiddle too much with their bit, as it lies very still in the mouth.

Snaffle bits with **cheekpieces** in varying designs can be useful for horses that are difficult to turn or tend to twist their heads, as the extra piece provides some guidance in the direction of the turn on the side of the horse's cheek. They are often used on school horses.

The **pelham bit** generally has a straight-bar mouthpiece but the cheeks of a curb bit, with a similar type of lever action. It is used either with two reins or with a leather link between the two rings on each side, allowing it to be used with one rein only.

Bits are effective only if used properly. If a problem continues to occur once a bit has been correctly identified and fitted, the first attempt at problem-solving must focus on the rider's hands.

Bits should be regularly checked for worn parts or sharp edges that could injure the horse's mouth, and discarded if any are found. Bits are traditionally made from metal, but rubber or synthetics, such as nylon compounds, are increasingly popular, especially for horses with sensitive mouths as the less cold, more supple material promotes 'mouthing' on the bit.

Competition rules specify which bits can or cannot be used at the various levels, and rule books should always be consulted for this information as using the wrong bit in a novice event, for example, could lead to elimination from the competition.

Bits

1. Double-jointed eggbutt snaffle
2. KK training bit
3. Double-jointed loose-ring snaffle (French snaffle)
4. Single-jointed loose-ring snaffle
5. Single-jointed eggbutt (D-ring)snaffle
6. Rubber snaffle
7. Cheek snaffle
8. Pelham with rubber mouth piece with curb chain
9. Eggbutt bridoon with curb bit and curb chain for a double-bridle

SADDLES

There are three main styles of saddle: general purpose, jumping and dressage. Whatever the style of saddle you use, however, a good fit is vital to enable the rider to sit in the correct position and give the aids effectively. Furthermore, a badly fitted saddle can cause the horse significant discomfort and injury. Saddle fitting is best undertaken by a qualified or accredited saddler.

A new saddle should always be fitted without a numnah (saddle pad). There should be an even contact with the horse's back, with the seat at the lowest point and enough clearance at the front (pommel) to prevent pinching the horse's withers once the rider's weight is in place.

The **general-purpose saddle** is an adaptable, all-round saddle widely used by novice riders throughout the world. It is suitable for any nonspecialized riding, and is also used for basic training in dressage and jumping. In design, it is midway between the dressage and jumping saddles in style.

The **dressage saddle** has a longer, straighter flap than the general-purpose saddle, to accommodate the rider's lengthened leg position.

PARTS OF THE SADDLE

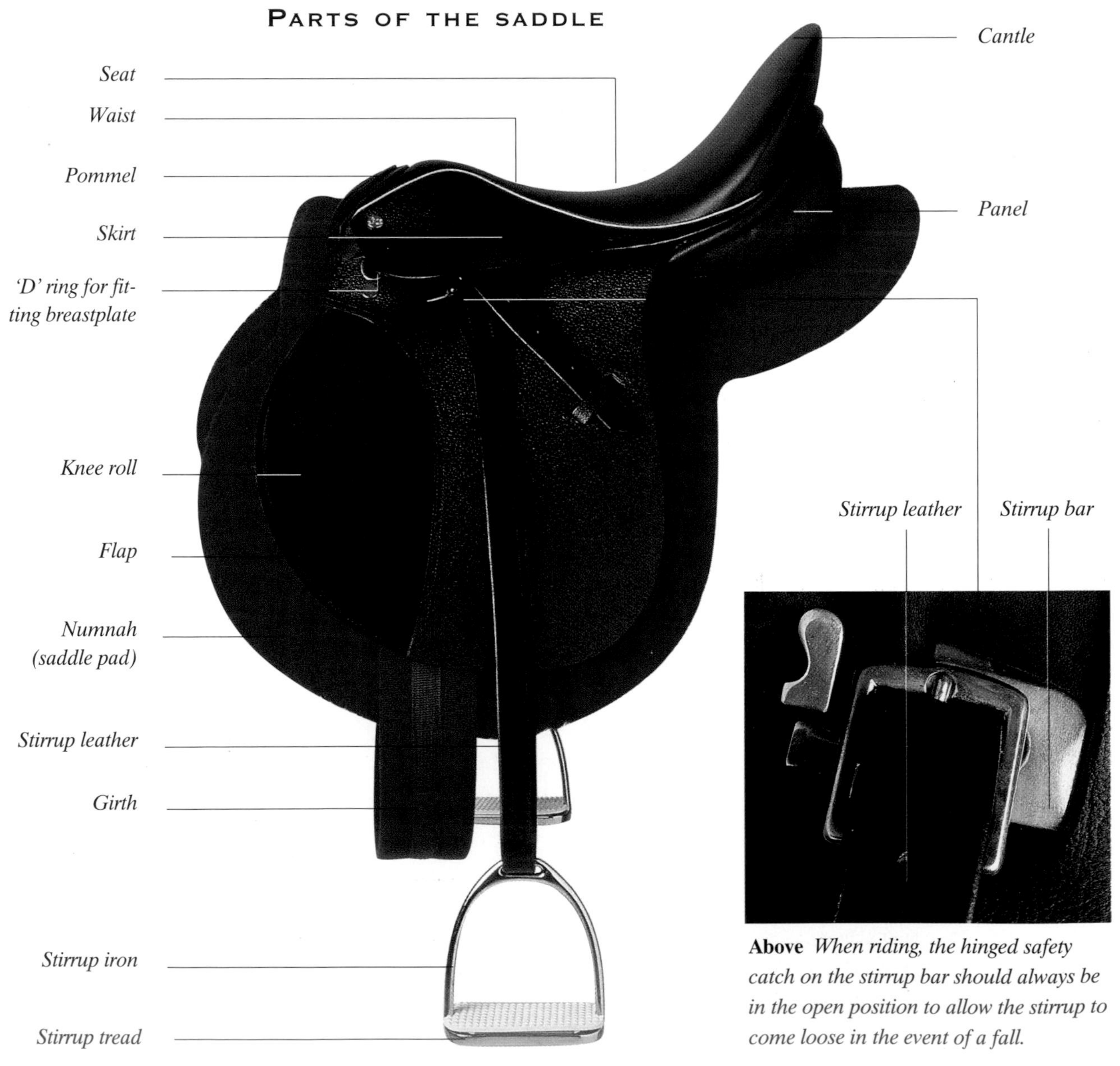

Above *When riding, the hinged safety catch on the stirrup bar should always be in the open position to allow the stirrup to come loose in the event of a fall.*

The traditional dressage saddle has long flaps to accommodate the rider's length of leg.

Below *The jumping saddle helps the rider to go with the horse's forward movement over the jump. The knee rolls support the rider in the lighter seat.*

The **jumping saddle** has a longer seat and forward-cut flaps to accommodate the light or jumping seat. Styles of seat vary from the 'deep seat', which supports the rider by means of a higher back and substantial knee rolls, to the 'close contact' or continental seat with less padding and wider panels which allows, as it suggests, closer contact with the horse.

The specialist **endurance saddle,** designed to give support to riders who spend many hours in the saddle, combines features of the general saddle with those of the **Western saddle,** such as the deeper seat shape, extra padding and the 'box stirrup' which supports the foot and is less tiring on a long ride.

A saddle is constructed over a base, or 'tree', made from steel, leather or synthetic matcrial which is then padded and covered. Traditional leather can also be replaced by synthetics, which are easy to clean and maintain and prove cost-effective for busy riding schools or the recreational rider.

Girth – a separate component available in various styles and materials, ranging from padded leather or webbing to synthetic. Some girths may have elasticized inserts to improve the fit. Double girths are often used for cross-country. The most important factor in fitting a girth is that it should be wide enough not to pinch the horse.

Stirrup bar – located under a small flap or skirt, this has a hinged safety catch which should always be left in the open position to allow the stirrup leather to come loose in the event of a fall.

Stirrup leathers and **stirrup irons** are separate components attached to the saddle at the bars. The stirrup should be wide enough and sufficiently heavy to ensure it can be released and picked up easily by the mounted rider. However, it should not be wide enough to cause the foot to slide around. Rubber treads on the stirrup irons provide extra grip.

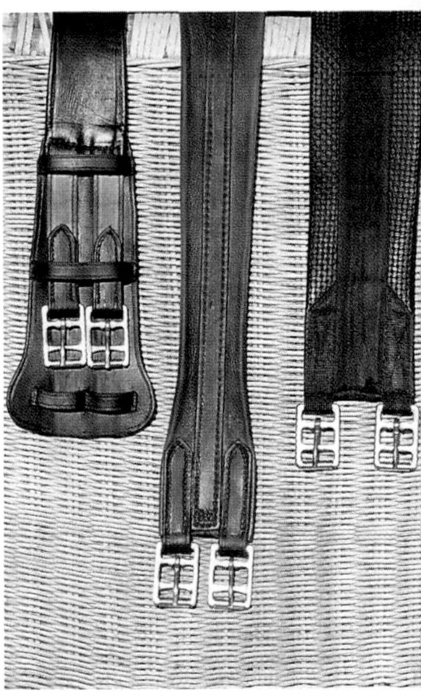

Girths come in many styles and materials, from padded leather to synthetics.

A numnah (saddle pad) fits under the saddle to absorb sweat and help keep the horse comfortable.

Numnahs, or saddle pads, are used for comfort and to absorb sweat from the horse in work. They should never be used for padding out an ill-fitting saddle. Saddle pads can be either shaped to the saddle or, as used traditionally with a dressage saddle, in a rectangular or square shape. They are made from various materials, such as padded or quilted cotton and sheepskin. New products, such as synthetic gel pads and remedial numnahs (therapeutic saddle pads), have both pressure-relieving and shock-absorbing properties.

ADDITIONAL EQUIPMENT

Among the many items of tack and equipment used in riding and training horses, auxiliary reins are used in lungeing, training and for other specific purposes.

Side reins are attached from the girth to the bit for lungeing. When correctly adjusted, they encourage the horse to lower its head and neck and promote a soft, swinging back. Side reins are therefore useful in instructing novice riders on the lunge rein to establish a correct seat, as this is much easier when the horse is soft in its back.

Running reins (draw reins) fit in a triangular shape from the girth, through the bit rings and back to the saddle, roller (surcingle) or the rider's hands. This is a much maligned piece of equipment due to its incorrect use for 'pulling' the horse into a falsely round shape. However, in sympathetic, experienced hands, running reins can be a useful piece of equipment for lungeing as they allow the horse more flexibility to stretch down and round.

In expert hands running reins can be useful for correcting some horses which have been badly trained, as they allow the rider to keep a still hand when re-educating a strong horse, or one that has learned to fight the rider.

There are various patented training aids on the market, consisting of some form of auxiliary rein. These can all be useful in expert hands, but should never be used as a shortcut or substitute for correct training under instruction.

The **running martingale** is most commonly used in jumping. It is permitted in show jumping competitions and the jumping phases of eventing, but not in dressage. A running martingale consists of a neck strap with another strap linking its base to the girth, and two straps ending in rings, through which the reins are passed. A martingale stop should also be added to each rein to prevent the rings sliding over the rein mounts near the bit.

Correctly fitted, this piece of equipment does not have continuous action, but only comes into effect if the horse throws its head up past the rider's point of control, hence its use in jumping where quick adjustments on the way to a fence are necessary.

Right *Nick Skelton of Great Britain rides Hopes Are High in a running martingale at the 1998 World Equestrian Games.*

Far right *Mark Todd of New Zealand, on Stunning, uses an elastic breastplate/martingale to keep his saddle in place during a cross-country event at Bramham, UK.*

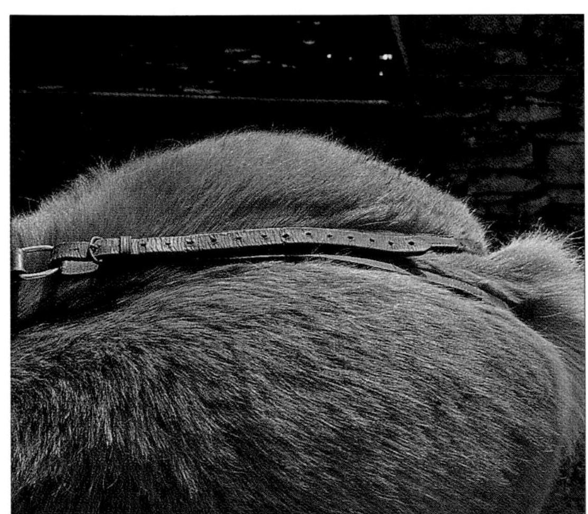

On ponies and short-backed horses, the crupper stops the saddle from sliding forward.

The **standing martingale**, which has one strap running up from the neck strap to the noseband, or coupled to the bit, was often used on horses with serious bad habits such as rearing. It is not widely used in general riding as it acts only at the time and has little purpose in re-educating the horse.

Other auxiliary equipment, which is used according to the requirements of each individual horse, includes the **breastplate**, which fits from the front of the saddle. Its purpose is to help prevent the saddle slipping back when the horse is engaged in big jumping efforts or in exertion across country.

The **foregirth** is a padded extra girth which fits in front of a dressage saddle and prevents the saddle moving forward. It is usually employed on horses with a less defined wither.

The **crupper** fits from the saddle cantle to a loop under the horse's tail to stop the saddle riding forward. It is commonly used on ponies whose backs and wither shape may be less defined.

A **surcingle** (overgirth) is an auxiliary girth used over the saddle in cross-country as security in case the main girth should break or come loose.

The **head collar or halter**, together with a rope, is the basic piece of equipment for leading and securing horses. Made of leather, or synthetic material for easy care, it consists of a headpiece, cheekpieces and noseband either buckled or stitched together integrally, and fastening from the headpiece or from the throatlatch. A head collar is usually the first piece of tack introduced to a young horse.

Left *The head collar (halter) is the basic equipment for leading or tying up a horse.*

Below *Mark Weissburger, of the USA, competing on Best Seller at the Burghley horse trials, uses an auxiliary girth (surcingle) for extra security in the event of his main girth breaking.*

HORSE CLOTHING

LEG PROTECTION: BOOTS

Brushing boots are used on all four legs to protect them both in work or while turned out in the field. They are commonly made of easy-care synthetic material, with Velcro fastenings and extra padding on the inside. Specialized boots, with a higher degree of protection, can be used for cross-country.

Fetlock boots cover the fetlock joints of the hind legs and are commonly used in show jumping.

Tendon boots afford protection to the vulnerable tendon area. Those open at the front are used on the forelegs in show jumping.

Overreach boots (bell boots) give protection to the coronary area and the bulbs of the heels, especially when jumping or lungeing. They are usually made from rubber and either pulled on over the front hooves or fastened with Velcro. Overreach boots are often used when travelling.

Coronet boots fulfill a similar purpose to overreach boots but fit a little higher over the lower part of the fetlock.

Travelling boots (shipping boots) are long, thickly padded leggings that protect from the hock or knee area right down over the coronary band. Travelling boots should fit snugly, but should not be too tight or exert pressure, and all fastenings should be closed on the outside of the leg with the strap ends tucked away neatly and facing the back.

Overreach, or bell, boots protect the horse's heels when jumping or lungeing.

BANDAGES

Bandages (called wraps or polo wraps in the USA), are used for protection during work – most often for dressage training and during cross-country. They are normally made of wool or a cotton mix, with varying degrees of elasticity and are usually fitted over a layer of soft wadding or a purpose-made bandage liner. Bandages must be applied evenly and with the correct tension to avoid impeding the blood supply to the legs or causing a pressure injury, so less experienced horse owners may find boots a safer option. Travelling bandages are made of wider, thicker material. They are applied over a thick layer of padding and secured by adhesive tape.

When bandages are used over shock-absorbing material for cross-country, the Velcro or tie fastenings should also be taped for extra security.

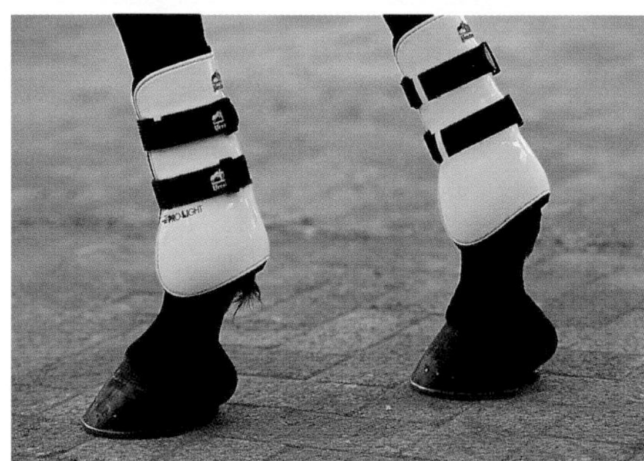

Top *Brushing boots protect the legs while in work.*
Above *Tendon boots are often used in show jumping.*
Below *Nick Larkin of New Zealand, on Red, uses bandages for protection during cross-country.*

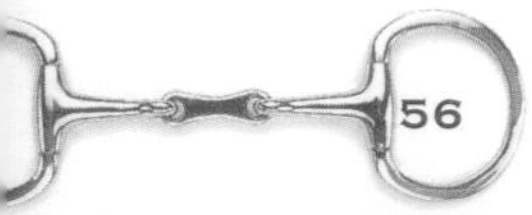

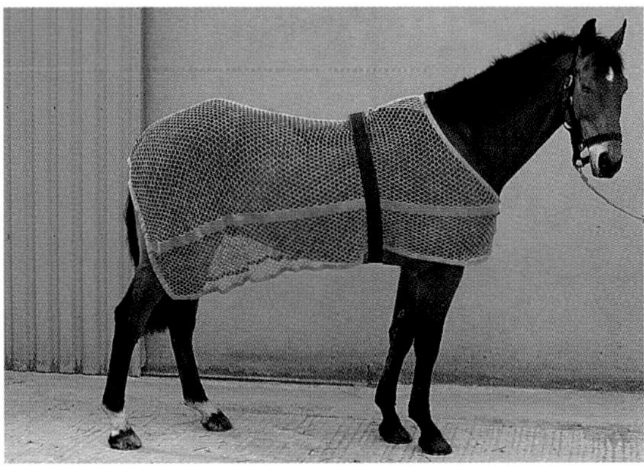

Top left *A weatherproof turn-out rug.*
Left *A stylish travel rug and leg protectors.*
Above *Sweat rugs are used after exercise.*

RUGS AND BLANKETS

In colder climates, horses in work are clipped when they develop their thick winter coats, then rugged-up at night and during periods of inactivity. This is done because a horse that has sweated under a thick coat could experience difficulties with drying off in cold wet weather, and is then at risk of catching a chill.

In the stable, the horse should not be excessively rugged-up (blanketed) as this can make it more susceptible to chills. Some horses feel the cold more than others, so much of the philosophy of rugging-up relies on common sense.

With the number of styles readily available, the well-dressed horse could be in possession of an entire wardrobe of rugs (blankets), but most owners will manage with just two or three.

As in most households, where sheets and blankets have been superseded by duvets, so it is in the stable. The quilted stable rug in various weights has generally replaced a night or day rug over blankets. Not only are modern stable rugs easier to maintain but they are lighter on the horse's back and, when secured with cross straps under the horse's stomach, do not normally need a surcingle or roller to keep them in place (other than for added stability), so there are no pressure points.

Turn-out rugs, all-weather rugs used in the field or paddock, not only help to keep horses mud-free and dry, but also enable the clipped horse to go out in colder weather. Turn-out rugs can be made from weatherproofed lined nylon or lined canvas. A popular version is generally known as a New Zealand rug.

Day rugs are made of wool blanketing and are most commonly used at competitions to keep the horse warm during waiting periods. They are often made in the owner's or sponsor's colours.

Sweat rugs (also called sweat sheets or coolers), are made in absorbent fabric and used in the same way as day rugs, as well as for cooling down after exercise or while travelling. Summer sheets, made from cotton or other light fabric, can be used under rugs, or while travelling in warmer times of the year, to keep the horse clean without providing warmth.

Exercise rugs generally fit under the saddle and keep the horse's back and loins warm during light exercise and riding out. They are made of blanketing or weatherproof material.

HOW TO BANDAGE

Bandages should be evenly rolled before application. The horse must be standing with its weight on the leg to be bandaged.

To apply a bandage, wind it down at a slight angle from the top of the cannon bone, just below the hock or knee, downward as far as the fetlock, then back up again. The material must be kept flat, unwrinkled and applied with consistent support all the way down.

Care should be taken not to wrap the bandage too tightly, yet wrap securely enough to ensure the bandage doesn't slip down. Any knots or Velcro should be fastened on the outside of the leg and the ends securely tucked in.

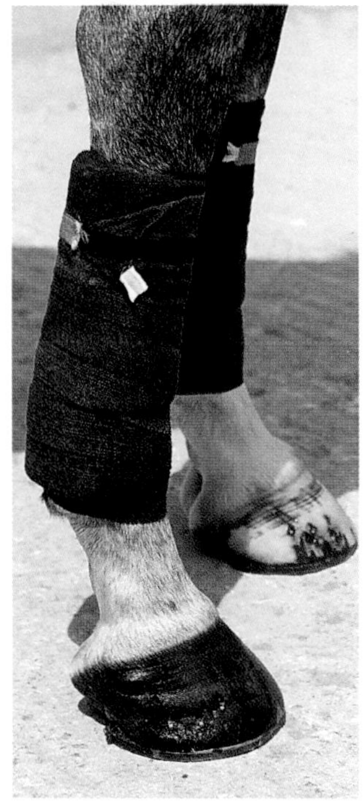

Exercise bandages are used for protection during work.

Rugs are used to keep the horse warm in winter, clean after grooming or help absorb sweat after heavy exercise.

Rugging up

Although modern lightweight rugs make rugging up (blanketing) easier than in the past, if it is not done properly, a flapping rug can easily startle a horse.

The best way to put on a rug (blanket) is to fold it in two, from front to back, with the lining uppermost, and place it over the horse, setting it higher on the withers than it will rest eventually (1). Then fold the back portion down over the horse (2). After checking that the rug is evenly placed and free of wrinkles (3), fasten the cross straps or surcingle (roller), before fastening the rug at the front (4).

Your horse should be tied up or in the stable with the door closed during this process, as in the event of a horse going walkabout it is dangerous to only have a fastened front strap; the rug could slip and make the horse panic, causing an accident.

Rollers and surcingles are sometimes used over a pad placed across the back just behind the withers. They should be secure enough to keep the rug in place but not so tight as to cause the horse discomfort or force it to hold its breath all night.

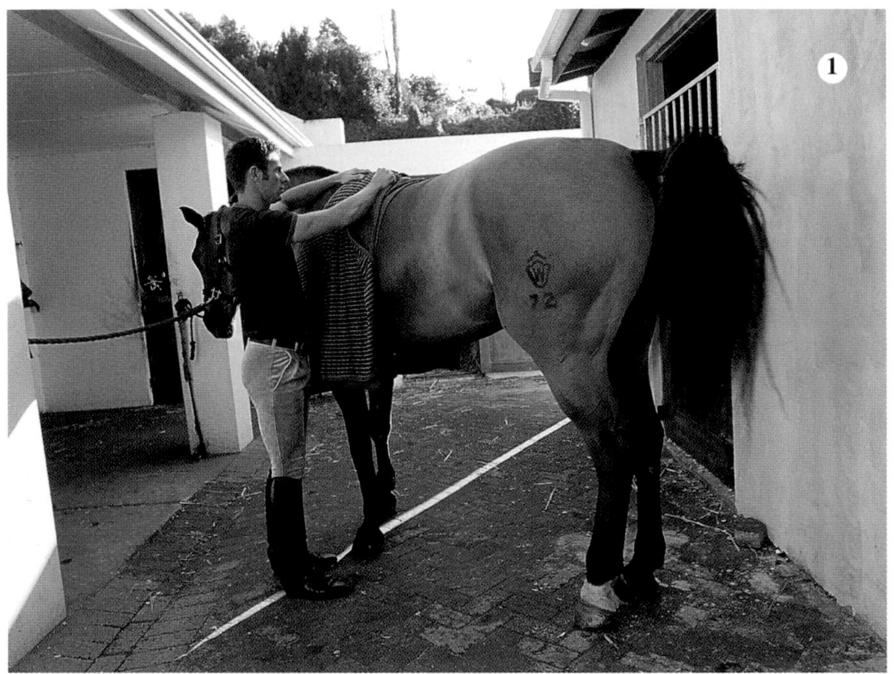
1

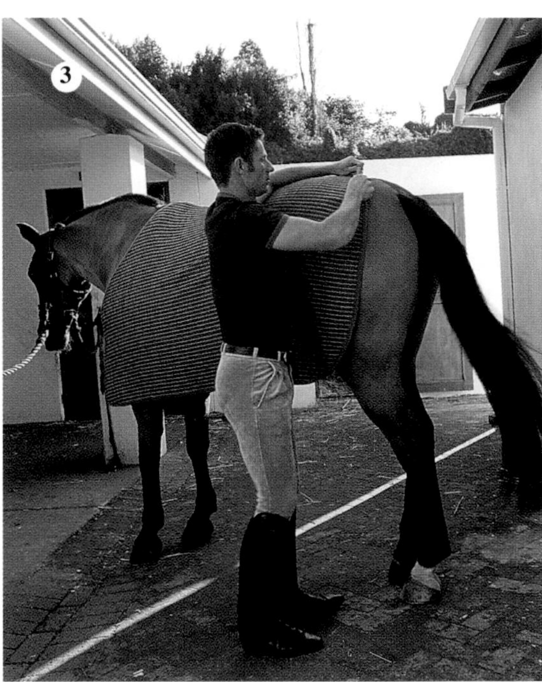
3

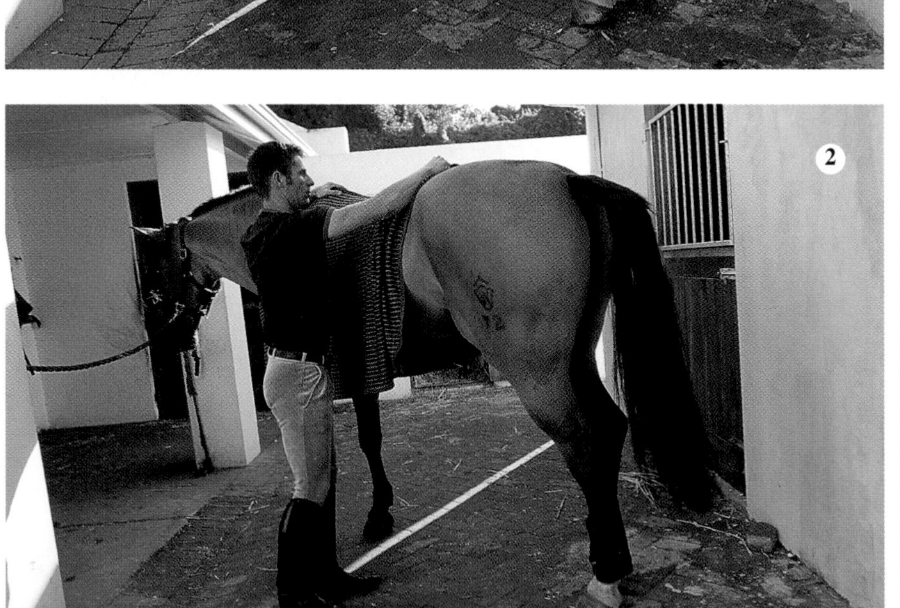
2

4

TACKING UP

The act of putting on the equipment used for riding a horse is called tacking up. If the horse is loose in the stable, the bridle goes on first; but if it is tied up with a head collar, the saddle can be fitted first.

PUTTING ON THE BRIDLE

To put on the bridle, which should be correctly adjusted beforehand, approach the horse from the left (or near) side and carefully place the reins over its head. Holding the bridle midway, remove the head collar, placing your right hand over the horse's nose and taking the bridle into your right hand.

With your left hand, position the bit under the horse's mouth (1). Exerting a light pressure on the corners of the horse's mouth will encourage the horse to open its mouth and accept the bit. As the bit goes in, with you taking care not to bang the horse's teeth, you can reach up and place the head-piece over one ear at a time.

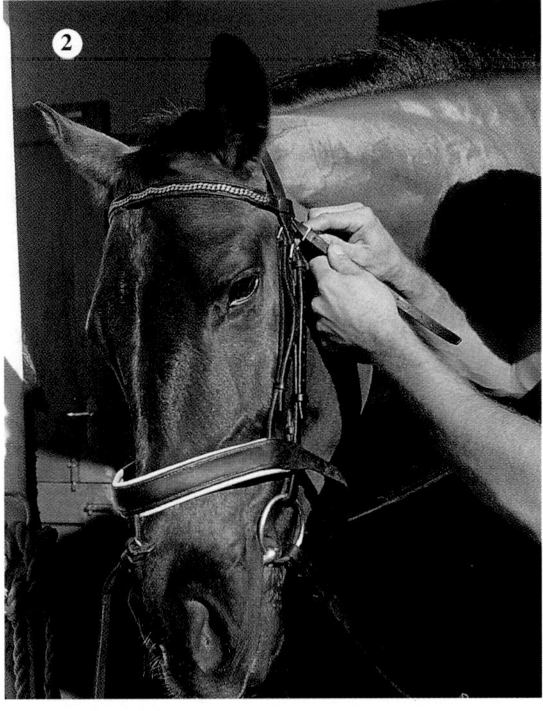

It is worth taking the time to learn how to put on and adjust the bridle correctly, as an ill-fitting bridle is not only uncomfortable for the horse, but could result in reduced control for the rider.

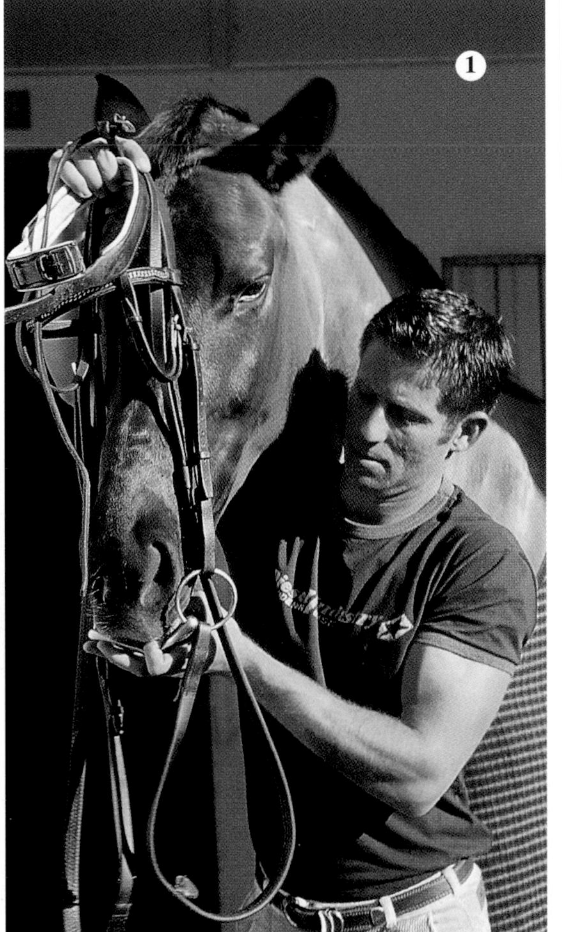

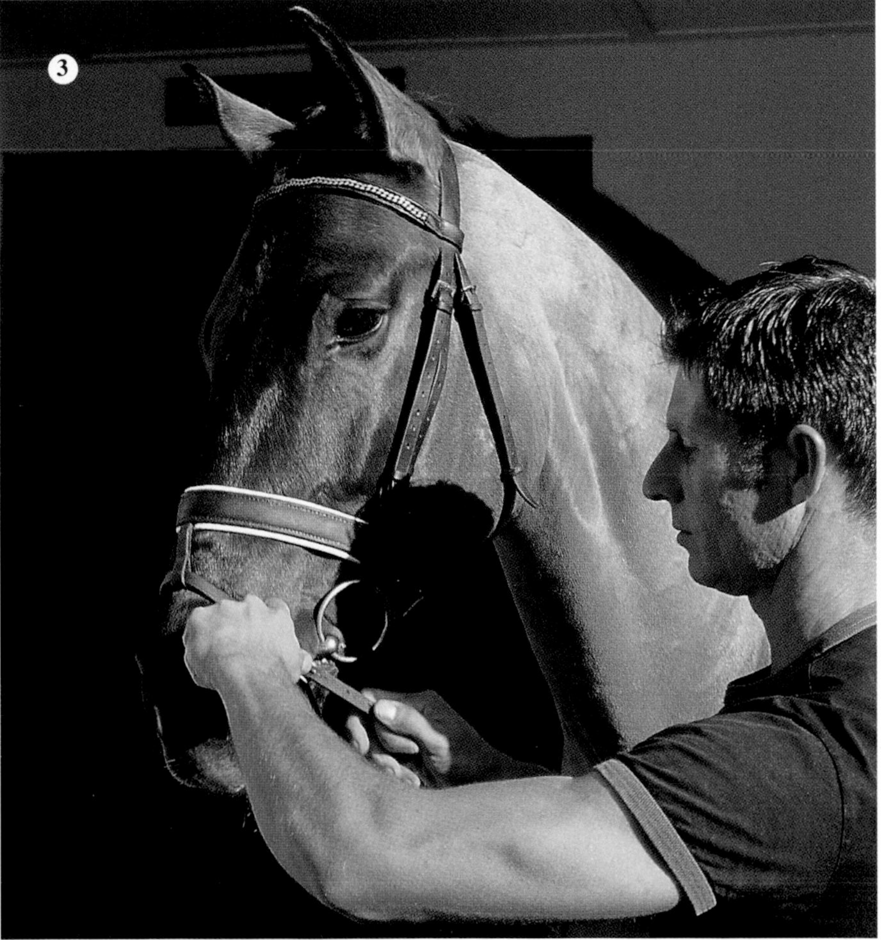

Horses come in a variety of shapes and widths. A well-made, professionally fitted saddle will improve the horse's comfort and prevent the formation of painful saddle sores.

After checking that no mane or forelock is caught in the leather work, and the bridle is lying comfortably and without twisting, you can fasten the throatlatch (2) (allow one hand's width between it and the horse's throat), then the noseband (3).

A cavesson noseband should lie one finger's width below the bottom of the horse's cheekbone and be fastened to allow one finger's width between the noseband and the horse's nasal bone. A drop noseband should lie four fingers' width above the horse's nostrils and should be fastened securely enough to prevent the horse crossing his jaw, but with enough room for the horse to be able to mouth the bit comfortably.

SADDLING UP

This is done from the horse's left, or 'near' side. If using a numnah, or saddle pad, place this on the horse's back first, a little further up on the withers than it will rest eventually.

With the stirrup irons run up and the girth (attached on the right side) placed ready over the top of the saddle, lift the saddle clear of the horse (1) and allow it to settle gently on its back, then slide both the saddle and pad into position (2). Check that the pad is flat, unwrinkled and evenly positioned on both sides before taking the girth down on the right. Return to the left side of the horse and fasten the girth securely enough to keep the saddle in place (3 and 4). When the saddle is correctly placed, the girth should lie flat about 10cm (4in) from the point of the elbow. The girth can be tightened later by degrees before mounting, but it is not fair on a horse to fasten its girth up to the riding position immediately. It can cause discomfort and abrasion and can also make the horse girth-shy.

2

1

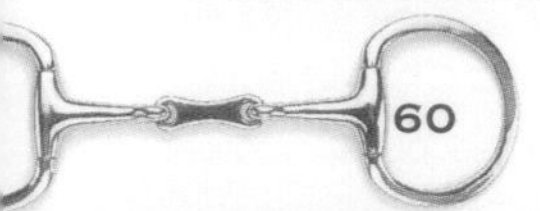

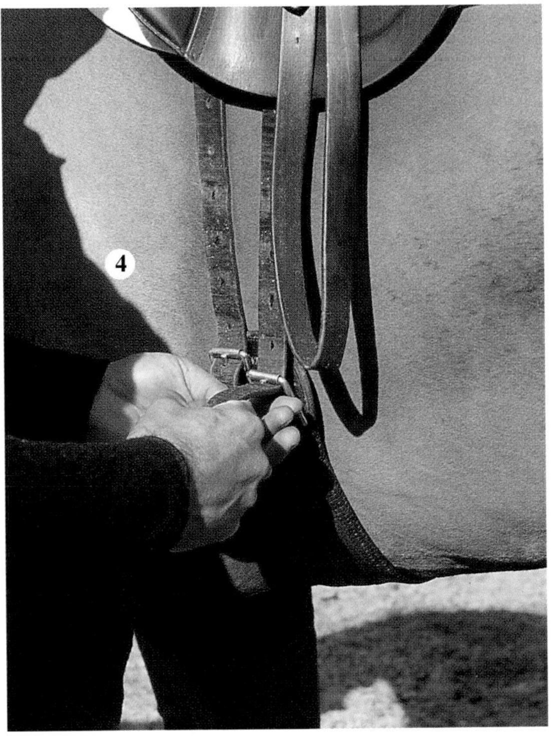

CARE OF TACK

Saddlery is generally very expensive, so it makes sense to look after equipment that, with good care, can last for decades. From a safety point of view, regular maintenance and checking can help prevent accidents and injury to both horse and rider.

Tack should be cleaned daily after use. Leather should be wiped clean with a damp (not wet) cloth, then finished with saddle soap. Leather needs to be kept supple to avoid cracking, and periodic applications of proprietary leather dressing can help prevent this. This is also an opportunity to take the tack apart and thoroughly check all stitching, buckles, etc.

After cleaning, bridles should be hung neatly on bridle pegs and saddles placed on saddle racks. Rugs (blankets) can be folded away or placed on special racks to air and dry before re-use.

Metalwork (bits and stirrups) can be washed in warm soapy water, rinsed, then finished with a dry cloth. Synthetic equipment should be cared for according to the manufacturer's recommendations.

Generally bandages, synthetic girths and rugs can be cleaned in a washing machine. Saddle cloths should be washed frequently, as dry sweat is not only unappealing, but can cause chafing. Tack should be stored in a ventilated, damp-free area to avoid mildew.

Regular cleaning and maintenance not only protects valuable tack, but enables the rider to spot potential problems before they occur.

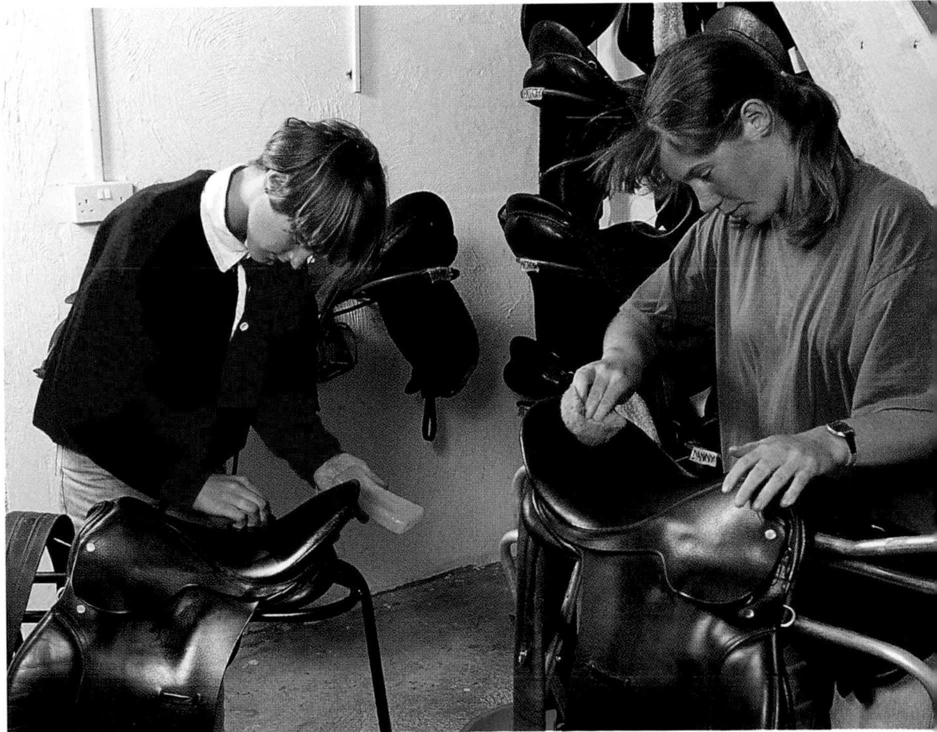

Top to bottom *A velvet-covered hard hat; dressage top hat; jockey-style skull cap and lightweight safety helmet.*

Clothing and equipment for the rider

The choice of casual riding wear has been revolutionized in recent years to incorporate a wide range of clothing in seasonally changing styles and colours. The influence of fashion makes a quick visit to the shops after your ride much less of a head-turning experience than it used to be.

In contrast, formal clothing for competitions still retains much of the original styling, which evolved from military uniforms and the traditional dress of the English hunting field, while encompassing new fabrics and designs that give the rider enhanced flexibility in the saddle, as well as improved protection in the more dangerous elements of the sport.

As with all risk sports, you can minimize the risk factor by using the right equipment. In this respect, safety first and fashion later is the wise rider's motto.

Hats and helmets

A hard hat with a safety harness or chin strap is an essential piece of equipment designed to protect against accident or injury and should be worn by all riders whenever they are around horses.

For a beginner, there are two types of riding hat to consider: the traditional velvet-covered, flexible-peak version, or the jockey-style skull-cap (crash helmet), which can be covered in any fabric or colour.

All reputable riding schools should insist that you ride in up-to-date, approved headgear, both from the point of view of your own safety and for their own liability and insurance requirements.

As there are various safety standards throughout the world, only buy a hat that meets the latest authorized standards (Europe: EN 1384, UK: PAS 015, USA: ASTM F1163, Australia/New Zealand AS/NZ 3838). You can be sure that any hat bearing these standards has been through rigorous testing and will offer significantly greater protection against potentially fatal head injuries than previous standards.

Finding the right standard hat is only the first step. It must also fit securely. An experienced supplier will ensure this, but if you are using borrowed equipment, you may have to try a number of hats to find one that fits you properly.

Bear in mind that any severe blow to a hat may damage it and reduce its shock absorbency, in which case it should be replaced.

Starting out

When starting out on your first lessons, it isn't necessary, or particularly wise, to invest in a whole new wardrobe. Many items, even hats, can often be hired or borrowed from your riding school until you are committed enough to riding to make the investment.

What you will need, however, is a stout pair of boots or shoes with a defined heel to ensure that your foot cannot slip through the stirrup. Ridged or all-in-one soles such as those on trainers (sneakers) are not safe riding footwear. A boot is more comfortable than a shoe, as it offers ankle support and better protection. If a horse places its foot on yours, it won't be aware of it but you undoubtedly will!

Trousers with a soft inside seam and preferably some stretch will be a lot more comfortable than jeans, where chafing from the double inner seam can do a lot of damage to the inside of your knees. Similarly, a pair of long socks is less likely to bunch up and cause pinching than shorter ones.

Wearing a close-fitting top will help your instructor ascertain and correct your body posture much better than if you wear a loose-fitting sweatshirt. Also, avoid choosing a top that is longer than hip length, as you'll be forever be pulling it out from under your seat.

Gloves are essential, and a pair of relatively thin leather gloves will do nicely for your first lessons. Thicker gloves will impair your feel and mobility in holding the reins.

The well-dressed rider

Once you have decided that riding is something you would like to pursue, you will want to 'look the part' by acquiring some items of conventional riding gear.

Boots

All riding boots should provide some protection against stray hooves, be well-fitting to avoid heel rubs, and should support the foot in the stirrup.

For everyday riding, ankle-length jodhpur boots and half-chaps are very popular. Ankle boots based on the traditional 'paddock boot' with laces, zips or elastic sides are much favoured by professional riders working at home, as they are designed to be comfortable for walking as well as riding, which is convenient for the occasional rider, as the boots can then also be used for general wear.

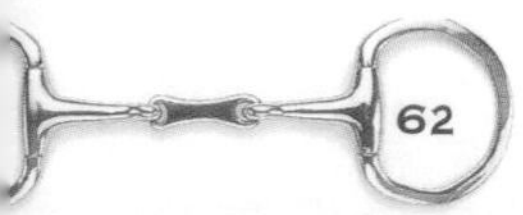

Half-chaps are leggings made of suede or leather, with extra padding for protection on the inside of the calf. An elasticized panel is often included for a closer fit. They are designed to give support, protection and a good contact with the horse.

As you become more accomplished, you may prefer to ride in full-length boots. Apart from the traditional black leather 'top' boots (or dress boots) used for competitions, several manufacturers produce the same style of boot in a range of colours and materials and it is even possible to buy boots finished in suede or denim for the 'leg' of the boot. Waterproof rubber versions are popular as they are hard-wearing and long-lasting. Zips in long boots have revolutionized riders' lives, providing an alternative to the struggle involved in getting long boots on and off.

Jodhpurs and breeches

Jodhpurs are full-length riding trousers designed to be worn with short boots. Breeches have a shorter leg, ending just below the calf, with a Velcro fastening to ensure a smooth, comfortable fit under long boots. Breeches and jodhpurs are both made from fabric that has a certain amount of stretch, whether of entirely man-made fibres or of cotton mixed with Lycra or Elastane.

No matter what other clothing you choose, gloves, an approved safety hat and a pair of boots or shoes with a defined heel are essential items for every rider.

WHIPS & SPURS

These constitute artificial aids and should be used primarily as a refinement of the rider's natural aids: leg, hand and voice. There are times when a horse needs a reminder, or reinforcement. For example, you should always carry a whip when riding horses on the road to ensure you have back-up if the horse shies, but punishment as such is no reason for carrying a whip or wearing spurs.

Spurs are made from metal and come in a variety of lengths and shapes. They require a steady leg and a secure seat and are therefore not suitable for the novice rider, although a blunt spur may be used for general riding and jumping.

In advanced dressage, spurs are compulsory. Dressage spurs have a wheel known as a 'rowel' that might at times look medieval, but its intended use is as the ultimate refinement of the rider's leg aid.

For jumping and general riding, a short whip is carried. To apply it correctly, the rider takes both reins into one hand and taps the whip behind his leg to reinforce his signal to the horse. The long, tapered whip, which is used in dressage and schooling on the flat, is either carried by the rider or employed from the floor by the instructor when training the horse in advanced movements such as piaffe and passage.

There are many different designs – pleated or smooth top, close fit or the 'baggy' design based on the original jodhpur shape – but all will incorporate reinforcement on the inside of the knee, known as the strapping.

Breeches with a 'continental seat' – where the whole seat is strapped with self fabric, leather, suede or a synthetic alternative – are particularly favoured by dressage riders. As with jodhpurs, the wide range of colours and designs has made breeches almost a fashion item among riders. Whatever the look, though, a good comfortable fit is essential.

Gloves

Specially designed riding gloves have reinforcement between the first finger and thumb and between the little and ring fingers. There are many varieties and styles of glove on offer, made of everything from hi-tech fabrics that provide optimum grip and warmth to soft leather. A knitted glove with synthetic 'bobbles' on the inside palm and fingers is effective, comfortable and competitively priced.

Tops

The choice of what to wear on your upper body will be determined by the time of the year and the type of work you are doing. The main guideline is that, whatever you choose, the garment should allow you to move your shoulders and arms freely.

Horses need regular exercise, so riders in extreme climates must be prepared for all weather conditions. Many casual jackets and other items of clothing designed for riders today combine ease of wear with the technological advantages of cold-weather fabrics such as Goretex and Polartec, or Coolmax, which is perfect for hotter climates. These new fabrics keep you warm (or cool) and dry, yet allow the skin to breathe, and because they are lightweight and flexible, they do not impede movement.

COMPETITION CLOTHING

Once you start entering for competitions, you will find that each aspect of the sport has its own set of clothing standards and requirements, which vary from novice to advanced levels.

Beginners are advised to borrow the required items until they are confident that the additional expense of acquiring their own will not be wasted.

Germany's Nicole Uphoff wears the formal clothing of a top dressage competitor.

Dressage

In the UK, a tweed coat can be worn for dressage tests at club level and in unaffiliated competitions, but beyond that the clothing requirements become more strict. At levels lower than Prix St Georges (the entry level for international competition), a short jacket in black or navy is worn with a shirt, and either a white tie or hunting stock (a specially tied cravat). Breeches of white, beige or cream are worn with long black boots and a velvet cap, bowler or short crowned top hat. Gloves should match breeches.

At Prix St Georges and higher level competitions, the elegant tail-coat (also known as a frock coat or, in the USA, a shadbelly) is worn with a top hat.

Most of the top international dressage riders favour a very high-cut boot with rigid outer leg shell that supports and enhances the longer leg position used in dressage.

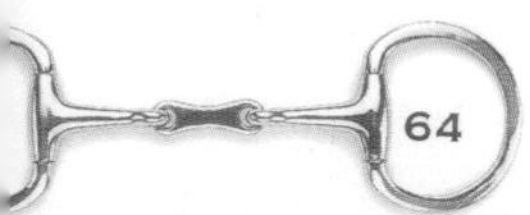

Nona Garson, on Loro Piana Rhythmical, riding for the USA, at the 1998 World Equestrian Games.

Stuart Black of Canada, riding Market Venture at Badminton 1998, clearly shows his body protector.

Show jumping

At club level in the UK, tweed coats are often worn. In higher level classes, as well as on the international circuit, the traditional outfit is a black, navy or dark green coat for ladies and a red coat for men, or national colours. Except in official championships, riders often wear coats in their sponsor's colours.

Although international rules permit riders to wear hard hats without a chin strap, it is inadvisable for novices to do so. Jumping riders often favour a softer boot, as it allows closer contact with the horse and more flexibility to the lower leg.

Cross-country

The demands of cross-country, even at a low level, require the highest attention to safety. Standard headwear for competitions is a jockey skull cap, which must be firmly secured.

Competition rules at both national and international levels require riders to wear a body protector, designed to protect the internal organs and rib cage. The British Equestrian Trade Association has introduced a three-class standard for body protectors, to enable riders to select one that is suitable for their needs. Class 1 (green label) is a lightweight protector for general riding; Class 2 (orange label) provides an intermediate level of protection and is also suitable for general use and novice cross-country; Class 3 (purple label) offers the highest level of protection for high risk situations, heavier riders, those with brittle bones or with previous injuries.

A sweater or shirt in the rider's colours goes under or over the body protector. A hunting stock offers some protection to the neck. Nonslip gloves are essential and riders frequently wear a stopwatch to check their progress over the timed course.

CHAPTER FOUR

GETTING INTO THE SADDLE

While it is true to say that you can take part in some sports without tuition, this is not true of horse riding. First and foremost is the question of safety. This is not unusual in many sports, but here we are dealing with a live animal rather than an inanimate piece of equipment, which means that prospective riders have to understand how to manage a horse, as well as learn the basics of riding.

In addition to knowing the basic correct signals to start, stop and steer a horse, the co-ordination, tact and timing that make riding a pleasure, and later an art, take time to develop. As with many other sports, the more experience and technical expertise you have, the more enjoyable riding becomes.

There are plenty of reasons for learning to ride: to acquire a new skill, for sport, fun and relaxation, as a different way of exploring the countryside, or simply to learn about one of the best friends man has ever had – but whatever your reason for taking it up, riding is more enjoyable if done properly.

Before you start learning to ride, it is worth working on attaining at least a reasonable level of general fitness and suppleness. Not only will this make the first few lessons more comfortable as you use new muscles (in some cases muscles you didn't know you had!), it will also most definitely help your overall balance and co-ordination.

Riding is not about strength alone. It is more about refining the signals the rider gives the horse. This is what makes top class sporting partnerships such a joy to watch, when horse and rider are working in harmony together, without any obvious signals. This level of expertise only comes with experience and training, but right from the start, good general muscle tone is the first step towards achieving the poise and posture that enable the rider to give those signals with refinement.

In riding, as with many other sports, there is 'training equipment' and 'advanced equipment'. A well-trained horse with a calm, laid-back temperament is the ideal mount for training beginner riders. However, this is not necessarily going to be the most beautiful horse in the stable. It is no rarity for a starter rider's face to fall on being introduced to his

Riding school pupils benefit from professional instruction and well-schooled horses.

or her first equine partner, having been led past the elegant head looking over the previous stable door, but your 'training' horse should be treated with the utmost respect, regardless of its looks. This capable, trustworthy partner is the horse that will help you overcome your nervousness, give you the confidence to try, and ignore your mistakes when you get it wrong. It will give you the right 'feel' when you get it right and you will be rewarded with the most wonderful sense of achievement. When you move on to a higher level of capability, and the opportunity to ride the horse of your choice, you'll never forget your first 'trainer'.

CHOOSING AN INSTRUCTOR

Riding is a risk sport, but it is a controlled risk if you put yourself in the hands of a knowledgeable and qualified instructor. When seeking a suitable person, riding skill in itself is not the sole criterion to apply. Certainly, a good instructor should be a skilled rider, but very importantly, he or she should be trained in how to teach. An accredited instructor should also hold a valid first aid qualification and have appropriate professional insurance.

A scheme to determine qualification levels for riding instructors across international boundaries has 28 member nations on four continents. In the

A qualified instructor is not just a good rider, but has also been trained to teach.

UK, the British Horse Society (BHS) administers the secretariat for the International Group for Qualifications in Training Horse and Rider, which issues 'instructor passports' in participation with national equine federations. Apart from monitoring the standards and qualifications of registered instructors, another advantage of this scheme is that if you fancy combining a starter riding course with a holiday in another country, you can be sure of finding a suitable venue and a qualified instructor.

For details of recognized and approved riding schools in your area, the first port of call will be your national equestrian federation, although personal recommendation is always a good indicator when sourcing a riding school.

A reputable riding school should welcome a visit from a prospective pupil before he or she begins a course of lessons. At a well-run school, your first impression should be of order and efficiency. It doesn't matter whether the buildings are state of the art or not, but wherever horses are housed, keeping yard equipment tidied away isn't just an indicator of pride in the place, but also of safety awareness.

The horses should be clean and tidy too. Horses ready for lessons might be having a doze, but they should look happy and well cared for. Tack should look clean and in a good state of repair; again, this is a safety essential.

Do ask to watch a lesson in progress. An enclosed arena, either indoors or outdoors, is a must for your early lessons, but any serious training in dressage or show jumping also takes place in an arena, so it is an integral part of reasonable school facilities.

A good riding instructor should appear confident and enthusiastic. The nature of the game demands that commands are issued and responded to by both horse and pupil, and so the instructor has to come over loud and clear across a large area. Expect a bold approach, but remember that this is a hobby, and you don't have to subject yourself to drilling from a sergeant major! Conversely, you shouldn't be left feeling at sea with your new sport as your instructor stands slouched in the corner with a cup of coffee.

The pupil who wants to ride only for fun and exercise is just as valuable an asset to a riding school's economy as the serious competition student. Discussing your aspirations will enable the school to partner you with an instructor and horse suited to helping you achieve what you want from riding. As your riding develops, keep up the assessment of your needs and abilities. If you are a bit nervous and feel you are being pushed too hard, say so – and do the same if you don't feel you are making as much progress as you would like.

If you walk away from watching a lesson feeling encouraged to give riding a try, you've found your school. As a prospective client, you should be welcomed with open arms. At schools recognized by an official national equestrian body, your checklist should be ticked with good impressions. If you have any negative feelings during your visit, extend your search in another direction, but if you are happy, sign up and get going.

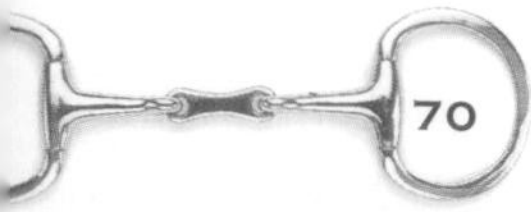

LEARNING TO RIDE

Until a starter rider becomes familiar around horses and gets a feel for how they behave, it is natural to experience a certain amount of nerves. Arriving at the stables a little earlier than your lesson and assisting with getting the horse ready helps form an acquaintance with it and build up your confidence.

When watching a proficient horseman around horses, it becomes clear that movements and actions are carried out smoothly and without a fuss. There is no pussy-footing around, just a quiet efficiency and a good application of attention to detail.

LEADING THE HORSE

The starter rider's initial moment of being in charge of the horse is to lead it from the stable to the arena or school under the watchful eye of the instructor. The stirrups should be run up on the saddle with the leathers passed through the stirrup irons to prevent them slipping, as dangling stirrups can easily frighten the horse or get caught on gates or stable doors.

Begin by taking the reins gently over the horse's head and stand by the horse's shoulder on its left side. With your right hand, hold the reins together near the bit, and take hold of the rest of the reins with your left hand to ensure they don't dangle free. Horses have a dangerous habit of becoming entangled in loose or dangling reins.

Leading a horse safely is ensured by encouraging it forwards as you stand by its shoulder. It then walks with you; you don't pull it along. Turning a horse while leading is commonly done to the right, with the handler on the outside, so you have more control and the horse is less likely to step on your toes.

When leading a horse, make sure that the you hold the reins clear of the ground so that the horse can't become entangled in them.

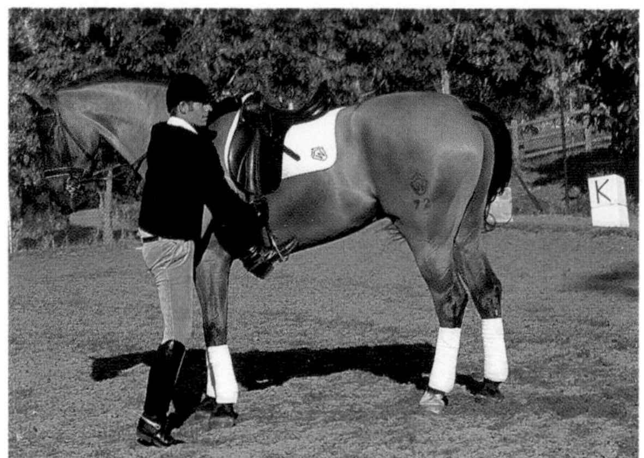

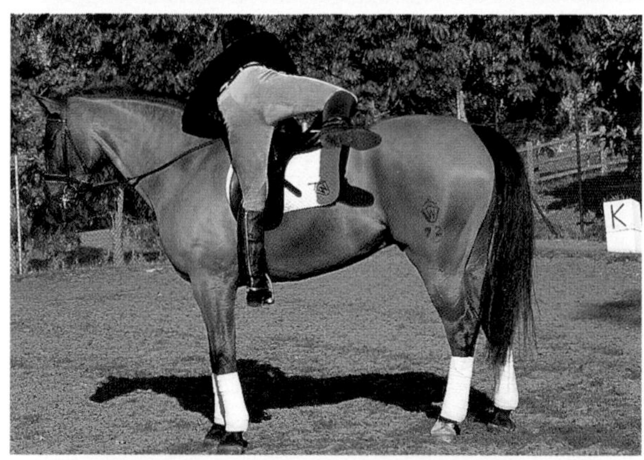

To mount a horse, stand on its left side and put your left foot in the stirrup. Grasp the back of the saddle, push off with your right foot and swing it over the horse's back, landing gently in the saddle.

Getting on and off

The standard way of mounting and dismounting a horse should be adhered to, simply because it is the safest way. A well-trained horse should always stand obediently for its rider to get on and off.

When pulling down or adjusting the stirrups or tightening the girth – which should always be checked before mounting – keep hold of the horse, even when the reins are over its head, by putting an arm through the reins. Loose horses can be dangerous to themselves and others.

Your instructor will advise on stirrup length, but generally, if you stretch your arm out along the stirrup, the correct length for you will be the approximate distance from your armpit to your fist.

When you are ready to mount, stand on the left side of the horse with your back to its head. Hold the reins in your left hand with slightly more contact on the right rein in case the horse starts to move, and place your left hand on the base of the horse's neck. Turn the outside of the stirrup iron towards you with your right hand. As you place the ball of your left foot in the stirrup, lean your knee towards the horse so your toe does not dig into its side. Grasp the back of the saddle with your right hand, then hop up into the saddle by pushing up from your right foot. Swing your right leg carefully over the horse's back, taking care not to kick it. As you land softly in the saddle, put your right foot in the stirrup and take up the reins in both hands.

This should be one smooth movement, which takes practice. However, never think of it as cheating to use a mounting block, or to ask someone else to give you a leg-up. It is easier on both your own and the horse's back and the saddle.

The normal way to hold the reins is so they run up between the third and fourth finger of each hand and out between the thumb and index finger, with the thumb on top.

When dismounting, rest the left hand, holding the reins, on the horse's neck. Put your right hand on the front of the saddle (the pommel), take your feet out of the stirrups and swing your right leg carefully over the back of the horse. As you do this, your body should turn towards the saddle as you slide gently to the ground. It may sound like a major gymnastic exercise, but it is easy, and with a bit of practice will soon become second nature.

FIRST LESSONS

Ideally, your first lessons should be on the lunge. The instructor, on foot, has the horse on a long lead, called a 'lunge line', and controls the horse, which is moving in a large circle around him or her, by means of voice commands and a guiding lunge whip.

Lungeing allows the novice rider to concentrate on developing a relaxed position without having to worry about steering or controlling the horse. If you are anxious to be off riding on your own, this first stage might seem a bit of a 'cop-out', but establishing a secure seat and developing balance on the lunge will enable more rapid progress to be made later on. Once security has been established at walk, trot and canter, and you can apply the signals (aids) that ask the horse to go forwards and backwards or change pace, joining a group of riders of a similar standard is the next progression.

One on one lessons are not always the best policy for a beginner at this stage. Instead, in a class situation, under your instructor's direction and mounted on your schoolmaster (an experienced horse used for training starter riders), you will begin thinking for yourself and developing a feeling for the finer points of riding and controlling a horse.

After a few lessons, when you start to feel more confident and in balance, you will be introduced to various exercises designed to improve your poise and control and further develop your security and confidence as a rider. These exercises will include short periods of riding with your feet out of the stirrups and with the stirrups crossed in front of your saddle. Your instructor may ask you to ride with your arms outstretched while on the lunge rein. You will also be taught how to check and adjust your stirrups and girth while in the saddle and how to handle and control your horse in the presence of other horses in the school.

Once you have established real security in the saddle in walk, trot and canter, you will be taught the jumping, or 'light' seat and be introduced to small fences. You will also begin riding in a group outside the confines of the arena or school.

Regardless of whether you just want to learn to ride for pleasure, or whether you have ambitions to be a dressage rider or specialize in cross-country, good all-round training and experience is the best grounding for long-term riding enjoyment.

To dismount, take both feet out of the stirrups, place your right hand on the front of the saddle, swing your right leg over the horse's back and slide to the ground in one smooth movement

Basic Exercises

There are various exercises that can be done on horseback to improve balance and control, as well as develop a sense of security and confidence as a rider.

Children are often taught exercises that promote suppleness and ease of movement, but most adults are better off preparing for riding by going to the local gym!

Right *Riding without stirrups, and with the instructor controlling the horse by means of a lunge rein, the novice can concentrate on developing a secure seat.*
Below *Holding the arms out to the side encourages the rider to maintain a sense of balance as the horse moves. Both the rider and instructor should wear hard hats or safety helmets, as well as gloves.*

Top and left *Bending and stretching exercises help to promote flexibility and suppleness.*

Above *Riding school classes give novices the opportunity to learn to control their horse in a group situation, among riders of a similar standard and level of experience.*

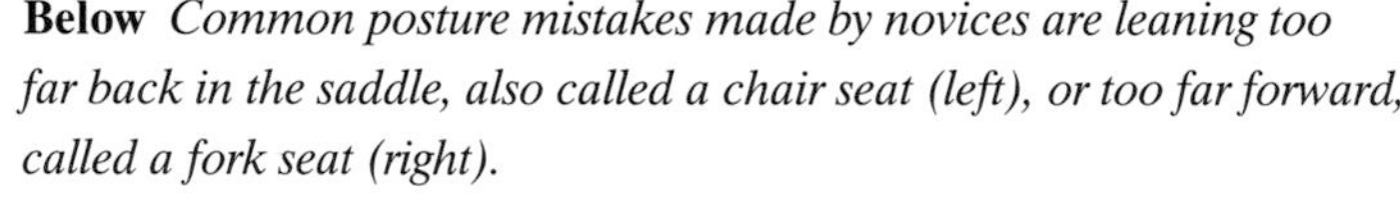

Below *Common posture mistakes made by novices are leaning too far back in the saddle, also called a chair seat (left), or too far forward, called a fork seat (right).*

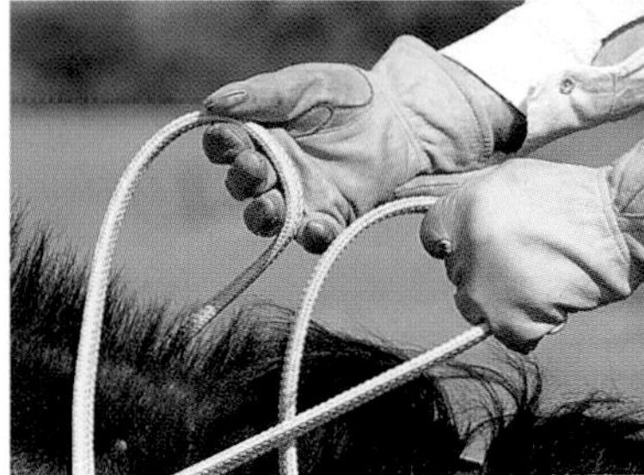

Above *The reins should run between the third and fourth finger of each hand and out between the thumb and index finger, with the thumb on top.*

Left *Keep your back straight, your legs close to the horse's side, your heels down and your hands low.*

RIDING AIDS AND CORRECT SEAT

The rider should always look straight ahead, with the head high and the chin up.

Sit 'tall in the saddle', with a straight back, but without any tension in the upper body.

The elbows should be bent and a straight line maintained from the bit through the reins to the forearm.

The seat should rest in the lower part of the saddle, with the weight evenly distributed on both seat bones.

The knees are bent slightly and relaxed, and should not be used to grip the saddle.

The lower leg should slope backward from the knee, with the calf in contact with the horse's side.

The ball of the foot, resting on the stirrup, should be under the rider's centre of gravity.

The rider's seat

There are two primary types of 'seat' (or posture): the basic, or dressage, seat used for general riding, and the light, or forward, seat used for riding across country and jumping. Whatever the type, the correct position, known as 'seat', is not just aesthetically pleasing, but essential for effective communication with the horse. The aids can only be applied properly if the rider is sitting securely, in balance, and with the suppleness needed to go with the horse's movement rather than stiffening against it.

The basic, or dressage, seat

The most commonly-used seat for all riding on the flat is the basic, or dressage, seat. You can use the basic seat with either a general-purpose or a dressage saddle, but in a specially designed dressage saddle the depth of seat and length of leg will be greater.

In the basic seat the rider sits upright in the saddle and a theoretical line can be drawn through the rider's shoulder, hip and heel. Other elements of the basic seat can vary as not all riders – or horses – are the same shape and size, but this line is constant.

Good horses and good riders come in all shapes and sizes, so if you have ever been told that to look elegant on a horse you have to be tall, slim and long-legged, forget it. Granted, longer arms and a short lower back will make it easier for a rider to carry the hands low and stable, while a round inner thigh will be less easy to rest flat against the saddle than a slim one, but every individual, with training and development, can make the most of their own shape to become an effective and elegant rider.

In a good dressage, or basic, seat the buttocks should be in the lowest part of the saddle and the rider's body weight should be distributed equally over both seat bones and thighs, with the muscles free of tension. Any tightness will raise the seat, which means the rider is sitting 'above' the horse.

The upper body should be 'tall in the saddle', with relaxed shoulders – poised but not tense – with the head proud and looking forward. The upper arms and elbows are carried close to the body and the lower arm low towards the horse's withers. The hands are held with thumbs uppermost, closed but not tightened over the reins. Clamped elbows will lead to stiffness in the hands, while sticking-out elbows destabilize the upper body, arms and hands. From the side, the bit, rein, and hand-to-elbow line should be straight and unbroken, as any break will affect the rider's ability to maintain a soft contact with the horse's mouth and give sensitive rein aids.

In later lessons, further development of this toned poise allows the rider to use the back muscles as a refined aid in the half-halt and in transitions. The phrase 'bracing the back' really means more of a 'hold-then-flex' reaction than an actual bracing.

The knee is bent so the lower leg slopes backward and the calf rests in contact with the horse. The foot is slightly behind the girth and under the rider's centre of gravity (the hip-heel angle), and the thigh should rest flat against the saddle. Turning the knee or thigh out causes tension and destabilizes the seat. In conventional riding, it is important not to ride with too long stirrups, as this reduces the movement-absorbing capacity of the knee and causes a lack of balance. The rider will end up sitting on his fork rather than his seat bones, and will not be able to control his lower leg. Conversely, stirrups that are too short will lead to a 'chair seat', in which the rider will not be able to sit deep in the saddle and his lower leg will be stiff and too far forwards. The ball of the foot, resting on the stirrup, allows the ankle to flex and the heel to lower slightly. 'Heels down' is often heard in lessons, but it does not mean with exaggerated pressure. With the leg in the right position, the knee and ankle absorb the horse's motion. The toes should face forward, not be turned too far in or out.

The light, or jumping, seat

For riding over fences, hacking (riding) out, or when schooling young horses, the rider needs, in degrees, to be able to take more weight off the horse's back and adjust quickly and smoothly to changes in balance and pace.

A jumping saddle or a general-purpose saddle with a shorter stirrup length allows for a more forward position of the knee. For a hack round the field after a schooling session, for example, the stirrups would be raised by just one or two holes. For a jumping or cross-country session, the rider may raise his or her stirrups between four to six holes. The shortest stirrup length is generally used for the fastest work, such as the steeplechase phase in a three-day event, when the rider's weight needs to be completely off the horse's back.

When jumping, the rider lifts his or her weight out of the saddle. The elbows, hands and arms must allow the horse's neck to stretch forward.

Components of the jumping seat: The rider's upper body is bent forward from the hips and the weight is absorbed more on the thigh, through the knee and down to the heel. Although the rider's weight comes mostly out of the saddle when jumping, when the light seat is used for riding on the flat, the rider should keep close to the saddle, with his or her upper body weight over the horse's centre of gravity, to ensure a secure position. As in the basic dressage seat, stability in the upper body and arms and elasticity through the hip, knee and ankle are vital.

With the foot a little more 'home' in the stirrup (further forward in it), the heel is deeper in the downward position as it absorbs more of the rider's weight. The knee is closed more securely to the saddle for stability. The lower leg should be secure, as if it slips back while jumping a fence this will destabilize the rider's position and lessen the flexibility he or she needs to go with the horse before, over and after a fence. The hands and arms will be more forward with the elbows slightly in front of the body, but the bit-to-hand line should be maintained.

The rider's seat over a fence: The rider needs to be balanced and secure in order to adapt quickly to the different phases of jumping – towards, over and away from the fence. On approaching the fence, the light seat needs to be adopted by lifting the weight out of the saddle, with the leg stable and effective,

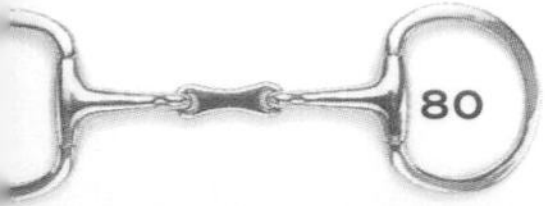

but not too far forward. He or she should also look forward, to the other side of the fence. Looking back or to the side affects not only the rider's balance but the horse's balance as well.

During take-off the horse's momentum should enable the rider to fold forward from the hip, the degree of forward bend depending on the height of the fence, while pressing down into his or her heel to keep the lower leg stable.

From the shoulder the arms should 'allow' forward as the horse's neck stretches forward. In the air, the rider's body should allow further stretch. How far out of the saddle he or she comes is largely dependent on the height of the fence, but the rider should follow the movement smoothly and allow with the hands. Flinging your weight forward will unbalance the horse. The rider's back should also be kept supple and straight through the horizontal position, as a 'bottoms up' posture will lead to lack of balance through the landing phase.

As the horse lands, the rider's upper body and, crucially, the contact with the horse's mouth, should adjust smoothly. Sitting up too quickly or being left behind the movement can affect the way a horse jumps. On landing, the rider should continue to ride forward in balance.

HOW WE RIDE HORSES

The signals by which we control and direct horses are known collectively as the 'aids'. The rider influences the horse through his or her seat (or weight), and leg and rein aids. In essence, weight and leg aids are forward-driving aids, while rein aids are restraining ones, but refined riding is a combination of influences, and none is ever used in isolation.

Ideally, all aids should be applied lightly and reacted to immediately. For a trained rider on a trained horse this is much easier of course, but in reality there are times when even an experienced rider requires stronger aids. The beginner rider will need to develop the seat and co-ordination to apply aids with increasing lightness and effectiveness.

There are two main points to remember. Firstly, an aid can only be responded to if the horse understands what you want. Secondly, if you have to ask a bit more strongly, it should be followed up with a lighter application when you get the right response so as to maintain and improve the horse's sensitivity.

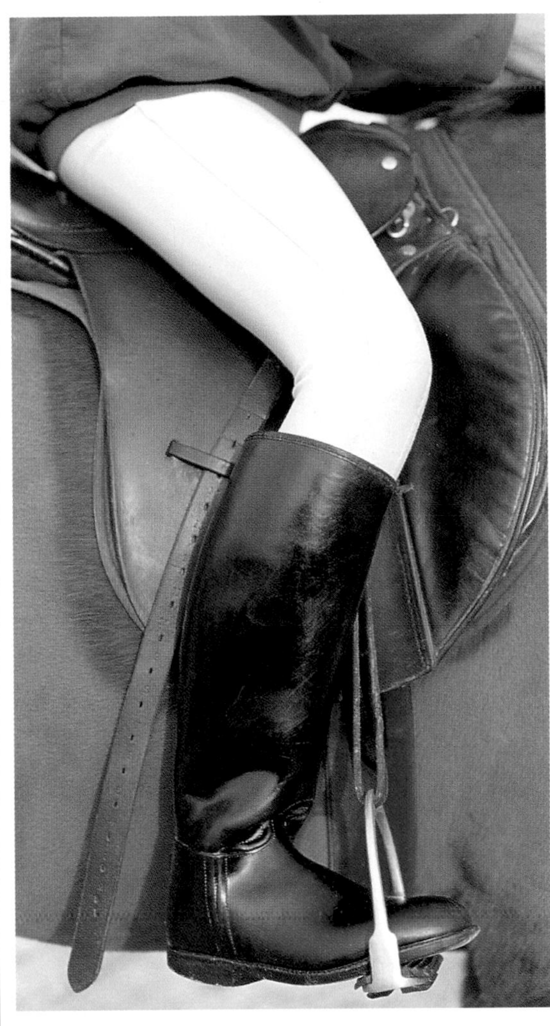

Leg aids are used to drive the horse forward, sideways and regulate pace. They can only be given if the proper position is maintained, with the lower leg in light contact with the horse's side.

LEG AIDS

Leg aids can be used in three ways: to drive the horse forward, to push it sideways, and to regulate.

To send the horse forward, the leg is applied just behind the girth as a nudging action with the lower leg. Once the aid has been responded to, the rider's leg should hang relaxed at the horse's side, retaining contact as the rider's shape fits around that of the horse. Clamping the leg to the horse's side or continuous kicking will only act as an irritant.

To push the horse sideways, the outside leg (the rider's leg away from which the horse moves) is taken back slightly more behind the girth and kept in position with a nudging aid as the horse moves sideways. In moving sideways (lateral work), and on all turns and circles, the inside leg, in the relaxed position, is the regulator, creating the degree of bend and maintaining the impulsion (forward energy).

REIN AIDS

Rein aids are given in co-ordination with leg and seat aids. Rein aids can be regulating, asking or allowing. The latter two are applied in tandem. For example, if an asking, restraining aid is applied in order to slow the horse, when the horse has responded the rider must also respond by yielding (or allowing) the horse to move forward in the new pace straight afterwards.

An **asking, restraining aid** is applied by the rider closing the fingers on the reins while the seat and back, instead of following the movement, goes into a slight bracing action. If the horse does not respond immediately, the restrain and allow action should be reapplied until it does. Pulling continuously on the reins has an entirely negative effect; the horse will brace against the rider's hands by becoming stronger on the bit, and stiffening in the neck.

An **asking, allowing aid** is used to guide the horse into a new direction, either on the straight or laterally. The rider indicates the new direction by opening the inside rein, while regulating the degree of bend or turn with the outside hand. Once the horse is established in the new direction, the rider should have more definite contact on the outside, regulating rein, than on the inside rein. Pulling on the inside rein into a turn is negative as it disconnects the horse, producing bend in the neck alone, and the rider loses control of the horse's hindquarters.

When asking the horse to change its outline (frame), such as lowering its head and neck into the relaxation position before or after work or in extended paces, the rider has to be ready to allow with the hands. In walk, for example, where the horse uses its head and neck more substantially than in the other paces, the rider's hands must allow forward movement to avoid blocking the horse's natural desire to go forward.

WEIGHT AIDS

Weight (or seat) aids are applied by either increasing or lightening the weight on one, or both, seat bones. They can only be applied correctly when the rider can sit, in balance, through every movement of the horse without relying on the reins for balance.

In downward transitions and with more advanced aids such as half-halts (asking the horse to change pace down), the rider's weight should have a slight bracing effect. In upward transitions (asking the horse to change pace up), the lightening of the seat encourages the forward urge, and the horse will respond by moving faster.

In lateral work the rider's weight distribution, while still always central, will allow the horse's hind leg to step further under. In half-pass, for example, the rider will sit with slightly more weight on the inside seat bone, in the direction of the movement, to allow the outside, propelling hind leg to step more clearly under the horse.

'FEEL'

Feel is a word often bandied around in riding circles. 'Oh, he's got such good feel' may be the comment on a particular rider, or the derogatory reverse may apply. It is not unusual for less-trained riders to experience some frustration at their real or perceived lack of this seemingly intangible talent or attribute.

This 'feel' is an essential component of an harmonious and confident relationship between a horse and rider. While it comes easily to some, if it doesn't come as easily to you, it is a fallacy to think you can never achieve it – with practice you can.

Feel is really the ability to judge the cause and effect of the horse's reaction to the rider. Examples are being able to give as the horse responds; being able to spot potential problems and deal with them before they become an issue; and being able to tell whether a horse is simply being disobedient or is just nervous. A lot of this comes with experience, but it has to be the right kind of experience.

A well-trained horse is the best professor of feel as it will teach a rider, literally, how good it feels when he or she gets it right. A good instructor will always communicate the idea to his pupil by asking, 'How did that feel?' The novice rider has to go through something of a learning curve of trial and error to find out what it takes to make it feel right and how then to achieve it consistently in the future.

The ideal feel: If you look at a very good horse and rider combination at work in dressage, jumping or cross-country, it almost seems as if the rider is doing nothing, while the horse looks happy, balanced, performs with brilliance and is in complete harmony with its rider, who will feel as if he or she only has to think and the horse reacts. It takes a combination of attributes, one of which is good

training of both halves of the combination, to achieve this 'state of grace'. Feel in a rider can be described as a mix of concentration, quick reaction, sensitivity, adaptability and a feeling for rhythm and movement, with the added ingredient of a relaxed and sympathetic attitude.

Contact

This is a big part of the feel and co-ordination that makes the aids work smoothly and effectively. The rider has to develop the ability to always allow the horse relaxation in its head, neck and mouth, while maintaining contact with the bit.

There are three basic rein positions. When the horse is 'on a contact' or 'on the bit', there is a consistent, soft connection from the horse's mouth to the rider's hands at all times and the horse is happy to accept the rein aids without resistance. When the horse is 'on long rein', its head and neck are carried in the natural rather than rounded position, while the rider retains a soft allowing contact. When the horse is on a 'loose rein', the rider has given the reins away completely, holding them on the buckle rather than on a contact.

Riding is really the art of communication between a willing horse and a sympathetic rider. It is never a matter of force. Instead finesse, skill, training and co-ordination result in perfect partnership and harmony. Ideal examples are dressage rider Nicole Uphoff of Germany and Rembrandt, show jumper Rodrigo Pessoa of Brazil and Gandini Baloubet du Rouet, or three-day eventer Blyth Tait of New Zealand and Chesterfield. Their level of horsemanship may seem unattainable, but that is the fascination of learning to ride. It is a process that never comes to an end.

No one has ever learned all there is to know about riding, but learning a little more each day brings its own sense of achievement and reward.

Left *When you get the right 'feel', it will be as if you and your horse are thinking and acting as one.*

Right *Constant schooling is the key to success. Top UK dressage combination Carl Hester and Donner Rhapsody practise shoulder-in.*

WALK

The walk is a four-time gait, with each leg moving individually and a clear one-two-three-four beat being heard. In walk the rider maintains the basic seat, keeping a straight line between the shoulder, hip and heel. The lower back and hips and forearms are relaxed and able to move with the horse's natural rhythm. The horse uses its head and neck more significantly during each walk stride than in the other paces. If the rider prevents this, it can spoil the rhythm. This rider could allow a little more with her hands.

TROT

The trot is a two-time pace, with the horse's legs moving in diagonal pairs. In a rising trot, the rider sits and rises in time to the up and down movement. In a sitting trot, the rider must allow his or her body to absorb the movement, sitting deep in the saddle in the classic position. This horse is a little behind the vertical in its head carriage. Some more forword strides ridden in rising trot with lowered hands will refresh the quality of both the trot pace and the horse's outline as it is allowed to stretch its neck more.

CANTER

This is a three-time pace with the horse's legs moving in the sequence: outside hind, inside hind and outside fore, inside fore, followed by a moment of suspension, when all four legs are off the ground, before the sequence repeats itself. The rider should maintain the classic shoulder-hip-heel line while keeping the arms and lower back relaxed and following the forward movement of the stride. A brisk canter on grass will give the horse renewed enthusiasm during a schooling session. The rider will often find it easiest to adopt a lighter seat position.

GALLOP

To ride a horse at this fast, exhilarating pace requires a secure seat and confidence in your ability to control your horse. The stirrup leathers should be shortened, so that the body lifts more easily out of the saddle, allowing the weight to come forward. The heels are well down, while the lower leg remains in the normal position. The rider should take care not to use the hands for balance in fast work.

Above *Riding schools that offer the convenience of an indoor school enable training and lessons to continue during periods of bad weather.*

Right *Fine weather provides an opportunity for riders and horses to exercise in an outdoor school or open field.*

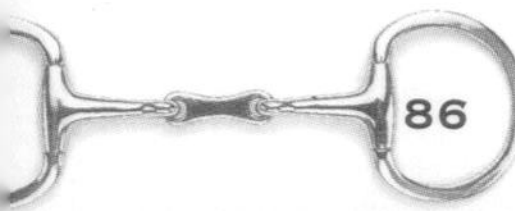

Riding with others

Once you have progressed from your initial private lunge lessons into a school (arena) situation, you are likely to have to negotiate other horses and riders as well as control your own mount right from the start.

Apart from allowing other riders to get on with their work harmoniously and with respect for each other in the school or the warm-up area at competitions, the protocols used (the 'school rules'), as with driving on the road, are there to prevent collisions! They might initially seem hard to digest but once practised a little, the school rules become second nature, rather like the highway code.

In the school

Before entering the school, regardless of whether it is an outdoor school or an indoor arena, announce your presence loudly to warn other riders, who can then circle away from the door to give you clear access. 'Door please' or 'door clear' are commonly used announcements (in the USA, it is 'heads up'). Offer the same courtesy also when leaving the school as you can't assume everyone else is anticipating your next move. Riders can be very focused when they are concentrating on their work.

If you are entering the school already mounted, walk the horse onto the centre line or to the centre

Above *Riders do not always have the luxury of the school to themselves, so it is important to learn the school rules.*

Above *When working in the school with others, riders should use the inner track for walking and to halt.*
Above right *Practising passing left hand to left hand as part of a group helps you to gain control of your horse.*

of a circle if you intend to stop and make any adjustments to the girth or stirrups. Similarly, if you are leading the horse, and intend to mount only once you are in the school, move it well clear of the track before getting on.

Horses in walk should always be kept off the main track and walked on the inner track, out of the way of others in trot and canter. When the school is busy, downward transitions to walk or halt are also normally performed on the inner track.

It is not only impolite, but also often unsafe to overtake another rider in the school. While working in a faster pace, if you have to pass another horse and rider, you should circle away and come back onto the track behind them, rather than pull out and cut in front of them.

When working in a school formation, a safe distance of one horse's length should be maintained between each horse and rider at all times.

During a lesson or schooling session, horses should be worked equally on both reins, so you have to get used to meeting other horses working on the opposite rein. If, for example, you are going to the right and the other rider to the left on the track, you should pass each other left hand to left hand. Therefore if you are going to the right, it is up to you to move your horse onto the inner track for a safe distance to pass the other rider, then return to the main track, as the rider on the left rein has priority.

The rider on the outside track also has priority over the rider on a circle, so the circling rider should come onto the inner track.

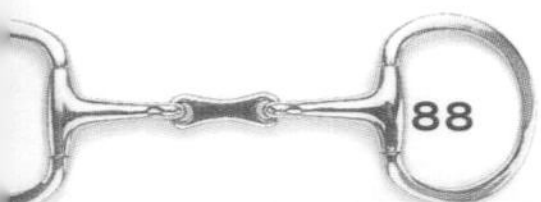

Above *Cantering over ground poles helps to achieve rhythm and balance.*
Left *Regular one-to-one sessions with an instructor will enable you to identify and correct faults. Note that hard hats or safety helmets should always be worn when training or riding.*

SCHOOL MARKERS

The arena used for dressage competitions is marked out with a series of letters (called markers), which denote where any given test movement is commenced or finished. These letters are also employed in the everyday training environment. There are two sizes of arena used in dressage competition: 20m x 40m (22 x 44yd) for lower level tests and 20m x 60m (22 x 65yd) for any level up to grand prix. The larger area is known as the long arena and has more markers.

Letters A and C mark each end of the school or arena, A being the point of entry and C the closed end. The half markers, letters B and E, are found halfway down each long side.

The other letters in a 20 x 40m arena are M, F, K and H, which are located on the long side, 6m (20ft) in from the short side.

In addition there are two 'invisible' markers. D is located on the centre line midway between F and K, and G occupies the same position between M and H.

The centre of the school, X, lies midway between E and B, and A and C.

Far from meaning you need a degree in advanced algebra to ride in a school, the markers are there to help you ride figures accurately. While it may take a while to learn the positions of the arena markers, they will soon become familiar.

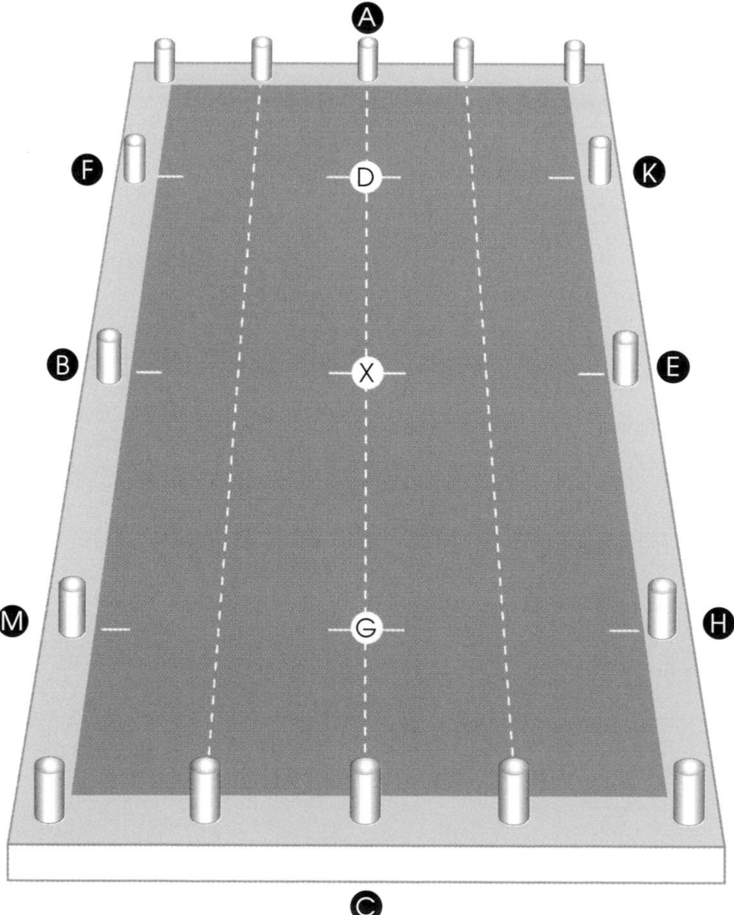

SCHOOL FIGURES

The classic school figures that form the basis of dressage tests also serve the purpose of training beginners to ride accurately, thus ensuring they are genuinely in control of the horse. When performed correctly, forwards in rhythm and balance, the school figures are training exercises promoting suppleness in the horse. 'Going large' is the term for riding around the school on the track. When going large, the corners of the school are ridden as quarter circles. In training, advanced horses, with a higher degree of balance, can be ridden deeper into the corners than novice or less experienced horses. Schooling the horse on the inner track helps the rider to assess whether he is honestly controlling the horse's straightness or bend, as the horse often feels more secure when being ridden on the outer track, due to the supporting presence of the perimeter fence or wall of the school.

Changing the rein

'Change the rein across the next diagonal,' the instructor commands. 'I can't, my brother's got my other ones and he's gone for a hack!' replies the small boy, displaying his own logic. Riding terms can sometimes seem arcane but this term simply means 'change direction' and when you are in a school situation, makes more sense than: 'Change direction and go right or go left'. As a rider changes rein, he should, if in a rising trot, change diagonal by sitting for two beats of the trot at the point where the new direction is assumed, such as on reaching the track, or passing over X. The rider should also change his whip into the inside hand. To do this, both reins are taken into the whip-holding hand, while the free hand grasps the whip at the top and neatly pulls it through to the new position on the other side, taking care not to give the horse an inadvertent whack. When riding in a school, unless it is specifically needed on the outside, the whip is generally carried in the inside hand, to prevent it dragging on the walls of the school. While any change of direction counts as a change of rein, using the classic school figures ensures that the movement is beneficial to both riding technique and the horse's way of going. Changes across the diagonal can be carried out on the long diagonal (FXH or KXM), or the short diagonal (from F or M to E, or from H or K to B).

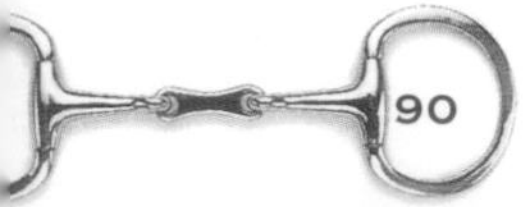

Changes of rein can be made either through two half-circles or one half-circle and return to the track, and are usually performed out of the corner at the end of a long side. The horse is ridden through a half-circle, then aimed at the track on a straight line with the new bend employed as the track is reached. A change of rein across the school, from E to B, for example, will be ridden as a quarter-circle, followed by a straight line, followed by another quarter-circle, before moving smoothly onto the track on the new rein.

Circles

The 20m (65ft) diameter circle is the preliminary circle for the novice rider to master while maintaining bend, balance and rhythm in the horse. The 20m circle is made easy by the markers, as one half of the circle will be naturally described by the short side of the school. If your instructor calls: 'At A, twenty-metre circle', you will know that in a 20m x 40m (22 x 44yd) school, the circle will touch X. Similarly, a circle ridden in the centre of the school will touch the sides at E and B. Other schooling circles are 15m (50ft) and 10m (32ft). Smaller circles, known as voltes, are only performed by highly trained horses as a greater degree of collection is needed to execute them correctly. A figure of eight, consisting of two circles with a change of rein, requires a change of bend through the centre of the figure.

Loops

A simple exercise in change of bend, loops are ridden on the long side of the school, as a curve off the track. The return to the track is made at the mid-point (E or B) with a change of bend at each change of direction. A loop 5m (5.5yds) in from the track is furthest away from the track – 5m – at the mid-point.

Serpentines

Serpentines help promote bend and looseness in the horse, and control, accuracy and 'feel' in the rider. The number of loops determines the difficulty of the exercise. Loops are ridden as a series of half-circles with straight sections in between. Serpentines can also be ridden as smooth bulb-shaped loops with changes of bend each time the horse crosses the centre line. With an even number of loops, the movement finishes on the same rein, whereas an odd number involves a change of rein.

Above *Schooling is a process of constant practice, until the basic exercises become second nature to both rider and horse.*

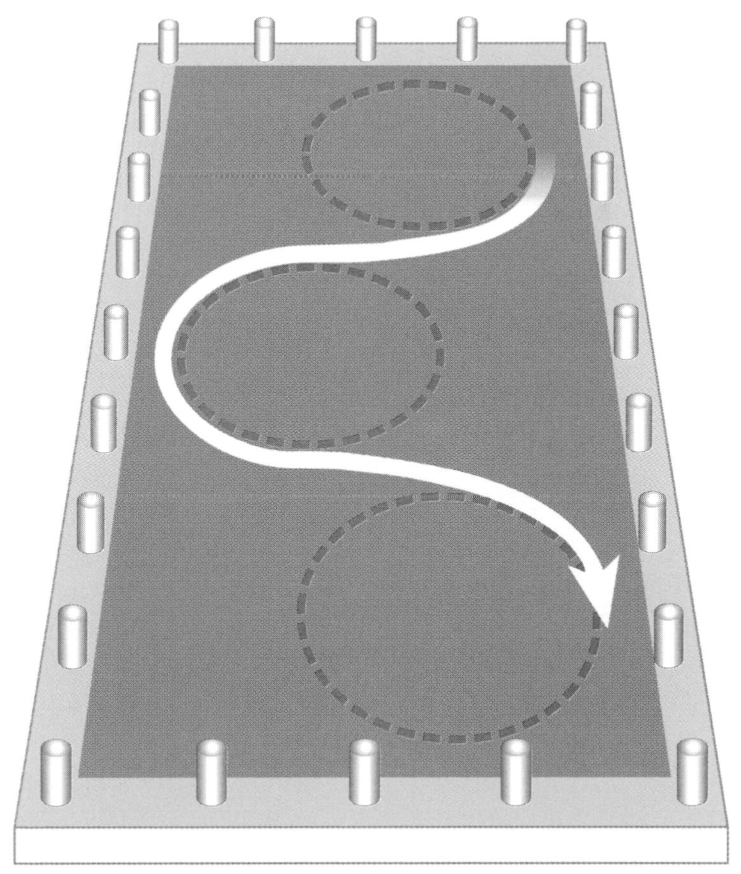

Above *The Serpentine*

CHAPTER FIVE

Riding for Pleasure

Once the basic skills of horsemanship have been mastered, and the learner rider is gaining experience and confidence, it is time to move out of the confines of the school. The true pleasure of riding is as much in the companionship and friendship it brings as in the establishment of a bond and relationship between rider and horse. While riding can be a solitary occupation (many competition riders spend hours alone in the saddle during training), most recreational riders enjoy the company of others.

Learner riders have a chance to practise new-found skills while on outrides led by a competent rider. More advanced riders have many opportunities, such as overnight trails and riding holidays, to have fun on horseback while expanding their knowledge and experience. The only limits are time, money and imagination.

Riding out

The first step towards expanding your horizons as a rider is to become competent at riding outside of the school environment. Riding in the open, or 'hacking out', is an important part of confidence-building and the education of both horse and rider.

While a young horse needs to be kept under control, and be sufficiently accepting of the rider to be safe enough to ride out, similarly the starter rider must establish security in the seat, and demonstrate enough ability to control the horse within the school, before being able to ride out in safety. It is therefore important that less experienced riders are mounted on steady, familiar horses that are accustomed to hacking out, as horses used to being in the school tend to be somewhat 'on their toes' and forward-going when venturing into the great outdoors.

Riding out unaccompanied is not something an inexperienced rider should attempt. When riding out in a group, more experienced riders should always be positioned at the front and back of the ride, and they should ensure that the duration, pace and the overall demands of the ride are tailored to the abilities of the least experienced rider in the group.

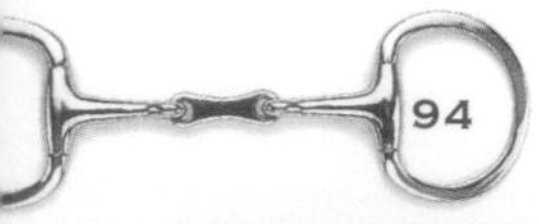

Riding out is a sociable experience, but novices should always be accompanied by more experienced riders.

What form riding out takes is dependent on your area. Riders who live in the countryside have more opportunities for hacking out than those in towns and suburbs, but even so, most riders nowadays will have some housing areas and busy roads to negotiate, so it is important to be as aware of the highway code as the country code, and a great deal of attention must be paid to all aspects of safety.

Before hacking out, tack should be thoroughly checked for wear and tear. All riders must wear an approved, correctly fitted hard hat or crash cap. Not only is this a precaution for the rider, but in the event of any accident involving an insurance claim, it is important that essential safety precautions have been adhered to. Furthermore, riders who disregard the basic elements of safety are less likely to be afforded respect by nonriding road users and may well incur unpleasant comments from passing motorists.

If the first part of the ride is through a busy area, it is advisable to ride the horse in the school for a while to get it relaxed and listening. For the benefit of the less experienced or infrequent rider, this is also a chance to relax and get the feel of the horse.

As a general rule, horses should always be ridden in walk on surfaced (hard top) roads. On a familiar, safe part of the road, riders may trot for short,

Horses should only be ridden in walk or trot on hard roads, to prevent damage to their legs as well as to reduce the risk of slipping on wet or oily surfaces.

controlled, steady periods, but if a horse is ridden too fast on hard roads, it can cause concussion and damage to its legs. There is also the risk of slipping. One expects wet roads to be slippery, but oil build-up can mean that dry roads can be slippery too.

Vehicles, cyclists, pedestrians and other riders should always be passed in walk, and horses brought to a walk whenever traffic approaches. Not all road users are familiar with, or sympathetic towards, animals on public roads. Courtesy is vitally important, not only to thank the considerate driver who has given your ride a wide berth at a slow speed, but also to promote the reputation of riders as sensible road users.

A driver who has slowed to pass you is likely to be less helpful to the next group of riders he passes if all he's received previously is a glum expression and no acknowledgement. A hand raised in thanks, along with a smile, goes a long way towards keeping drivers on the side of riders.

For communicating changes of direction and pace, hand signals are used. The lead rider should indicate a turn via an outstretched arm to the right or left, which is then taken up by the rest of the ride. In a group ride, the front and back riders should be in charge of signals and an agreement made beforehand that this will not be the responsibility of the least experienced riders. A signal to the ride to slow down, or a request for traffic to slow down, is given by raising and lowering an outstretched arm. If the ride is going to halt at a junction, for example, the lead rider will raise a hand and hold the position until all the horses have come to a stop.

Riders should move in single file on busy roads, but on quieter roads and riding tracks they can ride two abreast with a sensible span between each horse.

Cantering on an appropriate track, or around the edge of the field, should follow several periods of walking and trotting so the horses are warmed up and less fresh. When cantering on a group ride, it is safest to stick to the single file formation with the lead rider controlling the pace sensibly to safeguard the less experienced riders.

If by chance any damage occurs on a ride, it is polite to report it as soon as possible. Farmers who allow riders to use the edges of their crop fields will soon put a stop to such favours if crops end up being trampled by out-of-control horses. Damage to gates or fences should be made good for the same reason

and good relationships with farmers and land owners should be cultivated if riders are to be allowed the privilege of riding over their land. Needless to say, horses should not be taken on tracks or routes which specifically say 'no horses', even if a grassy track looks appealing. On foot paths and public recreation areas, riders should be prepared, especially when in a fast pace, to slow down when approaching walkers, runners or cyclists. Avoid very wet, muddy tracks, not just because they can be dangerous for the horse's legs but because the impressions left in the mud by hooves will harden when the track dries out, leaving dangerous ruts.

The last part of a ride should be undertaken in walk to cool the horses before they return to the stables.

Riding out consists of not only being in control of the horse but also being aware of other conditions and situations that could affect one's enjoyment. The pace, duration and direction of the ride should always be based on prevailing weather conditions, as well as the level of training and competence of the least-experienced horses and riders in the group.

To some novice riders, the number of things to think about on an outride may seem daunting, while to others it may be stating the obvious.

Riding in the open is supposed to be recreational. It should be fun and a chance for less experienced riders to gain confidence in horses in a relaxed way, but even a Sunday afternoon drive through the country is only enjoyable if you are in control of your car and the situation on the road.

Drivers who slow down to pass you should always be courteously acknowledged.

Although some periods of an outride may be spent cantering or galloping, walking the horse back to the stables at the end of the ride allows it to cool down.

Learning to open and close gates without dismounting takes patience, and a horse that stands or moves when asked. With practice, however, it soon becomes a routine procedure.

OPENING AND CLOSING GATES

Gates should always be shut securely when the ride has passed through them, and this should be the responsibility of an experienced rider at the back of the group. Gate opening and closing takes a bit of practice for both rider and horse, but there is a specific way of accomplishing this task from horseback.

Approach the gate so the horse's body is more or less parallel to the gate, with its head towards the latch. With both reins and the whip in the outside hand, reach down and open the latch with the inside hand. When the latch is open, push the gate outward sufficiently for the horse to pass through without knocking itself, while keeping one hand on the gate so it does not swing away too far and you can retain control to close it. This will involve asking the horse to go forwards, then when its hindquarters are clear of the gap, stopping and turning the horse around its forelegs by using your inside leg behind the girth so the horse is back facing the gate as you push it to, and you are in position to close the gate with the new inside hand, having taken reins and whip into the new outside hand. Sounds complicated? With a bit of practice, and a horse that stands when asked, the manoeuvre becomes easier.

When a group has to pass through a gate, it is sensible for one rider to hold it open so the rest of the ride can pass. Never rely on gates staying open on their own, as a swinging gate can cause injury.

RIDING IN THE COUNTRY

Hacking in the open country forms the basis of the more formal discipline of cross-country riding and is an opportunity for the novice rider to develop and refine his or her skills and confidence.

On country rides, novices must always be accompanied by more experienced riders, who should lead the way over jumps and other obstacles, showing the less experienced riders and horses how to do it. They will teach the novice to take a systematic and safe approach over a variety of natural obstacles, not just jump them haphazardly or without thought.

Once the rider has sufficient control to ride a horse outdoors with safety, it is time to start tackling different terrain. Learning to ride on hills or through wooded areas, and to negotiate ditches or water crossings is the next step to becoming a confident all-round horseman.

All new experiences should be practised at a walk before going on to trotting and cantering. Riding on slopes and undulating ground requires both a secure seat and the balance to adapt the rider's weight to the horse's centre of gravity.

The light seat is adopted when riding uphill or downhill, with the rider's weight more out of the saddle when going uphill, to a degree that is dependent on the steepness of the incline.

Less experienced riders should use a neck strap when practising hill work, as it is very important that the horse has sufficient freedom of the head and neck to help maintain balance, and a rider hanging on for balance is counterproductive. The rider's heels should be kept down, while the knees and lower leg remain in secure contact with the horse's sides.

In deep, boggy ground, the rider should also use the lighter seat to take his or her weight more off the horse's back, and the horse should be given as much rein as necessary. If the horse is sinking into soft ground, it is better to dismount and lead it, allowing it plenty of rein for easier movement.

In icy conditions, dismounting and leading the horse is often the safest choice. Care should be taken to avoid steep turns in these conditions, as it is easy for the horse to lose its footing and slip.

When riding through water, always take a known path with a firm, level base. If you are unsure of the best route, dismount and lead the horse through, or at least take a careful look before asking the horse

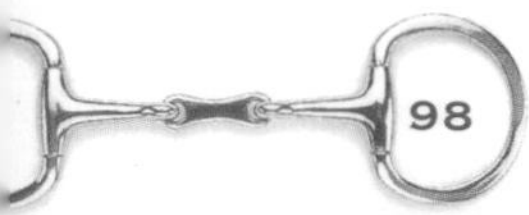

to step into the water. On hot, sunny days riders should keep the horse moving forwards, to avoid any possible inclination for it to stop for a refreshing roll. Pawing the ground is a definite warning sign!

When riding in wooded areas, lean well forward when passing underneath overhanging branches. If you have used a hand to sweep aside a branch, do not allow it to whisk back onto the rider behind you. Either stop and hold the branch until the rest of the ride has passed, or release it slowly and allow the next rider to take hold of the branch and move it out of the way for themselves.

One of the pleasures of riding in the country is the opportunity to jump natural obstacles, such as logs, ditches and small stone walls. Riders should have had experience of jumping in the school before tackling outdoor obstacles and on no account should any natural fence or obstacle be attempted if it is bigger than the fences the horse (or rider) is used to jumping in the school. All natural obstacles should be inspected first to ensure that there are no sharp edges or unseen dangers on the other side.

When approaching a natural obstacle, such as a fallen tree across a bridle path, the rider should decide in advance whether to attempt it or go around the obstacle. Once a decision is made, the rider must ride on with confidence and approach the obstacle straight on and at a suitable pace.

This wide, flat path in the Cotswolds, in the heart of the English countryside, provides these riders with the opportunity to enjoy a safe gallop.

Left *If a fall can't be avoided, try to keep hold of the reins, and roll over your shoulder as you land.*
Right *Before riding through a stream, inspect it to ensure the base is firm and level.*

COPING WITH FALLS

Sooner or later every rider comes off their horse. In most cases, the only damage will be to your pride, but in order to avoid the worst, there are ways to cope with a fall that will help to minimize any real injury to you or your horse.

Perhaps the most important thing to bear in mind is that, in any situation where you are feeling nervous or uncertain, slow down, and where relevant, move to the side of the ride. Firstly, slowing down may help you to regain control and in the second instance, you are less likely to cause an accident or be ridden over by following riders if you are on the edges of a ride rather than in the centre of a fast-moving bunch. Falls occur in a variety of ways. You might lose your balance in the saddle and simply slide to the ground; or be thrown as the horse trips or stumbles. Whatever the type of fall though, try to land sideways and roll over your shoulder. If you are not hurt, get up as quickly as possible and remount. This is important, both for your own confidence and to re-establish control over the horse, particularly if you suspect that it has been instrumental in your fall.

If you have managed to keep hold of the reins, the horse should be standing still, waiting for you, but if you have let them go, your first task may be to catch it before you can remount. In the case of a horse that is now relishing its freedom, this can be quite a job. If a loose horse decides to make capture into a game, never chase it. With the help of other riders, try and corner it instead. Once it realizes that all its escape routes are blocked, it will give in. If a fall is as a result of a horse having stumbled or tripped, check its feet and legs carefully, perhaps even trot it up, before remounting, to ensure that the horse is still sound and able to continue.

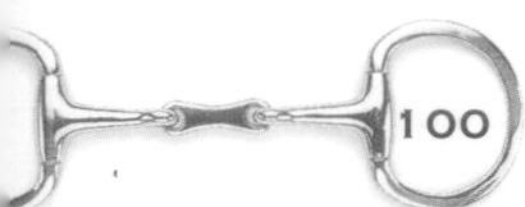

LONG-DISTANCE RIDING

This covers anything from a full day's ride through countryside close to one's home, to week-long trails in different locations. Day or weekend rides are an opportunity to explore new areas on horseback, either by taking your own horse by horse box or trailer to stay with friends, or booking up for a day's ride in a new location. Long-distance trails can also be a fun way to enjoy the sights in a foreign country.

The key to undertaking both types of trails successfully is careful planning and a sound knowledge of your own riding ability and limitations, as well as the capabilities of the horse involved.

Before contemplating any long-distance riding, it is important for both the rider and horse to be fit. A tired rider sits more heavily on the horse's back, but frequent extended riding sessions, particularly in trot, will help to build up the stamina required.

As riders must be prepared to dismount and walk alongside the horse, particularly on steep hills and long downhill stretches, comfortable boots and suitable clothes are a must.

All the tack and equipment used on long-distance rides needs special attention, as there is no quick recourse to the tack room for 'spares' should anything malfunction. In addition to the basic tack, the horse may also be asked to carry extra weight in the form of saddlebags containing the rider's gear, so much thought needs to be given to what to include.

On most recreational trails, all the gear and equipment is transported to the next overnight halt, but riders may need day-packs or saddlebags to take a warm sweater or jacket, snack foods and water, and basic first-aid items, including sunscreen in warm climates. You may also have to carry water and food for your horse.

Riding on slopes or undulating ground requires a secure seat. Riders should always be prepared to dismount and walk if a hill seems too tough for the horse.

Riding through a stream in the Snowy Mountains, New South Wales, Australia. Although bush hats are being worn as protection against the sun, novice riders should rather wear conventional hard hats or skull caps.

Before taking your horse on any long-distance ride, especially if it is overnight, it is wise to have it checked by the vet. The condition of the feet and shoes must be checked as well, and if required, new shoes fitted at least a week in advance of the ride.

Despite seeming daunting, long-distance rides can be easily accomplished if they are broken up into sections of suitable lengths. If you plan your ride sensibly, you will be able to structure the pace and energy required so that both you and your horse are able to enjoy the activity and turn out each morning feeling fresh and ready for the next stage.

TRAIL RIDING

Although there are many aspects to trail riding, such as competitive trails and endurance rides, most riders will focus on pleasure trail riding, which is a pleasant way of combining a vacation with riding.

Trail riding has a great following in the USA, but is gaining in popularity worldwide, with the choice of countries and trails on offer increasing every year. As the name implies, pleasure trails are just that – a group of riders and horses making their way leisurely from one overnight stop to the next. These are the equine equivalent of hiking trails and most trail organizers go to great lengths to ensure that their trails pass through interesting and attractive countryside. Overnight stops may be in tented camps, farmhouses or log cabins, and riders can generally expect hot showers, cooked meals and a chance to relax with a cold drink at the end of the day.

Most trails supply horses, and riders wishing to take their own horses should enquire well in advance whether this is possible. Trail instructors will attempt to match horse and rider and it is up to you to be honest about the level of your riding skills.

Riders on a safari trail in Botswana's Okavango Delta have the opportunity to view elephants and other big game animals from really close up.

Some trails offer different options for novice and experienced riders, so that groups with the same level of ability ride together. Other trails are taken at a slower pace throughout and are suitable for all levels of experience.

In the USA, many trail operators offer the chance to ride in either western or conventional style, but this is worth investigating before you commit yourself to a holiday and arrive with your breeches and top boots to find your fellow riders in jeans and chaps. On most trails riders opt for casual gear, and those used to a more conventional approach should find out ahead of time what the normal practice is.

American trails tend towards the 'cowboy' image, with many operators in states such as Arizona, Wyoming and Oregon. In contrast trail riders in Europe and the UK can take in the countryside, along with historic towns and villages, sleeping in castles, chateaux or country inns. In southern Africa and Australia, where the trails are often through wilderness and open country, riders can get close to big game, or take part in a cattle drive on an outback ranch, often camping out overnight.

To get the most out of trail riding, it is preferable for riders to have achieved a minimum skill level, to be competent at all gaits, including the gallop, and to be confident of controlling an unknown horse in the open. Fitness and the ability to sit in the saddle for some hours at a time are important, and most trails have a maximum weight limit.

As with any holiday, advance planning and booking ahead is essential for trail rides. Whether you want to improve your jumping, learn to round up cattle, or just sightsee in another country, there is sure to be a trail somewhere in the world to suit your riding skills, requirements and bank balance.

Western riding

While western riding is linked to the American Old West, it is rapidly growing in popularity throughout the world. Many new riders are drawn to western riding because they feel very secure in the large leather saddle with its horn on the front, riding sensible 'cow horse' breeds such as the American Quarter Horse, the Appaloosa, and the Paint. Some riders like the link between this form of riding and its frontier heritage, while others love western riding because there are plenty of high-energy activities to get involved in, from barrel racing to rodeos.

History of western riding

Western riding originated with the American cowboy, but it actually has a classical foundation. During the 1600s, Spanish explorers to the New World brought horses – fine Barb and Iberian stock – to help them travel through the rugged, unfamiliar land. Many of these European horsemen had military backgrounds, reflected in the classical riding principles used in the cavalry, and they rode with a classical deep seat that was modified over the years to suit changing needs.

These Spanish conquerors developed a saddle and way of riding that provided security and comfort during the long hours spent on horseback. Early versions of the western saddle had a high cantle and pommel and long stirrups, similar to the Australian stock saddles of today. The Spaniards settled not only in North America, but also travelled through Central and South America. Soon the Mexicans were adopting similar horsemanship principles, and Mexican *vaqueros* became experts with horses and cattle, as well as roping, riding and herding techniques.

This new form of riding was ideal for the American colonists who headed west in the 1800s. Ranchers modified the Spanish saddle to more workmanlike standards, added a horn in front from which to hang a rope for holding cattle, and deepened the seat for comfort and security, so that they could be comfortable whether they were tending cattle, going on hunting expeditions, or riding the range.

Techniques

Western riding required that the horse respond to the barest of cues. The cowboy rode with very little leg pressure at all, so the western rowelled spur was

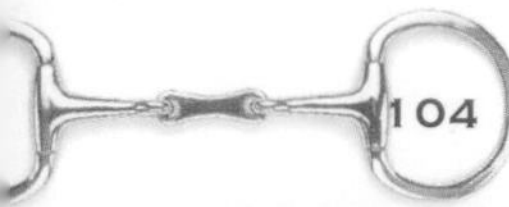

used to cue the horse without having to kick. The horse was guided with the rider holding both reins in one hand, usually the left, so the cowboy could hold his lariat (lasso) in his right hand. Western horses are usually ridden with a shanked curb bit for a greater degree of control and collection.

Even though western riding was developed for work, it soon turned into a leisure activity. Rodeos grew out of a need for ranch-hands to let off steam. Initially nothing more than an informal get-together to test the character of fellow cowboys, rodeos developed out of regular ranching skills. The tasks that were originally performed in order to break saddle horses, to rope and brand cattle and herd them have developed into competitive events, and today rodeos are held in the USA, Mexico and South America.

Travelling Wild West shows were popular at the turn of the century, and teams went from town to town, performing trick riding and roping, and shooting. The western competitions and gymkhana events that are popular today grew from these shows.

Riding differences

When a rider sits on a western horse, he or she will immediately notice differences. As in dressage, the rider sits deeply in the saddle, with a tall, upright posture and long leg. The rider's leg does not come into contact with the horse's side; instead, the horse is cued from the rider's heel or spur. Split reins (two reins unattached) are held together in one hand over the saddle horn, and the horse is guided through light rein pressure on its neck, called neck reining. The rider always rides with a loose rein contact, and the horse responds to light cues on the curb bit.

The rider sits all gaits of the western horse. The horse performs the walk, the jog – a trot that is a bit slower and more collected – and the lope, an easy swinging canter. For the pleasure rider, the aim is to ride in harmony with the horse, staying relaxed, balanced and solid in the saddle.

The western seat

For competitions however, the correct seat is with the rider sitting vertically, with a back that is straight, not arched. The shoulder, hip and heel should all align. The leg should be bent slightly at the knee, with the rider's weight in the heel. The rider's seat should be tucked underneath to absorb the horse's movement. The shoulders are back and the chin is looking forward. The rider holds the two reins in one hand, and steers the horse by laying the rein against the horse's neck; the horse moves smoothly away from the feel of the rein.

Showing and competing

Western show classes focus on the horse being willing, smooth and responsive, and the rider's equitation and horsemanship. Classes include western pleasure, where the horse is judged on its way of going at the walk, jog and lope. Using the selection criteria of a horse that would be the most pleasurable on a trail ride, each gait is performed in a slow, easy, relaxed outline. Horsemanship classes emphasize the rider, with the pair performing a pattern that demonstrates control and skill at the walk, jog, lope, turn on the haunches, lead changes, and rein back. A popular event is the trail class, which is like an obstacle course on horseback. The horse must not only successfully deal with each obstacle, but must also approach the obstacles in the correct order and at the right gait. Moves include a side-pass over ground poles, riding over an artificial bridge, manoeuvring through a gate while the rider opens and closes it from horseback, going up to a mailbox, and jumping a small cross-rail.

TRAIL RIDING

Most people who ride western do so because of the pleasurable experience of trail riding. Trail riding helps the horse become more sure-footed and builds up muscles in a way that arena riding cannot, but it takes skill to traverse varied footing, hills and slopes. Trail horses must have a sensible temperament, be well-balanced and athletic, able to traverse steep hills or carefully pick their way over a rocky path, and should be good in the company of other horses. Organized trail riding offers many options, from day rides to overnight camping trips through wilderness country only accessible by horseback.

Western riding enthusiasts can also holiday at specialized guest ranches, getting involved in cattle drives and taking lessons in cutting, reining or roping. These ranches usually have horses of varying ability, so that even novice riders will feel comfortable, and wranglers will often give lessons to beginners so that they can join in the fun.

Above *In trail classes, riders tackle unusual obstacles.*
Far left *Western riding has its own clothing, with chaps, spurs, wide-brimmed hats and informal shirts the norm.*
Below *A western saddle with its typical horn, high pommel and box stirrup.*

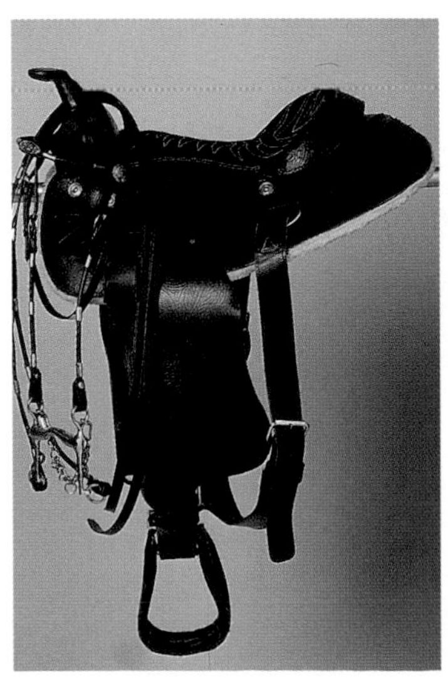

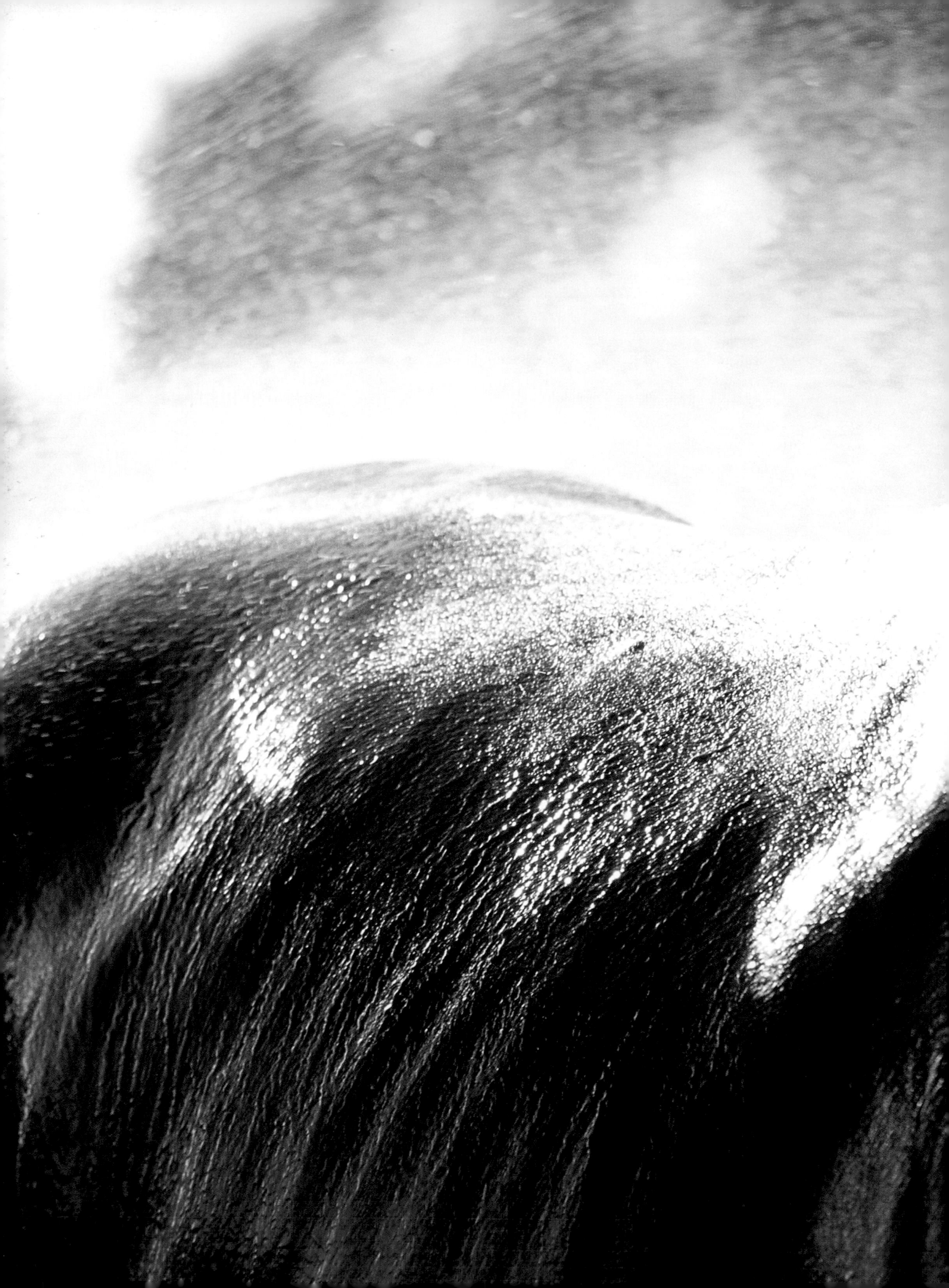

CHAPTER SIX

CARE, FEEDING AND HEALTH

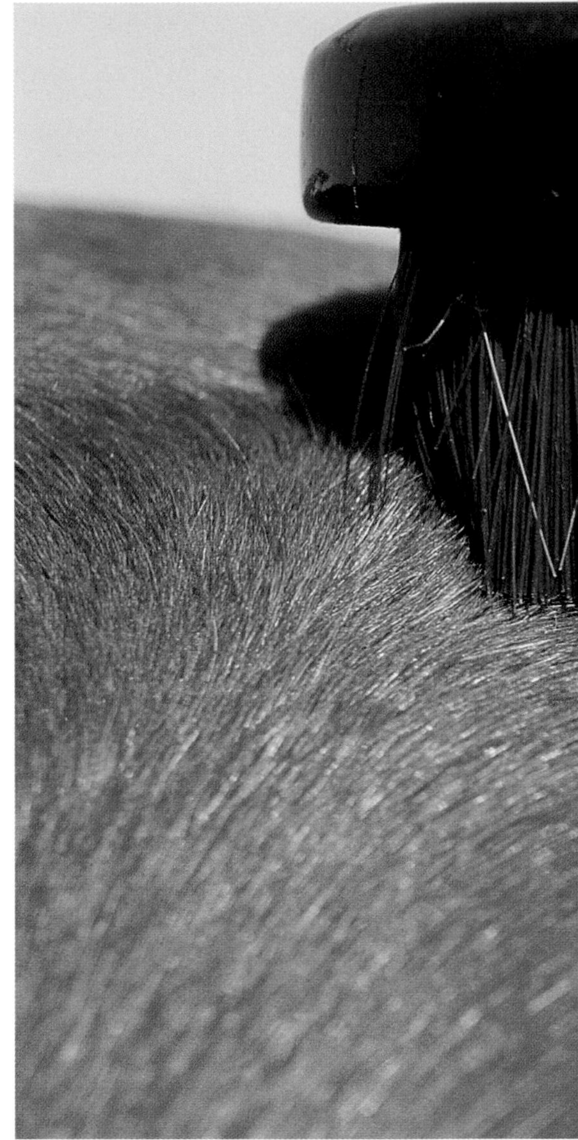

Every horse is entitled to the minimum of care necessary to enable it to function. The majority of horse owners go much further than this, spending a great deal of effort, and often money, to ensure that their animal is maintained and looked after to the maximum of their ability. Grooming, feeding and caring for a horse takes time and commitment, but as any horse owner will confirm, the rewards more than make up for it.

GROOMING

Grooming is essential for maintaining a healthy coat and skin, it is no mere cosmetic process. In the wild, horses are 'groomed' by companions in the herd. You can observe horses in the field scratching each other, and on their own, rolling and scratching themselves to remove mud and dust as well as scurf, sweat and loose hair, which in combination with the massage action promotes circulation, and cell and coat renewal. In the wild, grooming is an enjoyable process for the horse as it includes relaxation and helps it 'bond' with its companions. The domesticated horse needs man to take over that role and task.

Even in a busy stable where handlers have several horses to groom every day, the grooming period is a chance for a pat and stroke, plus some affectionate words. For young horses, it is an important part of the process of getting to know and trust their new herd leader, the human.

New riders will find that grooming is a good way to get to know horses and build confidence in being around them. While the length of time required will vary according to the individual handler and horse, an experienced groom will take from 10 minutes for a quick brush-up to up to an hour for a full groom and trimming session.

The horse should be lightly brushed off and tidied before exercise. This provides an opportunity to check the horse over before riding. The main grooming session should come after exercise, to remove sweat and dirt and to generally make the horse comfortable before it is returned to the stable.

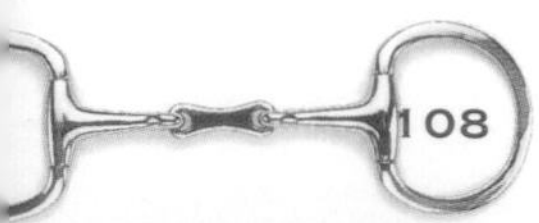

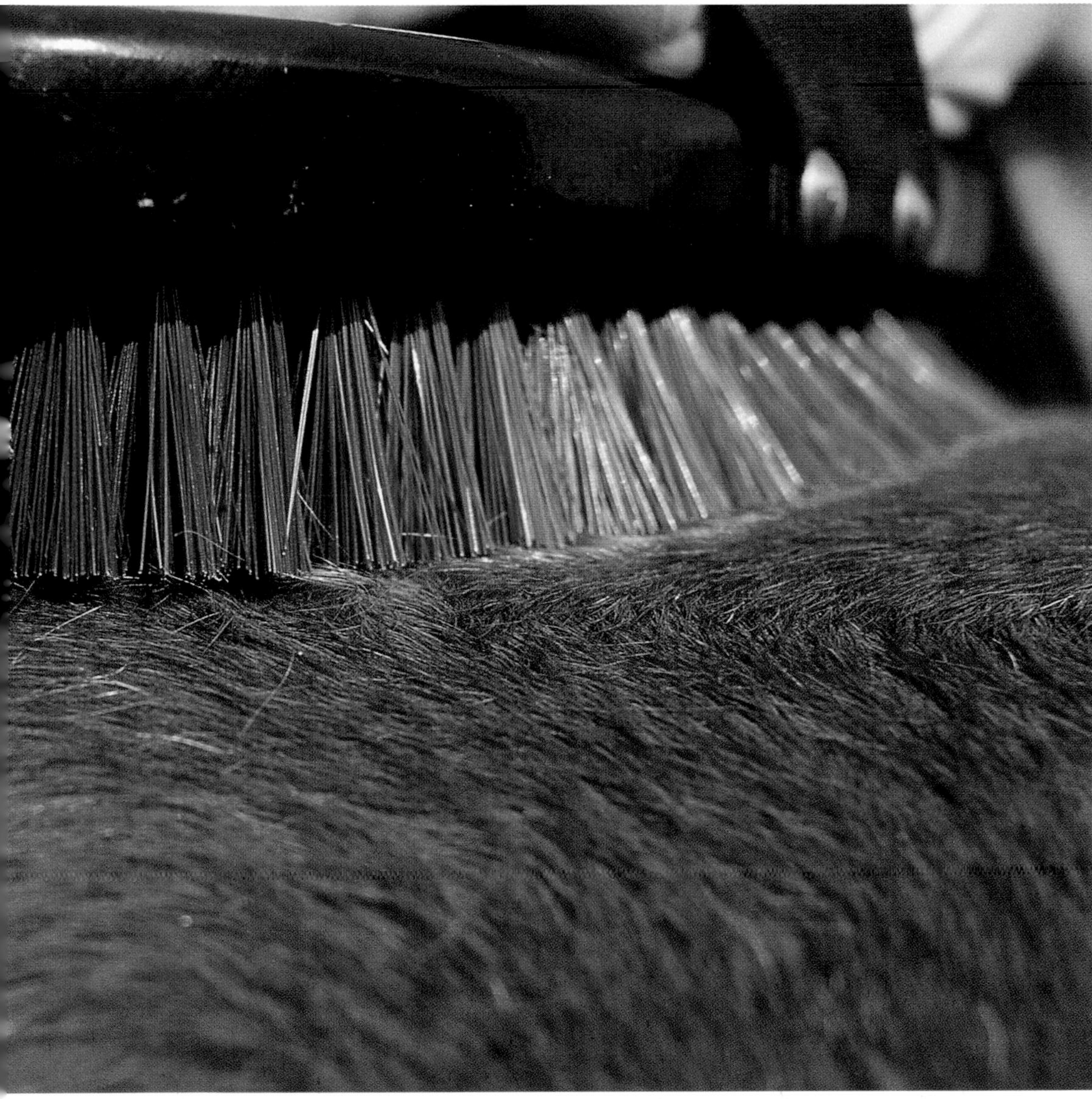

Regular and thorough grooming is essential for maintaining the horse's coat and skin in peak condition.

BEFORE GROOMING

Ideally, grooming should be carried out in a separate area, not in the stable. This ensures that dust does not clog the horse's habitat and also usually ensures more light for the groom.

The horse should be secured with a head collar and rope. Cross ties – where the horse is secured with two ropes, one on either side, attached to two points in a corridor or grooming box – are the ideal. These allow the handler equal access to both sides of the horse, and a mischievous horse cannot turn round and 'groom' its handler (i.e. nip him or her!). If this is not an option, then the horse should be tied securely using about half a metre's length of rope to avoid too much moving around.

All ropes and ties used in stables should be purpose designed, with easily released knots or clip fastenings, in case the horse is startled and pulls back. Ropes should always be tied using a quick release knot for the same reason. They should never be attached directly to a hook or wall ring. Wall rings are more safely utilized if a piece of twine or string is attached to the ring itself and the rope is then tied to this. If the horse pulls back hard, the twine will break easily whereas a wall ring won't give way, and the horse could injure itself or its handler.

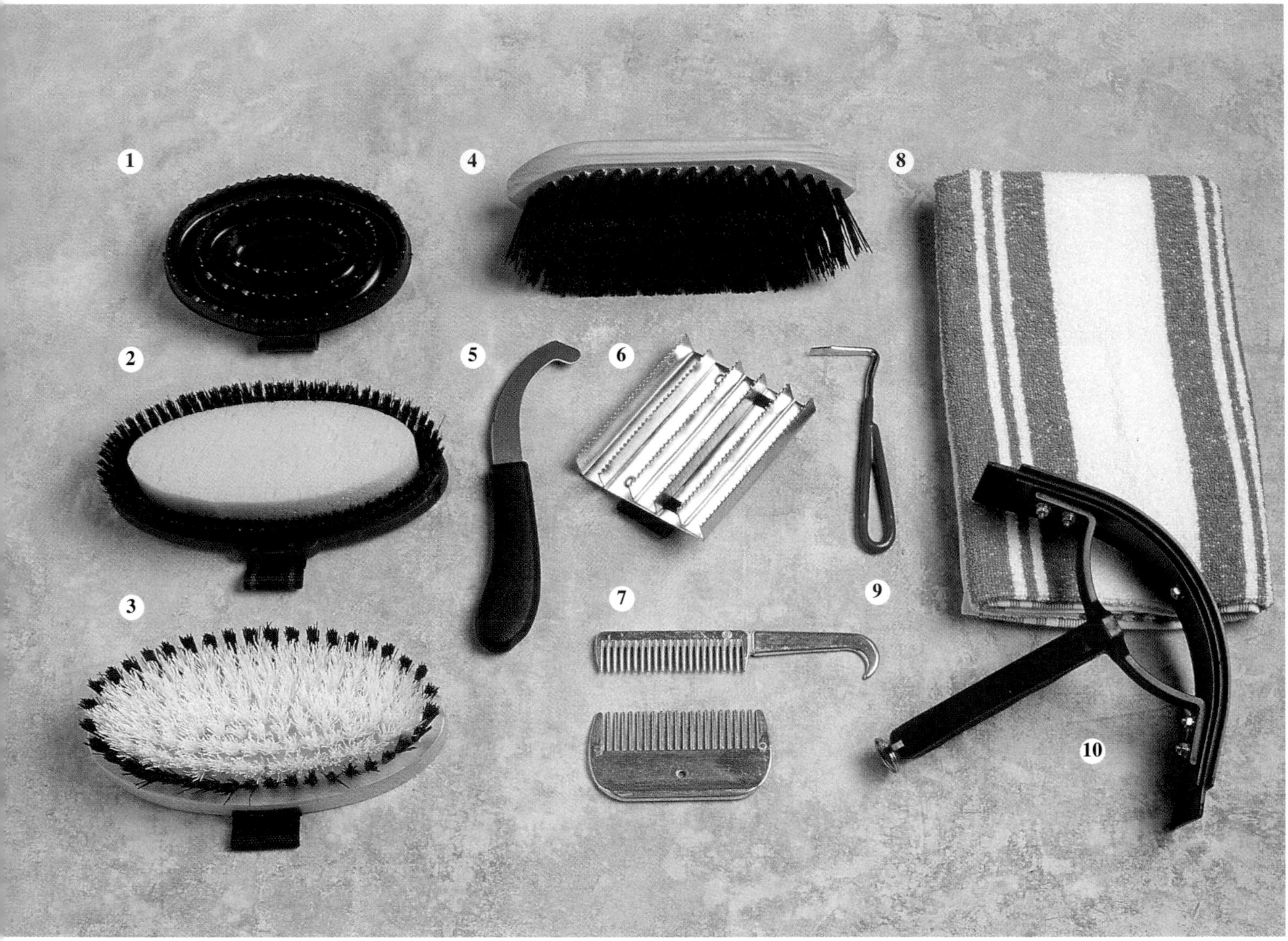

GROOMING KIT

1. Rubber curry comb
2. Body brush with sponge
3. Body brush
4. Water brush
5. Hoof scraper
6. Metal curry comb
7. Mane and tail combs
8. Stable rubber
9. Hoof pick
10. Sweat scraper

THE GROOMING PROCESS

The first task is to pick out the horse's feet in turn. With your inside hand, hold the hoof in a supporting grip around the base, near the coronet area, and use the pick to remove any bedding or mud, working from the heel to the toe, taking care when clearing the cleft of the frog, as this is a sensitive area.

Picking out the feet not only helps to keep a yard tidy, it is an opportunity to check that the foot is healthy and that shoes are secure before and after exercise. A skip should be placed in position to catch foot debris.

After exercise, the feet can be hosed clean, or if this is not practical, scrubbed lightly with a water brush and bucket of warm water. Care should always be taken that the heels are thoroughly dried.

It is important that the grooming process should not strip the coat of its natural oils. In many big training stables, horses are rinsed down after exercise. Excess moisture is removed with a sweat scraper and the horse is then dried off under sun lamps, which promotes relaxed and warmed muscles, before being groomed later. While this is a refreshing process, it is usually only practical in an indoor yard with these special facilities.

A patent shampoo can be used to wash the horse once in a while, such as before a show, but sustained use can strip the coat of its natural lubrication.

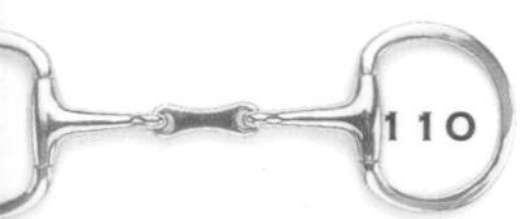

Washing a horse outdoors is to be avoided in anything but mild weather, even if it is walked around and allowed to dry under a sweat rug, as cold draughts can cause chills. In warm, sunny climates the horse should still be walked while the coat dries, as horses tend to roll when put back in the stable with a damp coat, defeating the object of the exercise.

Generally, the grooming process begins with the removal of sweat and mud, starting at the top of the horse's head and working down. When working on the left side of the horse, the brush should be held in the left hand, and vice versa. When working on the hind end, it is helpful to grasp the tail in your alternate hand. It not only avoids a potentially painful swish in your face, but discourages a ticklish horse from kicking out.

A rubber curry comb is the most effective tool for removing mud, dust and caked sweat. It is used in a circular, massaging motion (never scrubbing) on the soft parts of the body. It should never be used for the bony head or lower legs, where a softer dandy brush should be used.

Once the worst dirt has been removed, the main massage process can begin. A body brush is used in short but sweeping strokes over the muscles. After every few sweeps, swipe the brush over the metal curry comb (held in your free hand) to keep the bristles free from dust and loose hairs. Tap the curry comb periodically on the floor to remove the dust. Areas such as under the belly, under the mane and between the legs should not be forgotten.

When each side of the horse has been brushed, the head needs special care.

Release the head collar and re-attach it so it rests around the horse's neck only. Put the curry comb aside and with one hand held over the bony part of

Top left *A rubber curry comb is used to remove sweat and mud from the coat.*
Top right *The body brush is used all over the coat to stimulate and massage the skin.*
Bottom left *A metal curry comb removes loose hairs and dirt from the body brush.*
Bottom right *Picking out the feet removes mud and debris.*

Left *In warm weather, horses may enjoy a hosing down, but they must be allowed to dry thoroughly to ensure that they do not catch a chill.*
Right *A sweat scraper is used to remove excess water after washing.*

the horse's nose, gently work the brush around the head, taking special care around the ears, eyes and under the forelock. Work on one side at a time, not from the front and be aware that one inconsiderate bang with the hard part of a brush can make a horse fearful and head-shy, whereas gentle brushing can be both calming and enjoyable for the horse.

Brushing manes and tails should be avoided, as even gentle brushing can cause breakage in hairs that take years to replace. The base of the mane can be brushed at the roots to stimulate growth, but any hair tangles must be separated by hand.

To groom the tail, take it in one hand and release a small section at a time, separating tangles and strands with the fingers of the other hand. This process can be aided by the application of a proprietary conditioning spray.

Dip one sponge in warm water and wring it out, then gently wipe the horse's eyes, mouth and nostrils. With a separate sponge, wipe the dock, including the underside of the tail.

The horse's body can then be 'polished' with a folded stable rubber, and the mane and tail neatened into place with a damp water brush. The final touch is the application with a brush of hoof oil on the inside and outside of the hooves, not only for appearance but to improve their condition. Once the rugs are replaced, the horse can return clean and relaxed to its stable.

Grooming for grass-kept horses has to be modified, as horses living out need to retain more of the coat's natural grease for warmth and waterproofing. The eyes, nose, feet and dock should be attended to, but grooming as such should be limited to the removal of mud with a dandy brush or rubber curry comb.

Trimming

The stable-kept riding horse will have a trimmed mane and tail. The mane is 'pulled' to a length of approximately 10cm (4in) to facilitate general neatness and ease of plaiting for competitions. Pulling a mane basically means plucking out the longest hairs to regulate the overall length. It takes practice so as not to cause the horse too much discomfort. Manes should not be cut as this tends to make them bushy.

To pull a mane, start at the top of the neck, take a firm hold of a few hairs and with a mane comb, push the shorter hairs up against the lie of the hair. Wrap the longer hairs around the comb and, with a swift jerk, pull them out. Work down the mane to create the required length. If the horse is sensitive, pull the mane in short bouts over a period of a few days to avoid soreness. The idea is to make the mane lie flat and uniformly over to one side. This is usually to the right, but like human hair, horse hair parts naturally in different places, so if the mane falls over to the left, deal with it on that side. Plaiting the mane over will encourage it to lie flat.

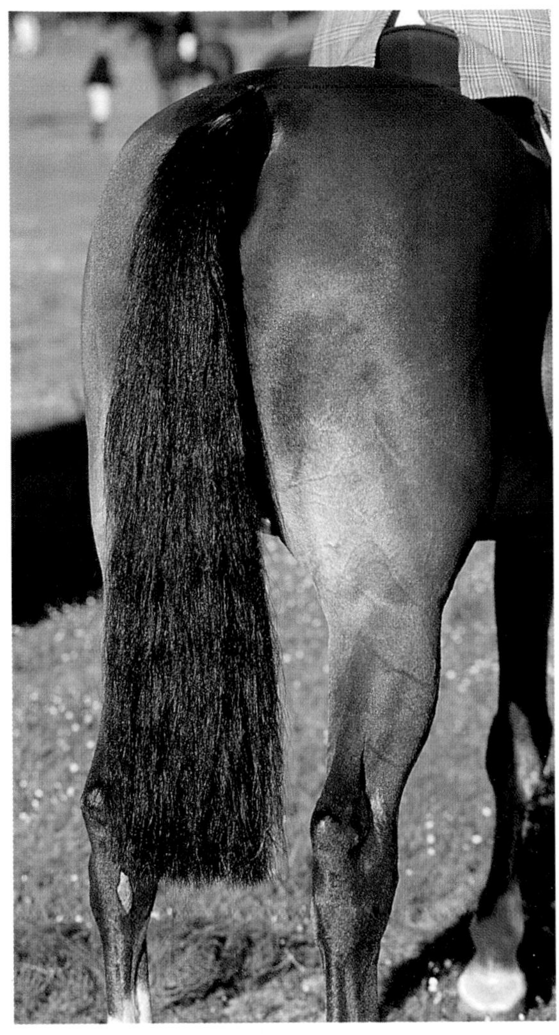

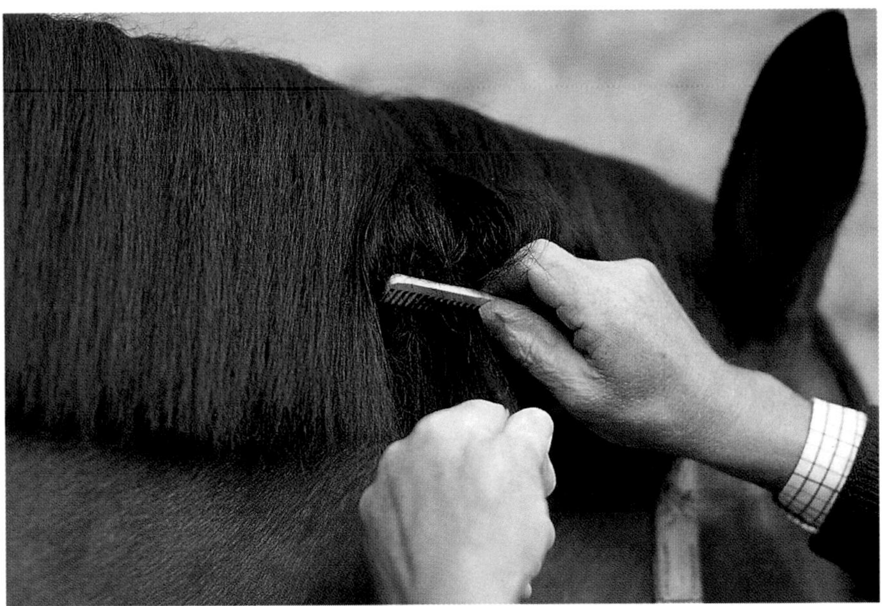

Left *A well-groomed tail is free of tangles and ends in a straight edge.*
Above *To pull the mane, wrap the longer hairs around the comb and give a firm tug to pull them out.*

If the mane is very thick where the headpiece of the bridle fits, a small gap can be clipped to allow the headpiece to rest more comfortably in this area.

A well-tailored tail should be narrow at the top (the dock end), and taper to fullness, ending in a straight-cut 'bang'. To create this effect, the long hairs under the dock are removed either by careful pulling or trimming with clippers, to a point usually about one-half to two-thirds of the way down the dock. The ends of the tail are cut so that when the tail is carried while the horse is in motion, the end of the tail will be level with a point about 10cm (4in) below the hock.

Before competitions and while travelling, applying a tail bandage prevents rubbing and ensures the tail is kept neat. A tail bandage should, as with all bandaging, be applied securely but not too tightly, with uniform pressure all the way down. The fastening should also be secured with tape, and a tail guard applied over the top while travelling, to avoid the horse rubbing the fastenings loose.

Hairy heels can be trimmed carefully, cutting the excess hair with curved scissors pointed downward or with hand clippers. Long hairs from inside the ears may be trimmed flush with the outside of the ear, but the protective inner 'fur' should never be touched. And while the long hairs at the back of the jaw can be trimmed, the long whiskers around the horse's muzzle are feeler hairs, and it is very unfair to remove them for the sake of appearance.

Clipping is an acquired skill best undertaken by experienced handlers. The style of clip is dependent on the amount of work the horse is doing, as this determines how much it is likely to sweat. Horses in full regular work can be 'clipped out' (given a full body clip) or clipped only to the elbows and thighs. The latter, with a saddle patch left on, is known as a hunter clip. Hair left on the legs affords protection from the weather, and the saddle patch can be useful on particularly thin-skinned, cold-backed or sensitive horses. A blanket clip, where the legs and an exercise blanket shaped area over the body are left unclipped, is a good option for the horse in lighter work. A trace clip involves clipping a strip from the horse's belly to the gullet, and is often used on ponies in less regular work.

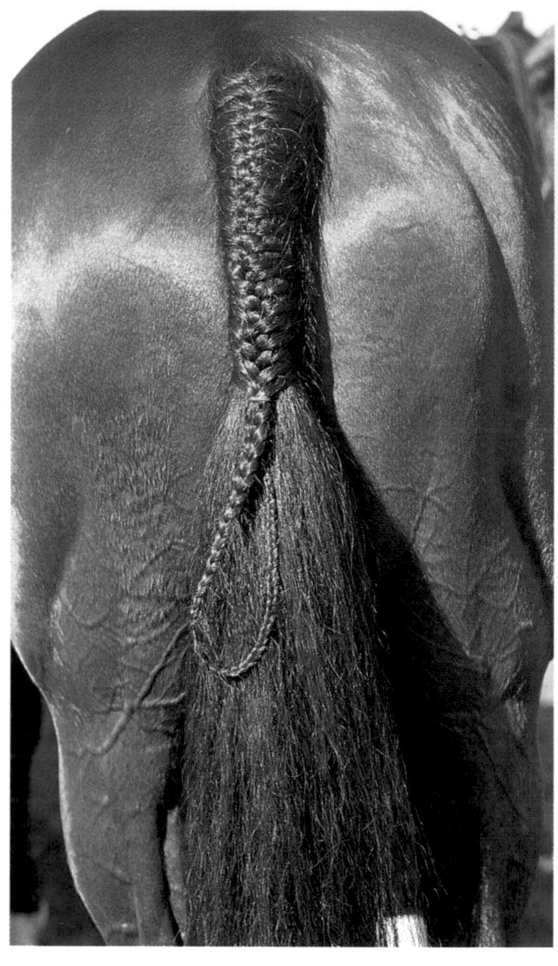

Above *A blanket clip is a good option for a horse in lighter work.*
Below and right *Manes and tails are frequently plaited for competitions.*

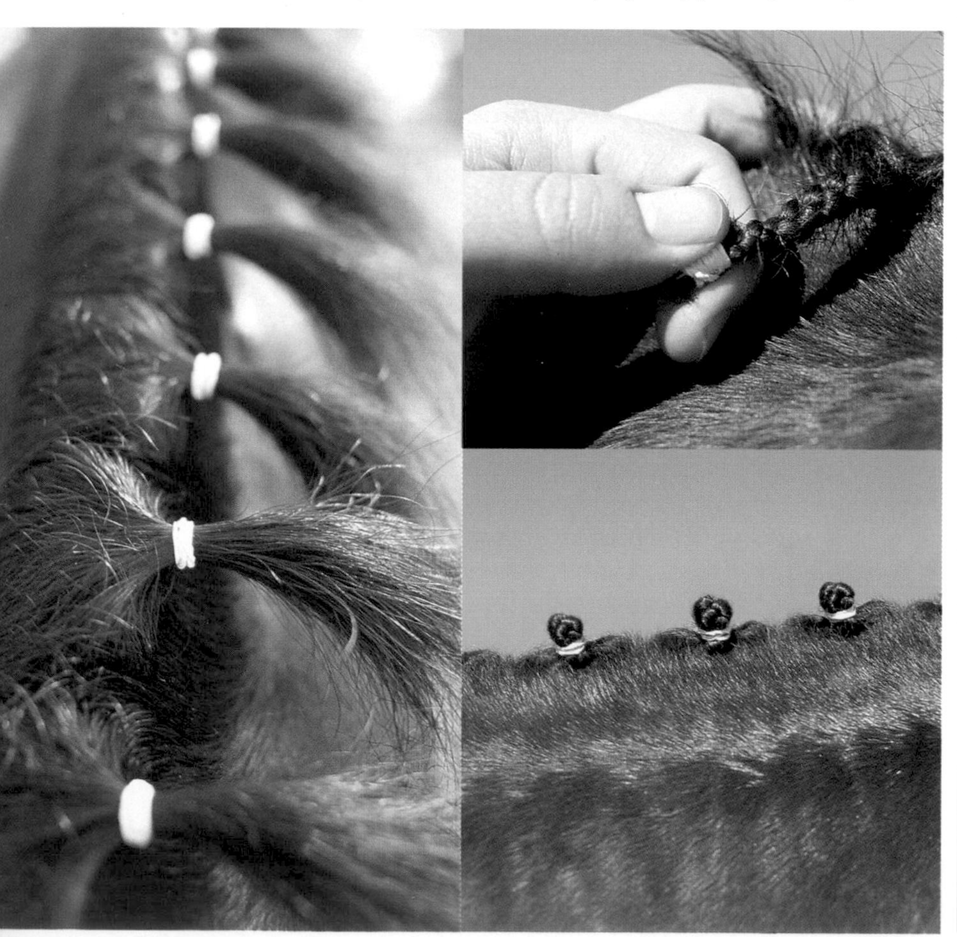

Plaiting

For shows and special events, a plaited mane is considered a sign of good turnout and of respect to judges or officials. For show classes, dressage and event dressage, you will feel out of place if you don't plait. In top class show jumping, however, plaiting is less common as horses are often jumping late into the night and on several days a week.

Basic plaiting involves sectioning the hair in widths roughly equivalent to one mane comb, then plaiting uniformly down to the very end of the hair, and securing with a rubber band before rolling or folding the plait under neatly and finishing by securing with another rubber band, or stitching with a needle and thread. Dressage plaits are often graduated in size to show off the outline of the neck, and finished with a covering of white tape.

Full, that is, unpulled tails can be neatly plaited to improve turnout on competition days.

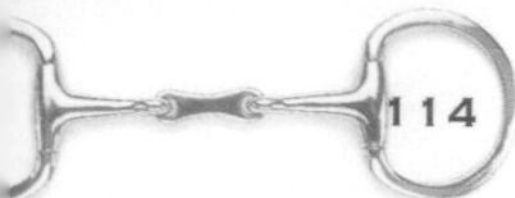

FOOT CARE

The saying, 'no foot, no horse', could not be more accurate. In the wild, as the horse moves around grazing from dawn to dusk on varying surfaces, the hoof is trimmed naturally, and growth and wear are kept in balance. In the domestic horse – particularly one that lives out in a restricted area – that level of natural wear does not occur, so feet need regular trimming and balancing. Adaptations are also needed for horses to walk on man-made roads and surfaces, plus help them cope with the conditions of being ridden. This involves shoeing.

Shoeing requirements depend on the level and type of work being undertaken, and there are many types of specialist shoes for use in all facets of equestrian sport, from racing to dressage. From birth, foals should have their feet checked regularly so that any problems with shape or alignment to the leg can be redressed. When the young horse starts work, it will require shoes for protection.

Daily foot care, such as removing debris and applying hoof dressing, helps promote healthy horn. Trimming and shoeing every four to six weeks, depending on the level of work, should be carried out by a qualified, professional farrier.

The farrier is an owner's accomplice in ensuring that a horse's feet are kept healthy and in good condition, and it helps to have these experts on your side. Appointments should be made on a regular basis, not the night before a show when you realize your horse has a loose shoe because you are two weeks late in getting the farrier.

He will remove any old shoes, then check the alignment of the feet in comparison with the conformation of the horse, before applying controlled trimming known as 'balancing'. The principles of a balanced foot are that the foot should align down in a continuous angle from the pastern (see 'Points of the Horse' pg 33); that the foot should be trimmed only to its natural shape and size; and that the bearing surface should be level.

A shoe is made up of two heels, two 'quarters' and the toe, and is secured by nails to the insensitive wall of the hoof. To give the shoe a better hold on the hoof, it is also secured with toe clips, traditionally one on the front and two on the hind shoes.

You should always keep the farrier informed of any changes in the way the horse has been moving.

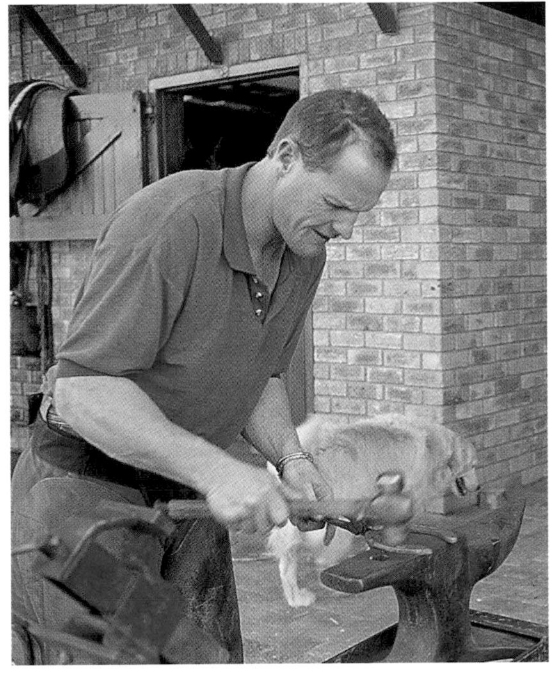

For example, 'brushing', the term used for when a horse strikes into its opposite limb while in motion, can have many causes, including weakness, excitement or faulty conformation. Protection can be afforded by using brushing boots, but brushing can also can be alleviated by special shoeing.

Overreaching, when the toe of the hind foot strikes into the forefoot, can happen when the horse is galloping, jumping or in extended trot. Overreach, or bell, boots offer protection, but if the horse is predisposed to overreaching, special shoes can help.

To prevent slipping on wet ground, studs can be used. The farrier will make holes in the shoes to accommodate studs, which should be screwed in place only for use during the work they are designed for, such as cross-country courses or road work. Studs should be removed immediately after work as a stabled horse could lie down and puncture itself with the stud. When studs are not being used, the holes should be plugged with greased wadding.

When the farrier arrives, have the horse ready to be tied up in a well-lit area with a hard floor and space for him to work. Shoeing horses is hard work and can be dangerous, so inform the farrier in advance if the horse is likely to be tricky at any stage. Traditionally, it is customary to keep the farrier supplied with cups of tea or a favourite beverage!

Top left *Shaping the new shoe to fit the hoof.*
Top right *Hot shoeing enables the farrier to shape the shoe to the horse's foot.*
Above *A new shoe should fit properly and be suitable for the work expected of the horse.*

Fresh grass provides naturally succulent food.

FEEDING

The horse has a complicated digestive system, including an intestinal canal approximately 30m (98ft) long. This convoluted system is prone to blockages and colic problems if not kept in good working order. In the wild, horses graze constantly, and this 'little and often' process has to be compensated for in the stabled horse. The horse takes up its food with its lips and tongue, and the incisor teeth pull up grass and hay, but the careful process of chewing food is carried out further back by the cheek teeth.

Horses grind their food, which is why the teeth, which continue to grow throughout the horse's life, should be kept in good order. If for any reason they are not, regular checks by a vet or specialized equine dentist will ensure that any rough or sharp edges or hooks are dealt with before they interfere with the chewing process.

FEEDING INGREDIENTS

1. Whole maize (corn) kernels
2. Green pellets (alfalfa pellets)
3. Fibre pellets
4. Soyabean meal
5. Crushed maize (corn)
6. Oats
7. Barley
8. Linseed
9. Chaff
10. Bran
11. Molasses

Good-quality hay should be fed at least twice a day.

To keep its digestive system working properly, it is essential that the horse has access to bulk roughage in the form of hay, hay replacement (haylage), or grass. Nutritionally, a healthy horse is one that has a balanced diet that incorporates the recommended levels of energy, protein, fibre, minerals and vitamins for the work required of it. This should be reflected in the horse's appearance.

A healthy horse should be neither too fat nor thin, and the coat should not be rough but have a soft, shiny appearance. A horse should always perform willingly at the level consistent with its training.

There are four main types of foodstuffs:
Green succulent food: grass, natural pasture
Forage: hay or hay replacement such as haylage
Individual cereals: oats, barley, maize, wheat, linseed, bran, sugar beet pulp
Compound foods (concentrates): mixes, cubes
The horse needs a combination of all these categories, plus vitamin and mineral supplements, to ensure a balanced diet.

FORAGE

Hay should be available for the horse at least twice a day, morning and night. The horse in light work can be fed hay as required, but for the performance horse in serious training, the digestive system should contain as little bulk as possible, necessitating an increase in concentrated food.

Dusty hay should not be fed, as the spores found in dusty hay can cause severe respiratory disease if inhaled over any length of time. If hay containing any element of dustiness has to be fed, the slices (flakes) should be pulled apart and soaked fully for 20 minutes to wash out the dust spores. Any spores that are not washed away after this time will expand and be ingested by the horse and not inhaled. In areas where hay quality is not good, for example, in late-cut crops, commercially branded hay substitutes can be used, with a compensatory adjustment to the concentrate ration, as these products are usually higher in protein and energy values.

Hay or forage should never be eliminated from the horse's diet, and owners should not be tempted to feed more concentrates to replace hay, as this may well disrupt the digestive system, resulting in colic.

CONCENTRATES (CUBES OR MIXES)

The old tradition of feeding a mixture of oats and barley or some other combination of individual cereals has largely been overtaken by the development of cubes and mixes. These products have an added viability for the one-horse owner, in that a complete food can be bought by the bag, so no storage is needed and freshness can be ensured.

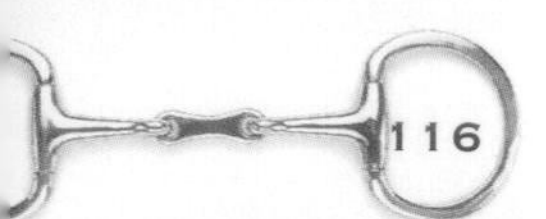

They are also useful in large stables where mixing a number of individual 'recipes' is time-consuming.

Cubes: In the wild, horses eat a variety of grasses and very little else, yet cubes are sometimes perceived as being too plain and owners believe the horse will become bored. The domesticated horse, in truth, will not become bored from eating cubes if that is all it knows, as what it doesn't know it will not miss. If bought from a reputable manufacturer, cubes will contain only quality ingredients. Cubes tend to have high fibre and low starch levels, making them ideal for hyperactive horses. The ingredients in cubes are thoroughly ground by the pelleting process and have been fully cooked, so they do not stress the digestive system. They are also effective in putting weight on the horse when required.

Mixes: At least one major feed manufacturer claims that coarse cereal mixes are designed solely for the horse owner, on the basis that if he or she does not like a particular feed (a preference usually determined by smell and appearance alone), it will not be fed to the horse! Mixes smell better than cubes due to their higher molasses level. Many feed companies now add herbs to the product, to appeal first of all to the owner. The main ingredients of a mix are easily visible – bright yellow flakes of maize, the green of peas and the golden grains of barley, wheat and, in higher energy mixes, oats.

Low energy mixes will contain some pellets, in the form of fibre pellets (pale brown), and grass or alfalfa pellets (green). These green pellets are often quite sour and can be left in the manger once the horse has picked out the cereal grains. For many horses they are an acquired taste.

Compound feeds

These may contain both cooked and uncooked cereals. Although many countries still use uncooked cereals in their mixes, the horse's digestive system is not able to break down and utilize the starch from these cereals as efficiently as the starch from cooked cereals. It is rather similar to the difference we would experience from eating a raw potato and a baked (jacket) potato.

Cereals such as barley, wheat, maize (corn), and peas will have been cooked by one of several methods. These are usually described on the packaging and literature as: steam flaking, which is exactly as described; micronizing, where the cereal is passed under infrared lamps while on a vibrating belt (rather like microwaving); extruding, where the whole of the starch structure is broken down with heat and pressure, then reformed; or uncooked, usually applied to oats, which are not cooked as the starch they contain is easily broken down by the horse's gut.

Chaffs and chops

Chaffs and chops are traditionally fed to horses that are prone to bolting their feed (eating too quickly). Dried grass chaff is a natural product which has the goodness of spring grass that has been cut and the moisture removed. As chaff is very dry, the horse cannot eat it fast, since it has to produce enough saliva to swallow it.

Chaffs and chops are an additional source of forage or bulk feed, but if fed, the horse's diet should also contain a nutritious element to enable a cost-effective reduction in the hard feed ration. Chaffs were originally just oat straw, cut daily with a chaff cutter. Over time, a niche market appeared, dictated by the needs of the one-horse owner, and now there are many varieties of ready-prepared chaffs available, including molassed, honey, oil and herbal chaffs, plus dried grass and alfalfa.

Feeding in hot countries

In a hot country, cubes are a good choice of feed as they remain fresher for longer than mixes. This is due to the lower molasses levels. (A highly molassed product is more prone to mould than a lower molassed product, as molasses is 65 per cent sugar.)

In some warm, wet countries mixes are prone to mites, small animals that can infest a feed store very quickly. These very tiny (pin prick) white creatures move en masse and can cover a large area in a small space of time. There is a distinctive sweet smell to mite-infested feed and the horse will not eat it. Some people are allergic to mites and are able to detect them by streaming eyes and noses.

In hot, humid climates, salt intake will increase. Salt is often mixed with minerals, trace minerals and protein supplements and can be fed by adding it as a top dressing at feeding time, or as a home-made granular lick given ad lib (as required). Commercial compacted salt blocks are also available.

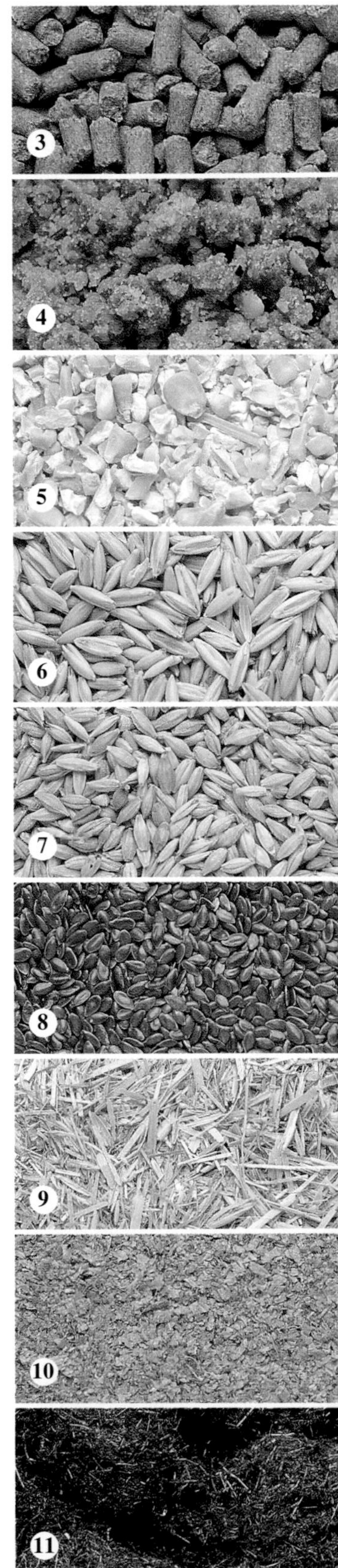

SUPPLEMENTS

Vitamin and mineral supplements are available on the market to cover every eventuality in the horse's life cycle. Herbal supplements are increasingly popular, from the calming variety to the extra energy versions.

There are supplements for increased mobility, for mares in season, you name it. What you have to watch, however, is that in reputable manufactured foods, the vitamin and mineral levels will be carefully balanced. Adding more vitamins can be a waste of time and money and can even upset the nutritional balance. Similarly supplements, especially the natural herbal variety, do need to get into the horse's system to have an effect, so be consistent. It is no good swapping supplements from week to week, or treating them as a universal panacea.

There may be another reason for your horse's excitability, for example, which cannot be cured by adding a supplement. Supplements do, however, have a valuable role to play in the horse's health. Probiotics, for example, which naturally restore the balance in a horse's digestive system, can be especially beneficial for the horse recovering from illness or injury. The key with supplements is to read the ingredients carefully and take advice from your vet and feed merchant.

FEEDING FOR BEGINNERS

With an inexperienced owner and a new horse, it is always wiser to aim for a low energy feed – if necessary lower than the work required of the horse. If the horse is new to the beginner, the last thing he/she wants is for the horse to be alert and frisky, and the rider on the ground! It is better for the rider to gain confidence by riding the horse calmly, rather than lose confidence by having to hang on. For this purpose, a Horse and Pony Cube or a Cool Mix would be the most appropriate feed. Once horse and rider have got to know each other, the rider has gained confidence and the horse has settled into its new surroundings, a higher energy feed can be provided as required.

CALCULATING AMOUNTS TO FEED

Especially for those new to horse-owning and feeding, the big feed manufacturers such as Spillers in the UK and Montana Pride in the USA, provide informative literature and run advice lines where queries are answered by a qualified equine nutritionist, so you never really need be in the dark on what seems a rather complex and scientific subject.

The advantages of buying ready-mixed compound feeds are consistency, as each batch is analyzed for content, and the constant availability of the different types of food required for various activities. In a compound feed the nutritional values are balanced, so there is no need to feed extra supplements, as you would to balance straight cereals (indeed you should not, as this will unbalance the ration). While they can be more expensive, compound feeds are simple for the novice owner to use. All you have to do is weigh the correct amount.

Your feed room should contain the following essentials: a spring balance (scale) for weighing haynets and feed; a weight tape to put around the horse's girth to assess its weight (use this weekly to determine weight gain or loss, see pg 122); a scoop, preferably jug-shaped rather than round (the jug shape's smaller surface area provides a more accurate measure). Measure a scoop of each feed you use, weigh it and record the weight so you have an accurate record of the weight of each food type.

Feeding to suit the workload

When choosing a compound feed, always buy a product appropriate for the level of work. Do not buy a competition mix, for example, if the horse is only hacking lightly. If you are feeding a low energy mix or cube and the horse needs more energy, do not increase the levels of your current feed, rather change to a higher energy feed. If you merely increase the level of feed, you can put more stress on the digestive system without creating the desired result. If the horse needs to carry more weight, choose a conditioning feed designed for the purpose of weight gain rather than more of the current feed.

Feeding the performance horse

The competition feeds on the market all depend on content, not feeding extra amounts, for effectiveness. They are based on high energy fibre, unlike traditional cereal mixes, which are based on high energy starch. With the new feeds, the high energy comes in a slow release rather than instant form, promoting stamina in the performance horse.

High energy chaffs are essential fibre sources. Oil, in a compound feed, is an excellent form of energy as it has three times the calories of cereals, is a slow release energy and provides condition.

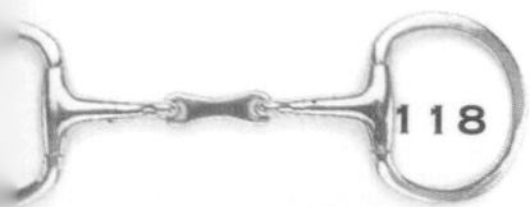

THE HEALTHY HORSE

The key to maintaining your horse's health is to remain observant. Being familiar with and recognizing all the signs of a healthy horse acts as a barometer for spotting signs of impending problems. Any change should be noted, as this provides useful information for your vet and makes early diagnosis easier.

There are four main types of health problems in horses: injury, physiological malfunction, nutritional disorders or invasion by germs or parasites.

The domesticated horse, whose lifestyle has been adapted from that of the wandering herd member, is reliant on good management for protection from injury and ill health. Vaccinations, where appropriate, and an effective anti-worming programme are preventative measures every horse owner should take in conjunction with veterinary advice. When a problem, or potential problem, occurs, an exact diagnosis and the ensuing treatment should be left to the professional veterinary surgeon. First aid equipment and an elementary knowledge of first aid are essential in a stable, but in any situation that calls for more than basic knowledge, the best course of action for an owner is to call the vet promptly.

WHAT TO WATCH OUT FOR

Changes in behaviour: If you know your horse, you will know when any behaviour seems out of character, possibly indicating pain – such as the normally ebullient horse that is standing listless at the back of the stable, or the normally calm horse that is restless and churning its bed up.

Above *A healthy, sound horse, such as Clinton, a six-year-old Holstein, is the goal of all horse owners.*

Left *In a large stable, mixing the correct feeds for each horse is part of the daily routine.*

The temperature is taken by inserting a thermometer into the rectum. The normal temperature range is between 37.7 and 38.6 degrees Celsius.

The coat: This should be shiny and lie flat. A winter coat should be even in length, not patchy. The skin should be pliable. If you pick up a fold of skin, it should go back into place as soon as you let go – this is a useful sign of hydration. A dull, staring (standing on end) coat, unexplained sweating or a feverish skin should be given closer examination.

Appetite and teeth: Some horses can be fussy eaters, but if a horse that normally clears its manger starts leaving feed or shows little interest in grazing while in the field, you have a good indication that something is probably wrong. The gums should be a pale salmon pink. Any deviation from this, such as too pale, too dark or patches of redness, are indications of various problems. Loss of appetite can also be due to soreness of the mouth due to teeth problems, which will be evident when the horse is ridden. The stabled horse's teeth tend to wear unevenly and need regular checks by an equine dentist. Specialist treatment may be necessary to ensure that wear is kept even, and horses, like humans, are susceptible to decay, scale and fractured teeth.

Eyes: These should be bright, slightly glossy and appear focused. Dullness, cloudiness or signs of discharge other than the normal morning 'sleep' in the eyes can herald a problem. The membranes surrounding the eye should be pale pink.

Nose: While a clear, runny nasal discharge after exercise or exertion is normal, a thick white or yellow discharge is abnormal.

Limbs: The healthy horse's legs and feet should feel cool and hard. Any swelling, puffiness or heat in the legs should be further examined, as should any heat in a foot. Hooves won't always smell sweet (nor do the soles of shoes) but an unusually foul smell is not normal and could indicate a foot infection.

Droppings: It is worth noting the colour (usually green-brown to golden-brown depending on the feed) and consistency of your horse's normal droppings. Horses regularly pass eight to twelve piles of droppings per day, which should be firm and moist soft 'clumps' that break open on hitting the ground. Changes in the normal pattern, diarrhoea, an absence of droppings or any sign of blood in the droppings should be investigated.

Urine: The horse should stale (pass urine) without any strain, passing yellow to yellowish-brown urine. Straining, or if the urine is darkened in colour, are signs your horse is not well, as is any indication that it is not consuming its regular water intake.

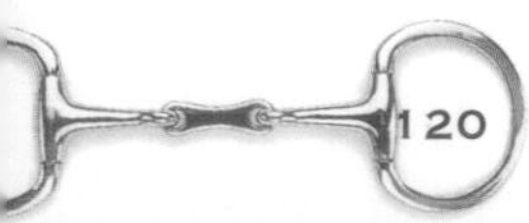

Using a stethoscope under the elbow to find the pulse: when at rest, the horse's pulse rate is between 30 and 40 beats per minute.

VITAL SIGNS

Having a record of your horse's normal pulse, respiration rate and temperature is extremely useful. To establish the average for your horse, readings need to be taken over several days, at the same time of day, while the horse is calm and at rest. Then, if there are any signs that the horse is off-colour, you have a point of reference for your vet.

Typical respiration rate is between 8 and 12 breaths a minute at rest; pulse rate 30 to 40 beats per minute; and temperature 38°C (100.5°F). A healthy horse may sneeze on occasions during schooling, as this is a sign of concentration, but coughing at the start of work is abnormal.

Taking the horse's temperature

Although this can be done with an ordinary thermometer, a specialized equine one is preferable. Get someone to hold the horse, and if you fear it may kick, they can pick up a foreleg to prevent this. Shake the thermometer and lubricate the bulb with petroleum jelly. Stand beside the hindquarters, lift the tail and insert the bulb gently into the rectum.

It is worth noting that the end you hold must be free of lubrication and you must hold it firmly. A horse's rectal muscles are very strong and it has been known for thermometers to disappear, necessitating a vet visit before you've even got this far. The thermometer should rest slightly to the side, otherwise you may end up taking the temperature of a dung ball, and should rest in place for a minute before removal for the reading to be recorded.

Taking the horse's pulse

A stethoscope is the easiest means of recording this. Place the stethoscope just inside the horse's elbow to find a pulse and record, with the help of a watch with a second hand, the number of beats per minute. If you do not have a stethoscope, you can find the pulse in the same place with your fingers. Press lightly until you feel the pulse beating. There is also a big artery under the horse's jaw that can be used for taking the pulse, but it is harder to locate.

Taking the horse's respiration rate

Using a watch with a second hand, count the number of 'in' and 'out' breaths per minute by either observing the rise and fall of the flanks or feeling this by placing your palm below the horse's nostrils and feeling the air blowing over your hand.

FIRST AID KIT

A well-equipped equine first aid kit should include:

- Equine thermometer
- Blunt-ended scissors
- Stethoscope (available from pharmacies and generally inexpensive)
- Large-volume syringe for flushing wounds
- Salt (to add to warm water to make a saline solution for flushing wounds)
- Veterinary antibacterial wash e.g. Hibiscrub
- Wound spray (obtainable from your vet) for minor cuts and grazes. Spray is preferable to powder as the latter tends to clog wound areas.
- Wound cream (such as Dermobion) for small grazes and sore patches
- Sterile wound dressings in various sizes e.g. Melolin
- Gauze-covered cotton wool e.g. Veterinary Gamgee
- Self-adhesive bandages in various sizes e.g. Vetrap
- Anamalintex poultice
- PVC tape (useful for holding hoof dressings in place)
- Stable bandages to support non-injured legs.

Measuring the horse's weight

To decide feed requirements and to gauge any change in weight, it is useful to record the horse's typical body weight using a proprietary weight tape (often obtainable from feed merchants). With the horse standing on a level surface, wrap the tape just behind the wither and to the back of where the girth normally goes. The weight can be read off the tape. Depending on its natural frame, a mature horse will weigh between 450 and 700kg (990 and 1540 lb).

VETERINARY VISITS

Having established any signs that the horse is off colour, further information that will be useful to your vet when you make the initial phone call is a résumé of your horse's work pattern and lifestyle. Is it stabled or turned out? Is it resting or in competitive work? What is the normal feed and, in the case of lameness, when was it last shod?

Generally speaking, the degree of pain the horse is displaying is a barometer as to how serious the condition is. However, severe colic indications (such as violent rolling and distress), acute lameness, choking, unwillingness to move or incapacity, breathing difficulties, injuries resulting in exposed bone, clear yellowish fluid (joint oil) leaking from joints, heavy bleeding, burns and eye injuries, can all be classed as emergencies.

Other conditions requiring veterinary attention include mild colic, diarrhoea, straining, heat and swelling in limbs or feet, and laboured breathing. Cuts longer than 2cm (1in) need stitching, but puncture wounds and other wounds, especially near joints, will also need veterinary attention.

If you have called the vet out, ensure that you have the horse ready when he or she arrives. Vets are busy people and won't appreciate waiting around while you collect the horse from two fields away.

Tie the horse in a clean, well-lit area and remove all feed. In the case of wounds, ensure the wound is clean and undressed. If the feet are involved, have them already picked out. Have a bridle ready, as the horse may need extra restraint while the vet examines a sore area. If the horse is lame, you will have to trot it up, so make sure an area is cleared for this, preferably on hard ground. In cases of suspected colic, it can be useful for the vet to be provided with a fresh droppings sample.

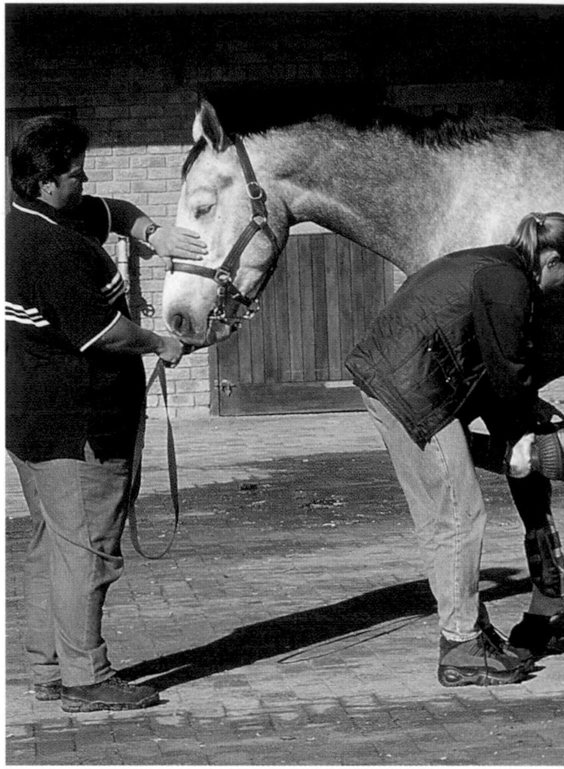

Top *The vet needs to examine the horse in good light and on a firm, clean surface.* **Right** *A well-equipped equine first aid box is an essential item in all stables.*

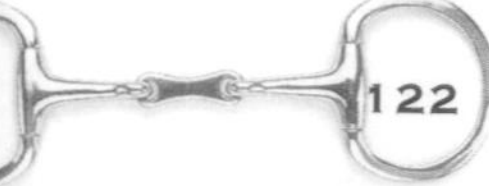

BASIC FIRST AID

The priority when applying first aid to a horse, which may possibly be in a distressed condition, is safety. The horse should be restrained with a head collar (halter) or bridle and help employed from another pair of hands to hold it, as well as help to keep it calm by talking to and stroking it. When looking over a hindleg, hold the tail firmly down and to the side, or get your assistant to hold up a foreleg, to help prevent kicking. Grasping a fold of skin on the horse's neck can also act as an emergency restraint. Whatever has happened, it is vital that the handlers keep calm in order to keep the horse calm.

Stopping bleeding

Put on a bridle or head collar and immobilize the horse, as movement will encourage bleeding. Ideally have someone else hold the horse. If blood is spurting from the wound, apply firm pressure with a cloth or dressing pad while the vet is called without delay.

If the blood is flowing more slowly, use a clean pad to apply pressure firmly to the area for about 10 seconds, then remove the pad. If the bleeding persists, reapply the pad and press firmly for longer. If the blood still flows after a few repetitions of this process, apply a clean pad to the wound and bandage it in place for half an hour. Remove and check. If the bleeding still has not stopped, apply a new pad and bandage for a further 30 minutes, but now is the time to call the vet if you have not already done so.

Wounds

After flushing away any mud and debris, clean the wound and surrounding area with saline solution or a veterinary antiseptic diluted to the required strength (a syringe is useful for this). When the area is clean check the extent of the wound. Any wound over 2cm (1in) long will need stitching by the vet. Small cuts can be treated with wound cream or spray. If the cut is in a suitable place, cover it with a sterile dressing, add a layer of Gamgee then hold the dressing in place with self-adhesive bandage secured with tape. Leg bandages can be finished with a stable bandage, but remember to bandage the other leg as well for support. Wise owners will always make sure that their horse's tetanus vaccination programme is up to date.

Bruising and swelling

Bumps, kicks, strains and sprains require treatment to reduce swelling. Hosing with cold water is the easiest method. When first applying the hose, direct it at the horse's foot and work it up the leg so the horse becomes accustomed to the idea. Continue to hose for about 15 minutes.

Alternatively, and in cases where there is no running water supply, apply a proprietary cold pack making sure it is not too cold, as it may cause a cold burn. Most cold packs consist of a gel that conforms to contours, so they can be bandaged into place. As a makeshift alternative, a packet of frozen peas is very effective.

Administering medicine

Powders and liquid medicine can usually be added to feed. If necessary, disguise powder in a little molasses, which will also prevent the powder getting left at the bottom of the manger.

Pastes, such as wormers and other medicine, come in syringes with dose markers. Determine the required dose with your vet or, in the case of wormers, by the weight of the horse.

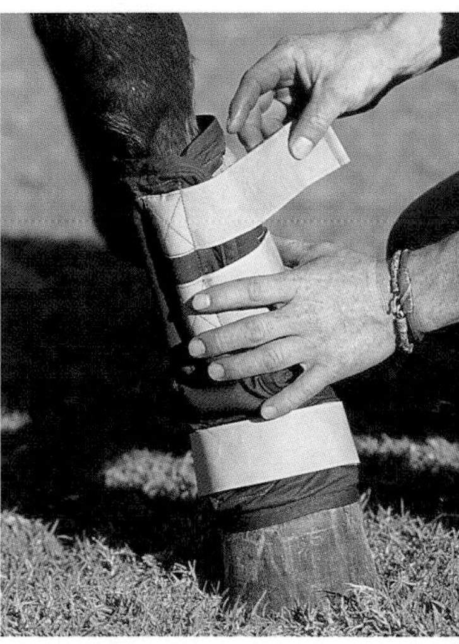

Cold-pack boots help to reduce swelling and are easy to apply. They can be kept in the fridge, ready for use.

A bright, clear eye is a sign of health, but a dull or clouded eye could indicate a problem.

Make sure the horse has nothing in its mouth. With one hand over the horse's nose, place the syringe in the corner of the mouth and squirt the dose with one efficient movement. Then hold the horse's head up to ensure that it swallows the lot. If you gently massage the underside of the jaw, you can encourage the swallowing movement.

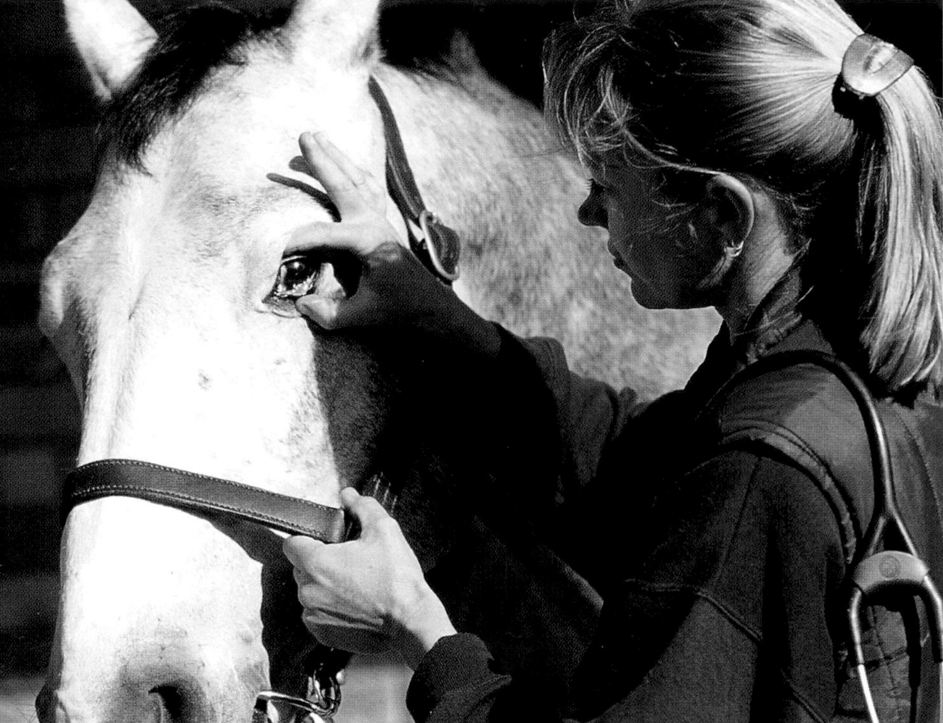

Eye ointments

These should be gently laid in a line inside the lid, accessed by carefully pulling the lower lid down or upper lid up with a finger. Close the eyelid. (This is often easier when someone else holds the horse.)

Below and right *While a poultice draws infection, a protective boot helps keep the foot dry and clean.*

Poultices

These warm, moist preparations draw dirt and infection from wounds and are often used for puncture wounds and for foot infections. They should never be used on a swelling without a wound and must be used with care near joints. Place the poultice, cut to the required size, on a plate and wet it with hot water for a few minutes. Drain the poultice (stacking another plate over the first and pressing firmly is a good way of doing this), and place a layer of plastic or cling film over the outside of the poultice. Position it over the required area, add a layer of Gamgee and bandage in place with a self-adhesive bandage. Foot poultices can be effectively held in place using a baby's disposable nappy (diaper). Applying wide adhesive tape over the bandage will preserve the base of the dressing as the horse walks on it. Alternatively, a purpose-made protective boot will protect the foot and keep it dry and clean.

Poultices should be changed two or three times a day as they are only effective while warm. They should not be used for more than a couple of days unless the vet directs differently.

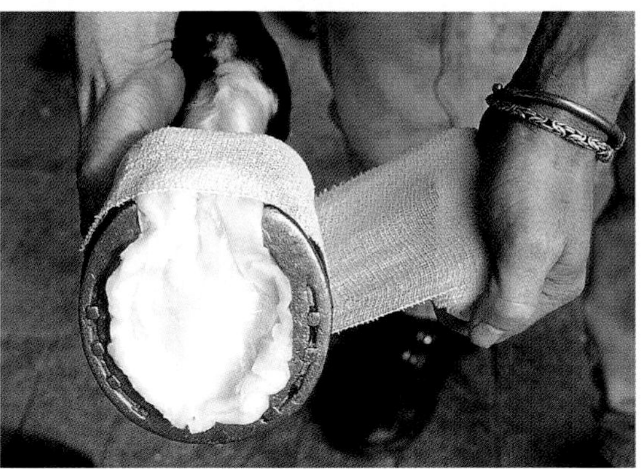

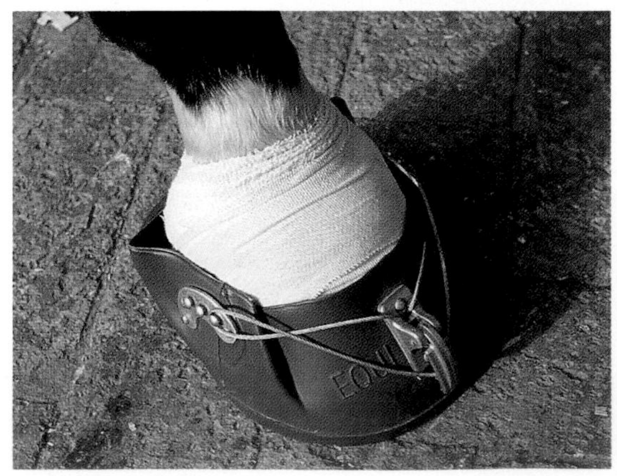

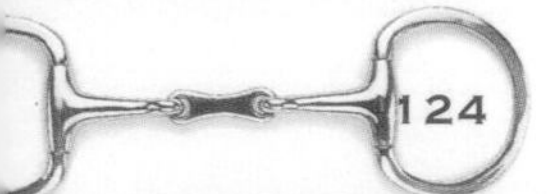

HANDLING EMERGENCIES

Horse owners must be prepared to deal with a wide variety of ailments and emergencies. Readers are advised to take professional advice in all instances where a serious illness or injury is suspected. If in any doubt, call the vet first.

ACUTE AZOTURIA

This condition, also known as 'tying up', is caused by the build-up of lactic acid in the muscles, and causes weakness, pain, and in extreme cases, muscle damage. The horse becomes reluctant to move, the muscles over the back and loins become hard and painful, and the horse may strain to pass urine; if it does it will be very dark red in colour. If you are riding, dismount. Put anything handy (such as your jacket) over the horse's loin area to keep it warm and arrange to get the horse home in a horse box. Once in the stable, keep the horse warm with a rug.

ACUTE COLIC

Any abdominal pain is referred to as colic. There are types and degrees of colic, from spasmodic colic (spasms of the gut wall); to flatulent colic (caused by excess gas); to impaction or blockage in the large intestine. Colic can be caused by worm infestation, stress, or sudden alterations in diet. Treatment varies from the administration of anti-spasmodic drugs and painkillers, to liquid paraffin to dislodge blockages, to surgery. Colic surgery is very serious, but only some five per cent of colic cases require surgery. If you suspect your horse has colic, remove all feed and ensure the horse's bed is thick enough to prevent injury if it rolls. Walk the horse gently if it is standing. If it is lying down, allow it to roll (it is a misconception that this causes the gut to twist); if it is rolling violently, keep out of the way to avoid injury to yourself.

ACUTE LAMINITIS (FOUNDER)

This occurs when reduced blood circulation in the foot causes the laminae holding the pedal bone to the front wall of the hoof to degenerate. Laminitis affects all four feet, but the front feet with more severity. In the initial stages the horse's movement will become restricted and 'pottery'; in extreme cases the pedal bone may start to rotate and drop. The condition can be caused by stress, and especially affects ponies on grass that is too lush. It is very painful. If the horse is in the field and able to walk, bring it into the stable. Remove all feed. If it is immobilized, just keep it calm until the vet arrives.

CAST HORSE

A horse is said to be 'cast' when it gets into such a position while lying in the stable that it is unable to get up on its own. If possible pull the front of the horse away from the wall. Once you have got the horse clear from the wall, move out of the way while it gets up. If it is still not able to get up on its own, you may need help, as rolling the horse over using ropes or lunge lines needs an accomplice. Once it is on its feet, check the horse for any injuries and remake its bed, adding fresh bedding.

CAUGHT IN BARBED WIRE

Get help, and get hold of wire cutters. This is a potentially dangerous situation as the horse is liable to panic, causing more injury to itself and possibly injuring those around it. If possible put a head collar (halter) on the horse to help hold it steady if it is standing. If the horse has fallen down, kneel on its neck and hold its head down to stop it struggling. Once the wire has been cut away, be careful to get out of the way when the horse gets up. Hose or wash the cuts and cover them with a clean, dry bandage or gauze pad. If stitches are required, keep the horse calm until the vet arrives.

CHOKING

If a piece of apple or dry food gets stuck in the horse's throat, it may be dribbling and attempting to swallow with its head down and neck tensed. Horses cannot vomit but it is unlikely it will suffocate. Do not give the horse water, as fluid could go straight to the lungs. Call the vet, but while waiting you may be able to feel the obstruction and gentle massage may help to dislodge it.

FOOT PUNCTURES

If possible, remove the object but remember where on the foot it came from. A nail, for instance, might be easy to remove, but any large or not clearly visible objects should be left in place until the vet arrives. Clean the area with water and, if possible, place the foot in a tub of warm water. Cover the area with a pad and bandage until veterinary advice can be sought.

FRACTURES

Broken bones occur most frequently in the horse's legs. A fracture may be indicated by sudden acute pain and swelling, often accompanied by the bone lying in an odd way. Keep the horse still until veterinary help arrives.

POISONING

Suspected poisoning may be revealed by symptoms similar to colic, along with diarrhoea, distressed breathing and sweating. If the horse is in the field, bring it into the stable. Remove all food and call the vet at once. Poisoning most often occurs from the ingestion of poisonous plants. If your paddock management is done properly, such plants will have been removed.

SEVERE TENDON INJURIES

Severe strain can cause the tendon fibres to tear or snap, which will drop the fetlock low to the ground. Keep the horse as still as possible, restrict its mobility and seek veterinary attention. In the meantime, hose the leg with cold water to reduce pain and swelling, and apply a cold pad and bandage for support.

CHAPTER SEVEN

Buying, Housing & Transporting

Once a rider has achieved a certain level of competence and feels committed to pursuing his or her interest in riding – whether for pleasure, towards competing, or simply for the chance to ride where and when he or she pleases – the prospect of horse ownership comes into the equation.

This immediately raises issues of which horse to buy, where to keep it and how to transport it. Setting out to become a horse owner means entering into a relationship with a living creature, which will not just be at your disposal but will also require you to be at its beck and call for feeding, exercise and overall care. A prospective horse owner needs to be aware of the responsibility he is taking on, as horse ownership makes riding more of a way of life than a hobby.

It is wise to have accumulated some experience of riding different horses with confidence before making a move towards horse ownership. Apart from acquiring the necessary skills, this means you will have some idea of the type and character of the horse that will suit you.

Keeping a horse

Before making the decision to purchase a horse, look at how owning one is going to fit in with your current lifestyle. How much time do you have, and how much money can you afford (this is not a cheap pastime). Where are you going to keep the horse, and who is going to look after it?

If the facilities are available, keeping a horse at home is fine in theory, but horses need and thrive on routine and company. It is not the happiest situation to leave a horse alone all day while its owner is at work. Land and stabling are costly to buy and maintain, so increasingly, boarding horses is the most logical option. Known as livery (or agistment in Australia, boarding in the USA), the arrangements for stabling your horse can take several forms. Full board entails the entire care of the horse being undertaken by the boarding establishment, including exercise if the owner is not around to ride it. Half board usually entails the stable undertaking general stable routine

A well-prepared horse is led into a trailer prior to travelling to a show.

and care, such as mucking out and feeding, with the owner responsible for riding and grooming the horse. Working livery is an arrangement used in teaching establishments, whereby suitable horses are boarded at a lower rate in return for use in lessons. With DIY livery, only the facilities are rented, while the owner does all the work.

With any boarding arrangement, however, it is essential to clarify the terms and responsibilities before the deal is entered into. Working livery, for example, is not going to be feasible if the owner turns up to ride on a Saturday morning to see the horse being ridden by someone else.

It is important to find an establishment where both you and your horse are going to fit in. A school that focuses predominantly on dressage, with the jumps stacked firmly in the corner of the arena, will be a frustrating environment for the keen jumper. Similarly, a rider who enjoys hacking in the company of other riders will miss out on this at a serious competition stable where everyone else is competing in shows every weekend.

As well as all-round suitability, the other criteria involved in finding a good boarding stable are very similar to those that are applied in finding a good riding school (see chapter 4).

What to look for when buying

Owning a horse provides an opportunity to form a bond with one equine partner, with the resulting build-up of confidence and trust enabling the rider to rapidly gain experience.

The main factors to bear in mind when buying a horse are suitability of purpose, all-round experience, size and weight, and the character and temperament of both horse and rider. In general, these factors should be matched. However, an inexperienced horse needs an experienced rider and vice versa. Learning together might seem like a nice idea but in practice it can lead to disaster, with neither horse nor rider benefiting. A rider who suffers from nerves should take this into account. You should look forward to riding, and feeling that you constantly have to steel yourself to ride an excitable horse is likely to remove any sense of enjoyment long before you have had a chance to develop a sense of achievement at overcoming your nerves.

A less experienced rider wishing to start competing seriously would be well advised to look for an older, more experienced horse that knows the ropes. To this end, the equine sporting bodies of many nations allow the 'downgrading' of advanced horses when a less experienced rider takes over.

At a riding school, the novice may have ridden horses of various shapes and sizes, but when buying your own horse, go for a close fit. With horses, it is not just size and weight-carrying ability that counts, but also a good match of temperaments. A heavy-set man will be better off on a solid hunter than on a light-boned Thoroughbred, while an older teenager may need a horse to grow into rather than a pony that will soon be too small. The shape of the horse should also suit the rider. For example, a narrow-hipped rider can experience considerable discomfort riding a wide-backed horse on a regular basis.

While much of this may appear to be stating the obvious, it is wise to be aware that emotions can cloud one's judgement when choosing a horse. Falling for a handsome face over a stable door which, when opened, reveals a tall broad body, is not a wise course of action for a petite woman, at least where horses are concerned. Romance can overcome many barriers, but not that of being unable to get back on when you have dismounted to open a gate while out hacking.

Sourcing your horse

There are various routes available to the horse buyer. Word of mouth is always a good starting point, but you may need to spread the net further afield. Buying from a breeder is a good source of proven young horses, but not always practical for the first-time buyer looking for a more mature horse.

Buying from an auction run by a breed association which prepares and trains young horses prior to sale is popular in Germany and, increasingly, in other countries. A reputable dealer or agent is another option that offers the first-time buyer the chance to look at a selection of horses. A good dealer will bear in mind that a first-time buyer is a potential second-time buyer and will offer sound advice and help.

Specialist equine agents will source a selection of horses for a prospective buyer to view; that is, they do all the hard work in finding horses that match the buyer's brief. Some trainers will also use their contacts to source suitable prospects for their pupils.

Riders come in a variety of different shapes, sizes and levels of experience. Finding the right horse to meet your needs and skills may take time, but it is a process that should not be hurried.

This process is commonly used for finding more expensive competition horses, but at any level, it should be made clear at the outset whether this is a business arrangement or favour, as an agent or trainer will usually take a commission from the vendor for introducing a buyer.

Buying via advertisements in the equestrian press can be time-consuming, as long distances may be travelled to view a 'paragon' which turns out to be completely different from its description. It is advisable to elicit as much information as possible during the initial enquiry before setting out to view. Conversely, the prospective buyer telling the vendor honestly what he or she is looking for will avoid wasted time spent sprucing up an event horse for viewing by someone who wants a quiet hack.

Viewing horses should not be regarded as an opportunity to ride lots of different horses either. Only view suitable-sounding prospects; anything else is both time-wasting and discourteous.

TRYING FOR BUYING

It is essential for the first-time buyer to take an experienced rider to view a prospective purchase. There are so many factors to take into account. An instructor who knows the purchaser's riding capabilities and future aims is the ideal companion. Don't expect a professional to give advice and time for free, but this will be money well spent.

On arrival, the horse should be viewed without tack, and trotted up so the buyer can get a first impression. If all looks well, ask for the horse to be tacked up. It is a good idea to be present during this process, or even help, as it gives a chance to see how the horse behaves while being handled.

The horse should then be put through its paces for you to view. Does it come up to the description so far? If everything is looking positive and you are interested, it is a good idea for your instructor or advisor to mount the horse. As well as his or her assessment of suitability, it gives you the chance to see how the horse reacts to a strange rider, but one with whom you are familiar.

The next step, if you are still interested, is to have a ride yourself. This is for your benefit, not that of anyone who is watching, to allow you to get a feel for the horse, so take your time and take it step by step. Don't feel obliged to try anything until you feel ready for it. If at any time during the stages of trying a horse you realize it is not for you, say so. A vendor is less likely to be offended that their horse doesn't suit you than to have a lot of time wasted and hopes raised in vain.

Having told the vendor you are interested in purchasing the horse, ask to see any breeding or registration papers and competition history. They should tally with the glowing references of your prospect that you were given over the phone originally.

By this stage you may well have found your dream horse, but you are only halfway there. It is often a good idea to try a horse a second time, perhaps dealing with it in the stable and riding it first yourself. At either the initial stage or at this point, try to do something different. For example, if you first rode the horse in an indoor school, ask to ride the horse outside, as the reaction can be significantly different. Try to ride the horse down the road or in an open field, not only in an enclosed arena. Your aim is to test as many eventualities as possible.

Some dealers may be prepared to offer a short trial period, but this is increasingly uncommon and not to be expected. Not only can accidents happen, but in the hands of an inexperienced rider, the horse's level of schooling may deteriorate with a consequent, even if temporary, reduction in its value.

If the purchaser likes the horse and everything is as it seems, the next step is to engage a veterinary surgeon to check the horse over.

VETERINARY EXAMINATION

Before going to examine the horse, the vet should be made aware of what the purchaser intends to do with it (for instance, general riding only, or participating in cross-country events or dressage).

An appointment should be made for the vet to view the horse, at your expense, at the vendor's establishment or at a nearby veterinary clinic, in which case you may have to provide transport.

Above *Before concluding the purchase, the horse should undergo a thorough veterinary examination to ensure it is suitable for the purpose for which it is intended.*

The extent of the examination depends both on the price and intended purpose of the horse. A top three-day event or dressage horse will be X-rayed and examined to a much greater extent than would be required for a children's pony, for instance. This is the vet's only interest in the price, however, and he should not be placed in the position of valuer.

The heart, eyes and lungs are the basic items checked and the vet will require the horse to be exercised under saddle or on the lunge to check both the heart rate and lung function. The vet will also look for any existing lumps or bumps, and may recommend some X-rays, such as of the feet, if any further probing is needed.

If the horse is clear on all these counts, the vet will issue a note or certificate to say so. This is often misconstrued as a sort of 'lifetime guarantee'. It isn't; it is a statement of the vet's findings on the condition of the horse on the day of the examination. It is also a certificate accepted by insurance companies as a health evaluation at the time of purchase.

CONCLUDING THE PURCHASE

Once a veterinary examination has been concluded positively, there is a tacit understanding that the sale will go through. If you have any doubts, do not go ahead with the veterinary examination. Of course, if the vet is not happy with any aspect, this negates the obligation to buy. In the case of a minor injury or temporary condition, the vet may recommend re-examination at a later date, and the purchaser must decide whether to wait or not to proceed any further.

Once the sale has been agreed and the price paid, the horse is the responsibility of its new owner. All papers and records should be handed over and updated with the new owner's details.

Insurance

There are various levels of insurance cover (for horses and riders) to suit both the value of the horse and the owner's pocket. Vet's fees, injury, 'loss of use' (if the horse cannot be used for the intended purpose due to injury, for example), saddlery and tack, and mortality can all be covered by insurance. It is always advisable to have third party insurance cover if nothing else, so that you are protected if your horse inadvertently causes an injury to another horse or person. This is often available at competitive rates through riding clubs, but you should shop around to meet your own specific needs.

Some countries offer specialist equine insurance, but elsewhere this may have to be taken as part of a standard household insurance plan. Before you first buy a horse, contact your broker for advice on equine insurance and third-party cover.

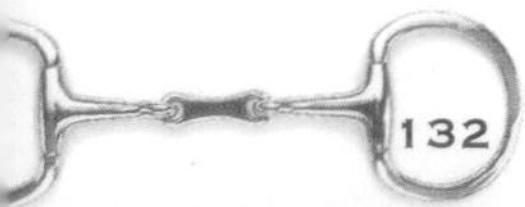

Keeping a horse

In its natural environment, the horse lives at grass with other horses. For a migratory creature of flight, this regime fits in with its desire to roam and graze freely, meets its social instincts to be part of a herd, and fulfils its need for space to exercise.

For young, growing horses, a free-ranging life in a large field or paddock is essential for healthy physical development – strengthening bones, joints and tendons as well as the muscles and internal organs. In reality, though, full time 'living out' is not always the most practical solution for the working horse, nor, frequently, for its equally hard-working owner.

The reasons for keeping horses stabled include protection from the extremes of climate, management time, the availability of suitable land, and the need to control and monitor the lifestyle of the performance horse.

Turning out

Certain breeds, notably hardy native ponies, can live out at grass all year round, or at least for part of the year while performing light work such as hacking, provided there is access to a constant water supply and a dry, wind-proof shelter.

As the workload increases, and feeding and work regimes become more controlled, the horse may need to be clipped and kept rugged up, so stabling is the only option. However, some daily turn-out time should be provided for every horse, even if space is restricted. It is not only unnatural for a horse to be confined to a stable for 23 hours a day, but turn-out is an important factor in keeping the horse's digestive system and circulation in good order, as well as being conducive to its general well-being.

Ideally, turn-out should have a social aspect for the horse. The natural urge to create a pecking

Although natural pasture and open fields are an ideal environment for horses, this is not always convenient for owners. However, stable-kept horses still need to be turned out daily for their own well-being.

order requires that groups be set up with forethought to avoid bullying. At a boarding stable with limited paddock space, it often takes a bit of management and effort to ensure your horse is turned out with suitable companions. No one wants their precious horse to need time off because of having been kicked in the field!

With valuable performance horses in peak condition, which are likely to burst into real 'whoopee time' when turned loose, it is understandable if turnout time is limited to sole occupation of one small paddock to prevent injury through high jinks. Some horses, when very fit, are so overjoyed when given a taste of freedom that it is considered only feasible to turn them out after the end of the competition season, when the horse is 'let down' to a lower level of fitness in preparation for a rest.

However, for many top riders, the level of relaxation gained by their horse being turned out for short periods outweighs their fears of knocks or bumps. Also, when the horse is used to a routine, it is less likely to race around like a mad thing. Instead, it will settle to graze after a buck and a roll.

With any horse that finds freedom highly exciting, being turned out with a quieter horse, often an elderly horse or pony that remains unimpressed and does not join in, tends to have a settling effect.

ROUGHING OFF AND BRINGING UP

When a horse is to be turned out for a rest – either full time or to spend days in the field and nights in the stable – a gradual adaptation needs to be followed to avoid upsetting the sensitive digestive system.

Known as 'roughing off' or 'letting down', this involves a gradual reduction in the ration of hard feed, a slow cutting down in the number of rugs worn by the horse in the stable, and a gradual increase in the number of hours the horse spends out, to get it accustomed to the change of lifestyle. Similarly, 'bringing up' involves the gradual introduction of hard feed while the horse is still living in the field, and a slow introduction and build-up of the amount of work. This is often advantageously begun with the horse being ridden at walk while living in the field.

Starting work with a calm, laid-back horse is much easier than with a newly clipped, newly stabled horse that will be relishing the effects of its hard feed and may well prove to be very much on its toes!

Before the horse is fully 'roughed off', its shoes – or at least the hind ones – should be removed (some farriers prefer to leave on the front shoes, especially in the case of brittle feet). When the horse is brought up the shoes will need to be replaced and anti-parasite medication administered. This is also a good time for the teeth to be checked and for annual inoculations to be carried out.

FIELD MANAGEMENT

The most important part of field management is the removal of droppings. Horses are just as migratory in their habits of excreting waste as they are in grazing, and laborious as it might be, removing droppings keeps down the levels of worm and parasite infestation and greatly extends the viability of any field.

The more time the horse is going to spend living in the field, the larger the area required. If horses are living out full time at one location, there should be enough ground for pasture rotation, so that areas can be rested. Pasture or meadowland consists of many different grasses, herbs and other plants.

Left *Trees provide valuable shade, as well as shelter from rain and wind.*

Above *Secure, sturdy fencing will help ensure that horses cannot escape from the field.*

Horses tend to head for areas containing the most succulent grasses, which are then eaten to the roots. If these die away and the less appetising plants take hold, the paddock becomes what is known as 'horse-sick'. Resting paddocks, or alternating horses with other livestock such as cattle or sheep that have different tastes in plants can alleviate this.

A horse-sick paddock will need ploughing and reseeding (which is best done after a soil analysis, and in consultation with an expert body, such as a ministry of agriculture or farmers' association). Paddocks can be rolled and harrowed each year before the grass starts to grow, and 'topped' to discourage the spread of less popular plants.

The ideal paddock has well-drained flat ground, is located away from busy roads or other potential hazards, and has natural boundaries of hedges and trees that give protection from the elements. However, most horse owners have to make the most of what is available and it is worth considering that some of the best race and event horses in the world are raised in New Zealand on hills of escarpment proportions. The vital elements are good fencing and a constant supply of clean, fresh water. Unless your paddock has a natural unpolluted running stream with a pebble bed, a reliable alternative water supply must be provided. A purpose-made trough, sited on ground prepared with a stone- and sand-drained area, is a wise investment. Old baths or other insecure stop gaps with potentially sharp edges can be dangerous for horses. Bear in mind that fields without access to mains water will entail several daily trips with buckets to ensure the water supply is fresh and constant.

Fencing

Horses tend to exercise their freedom to roam at any given opportunity unless they are securely and safely enclosed. Some ponies can be veritable escape artists when it comes to getting out of fields.

Fencing of at least 1.2m (4ft) high, with top and bottom spacing is essential. Good post and rail timber, treated to discourage chewing and built with rounded corners for safety, makes an excellent enclosure but can be costly.

Other fencing materials include plain wire narrowly spaced with strong pillar posts, wire mesh, or special products such as wire that has been reinforced and widened with nylon or strong synthetic material. Barbed wire is very dangerous, can easily cause injury and should never be used to fence in horses. Electric fencing can be used temporarily to cordon off a particular area, but is not reliable as the main means of enclosing horses.

Gates should be wide enough to lead horses in and out without any risk of catching themselves, and should be well secured, with enough ease of access so that a handler can get one horse through the gate while dealing with the fastening and probably a bucket as well! Anyone who has ever struggled in the pouring rain with slip rails, a bucket in one hand and yearling in the other, has learned to appreciate the advantages of a well-hinged gate with good ground clearance and a safety catch.

Field shelters

Where natural protection from the elements is not available, a field shelter should be provided. This is normally a rectangular wooden or metal construction, large enough to accommodate the number of horses that may use it, closed on three sides, with one long side left open to allow easy access. You don't want a narrow entrance where horses might catch themselves when barging in or out.

The open front should be positioned away from the prevailing weather, so that wind and rain do not blow straight in. A straw base should be provided in winter if the inside floor gets muddy or churned up.

If hay is to be provided as food or bedding in the shelter during the winter months, it is often a good idea to build a feed store as an annex to the shelter to avoid frequent trips carrying supplies. Such a store obviously needs to be well secured to prevent the horses from raiding it for extra rations.

Above *Electric fencing is suitable as a temporary paddock enclosure, but should not be used full time.*
Top right *An adequate supply of fresh water must be available at all times.*
Right *A simple, open-sided field shelter provides shade and a refuge from the sun in hot climates.*

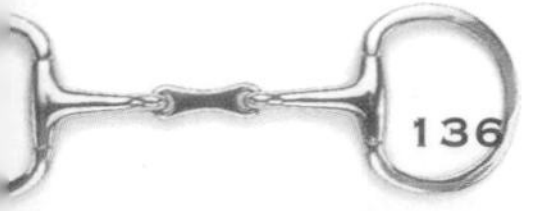

Stabling

Styles of stabling vary from area to area and from country to country. Stabling can comprise anything from modern timber constructions, to natural stone stables to purpose-built indoor barns.

Whatever the building style or materials used, and however humble or palatial the stabling may look from the exterior, there are several essential factors that need to be applied in order to create a good quality home for a horse.

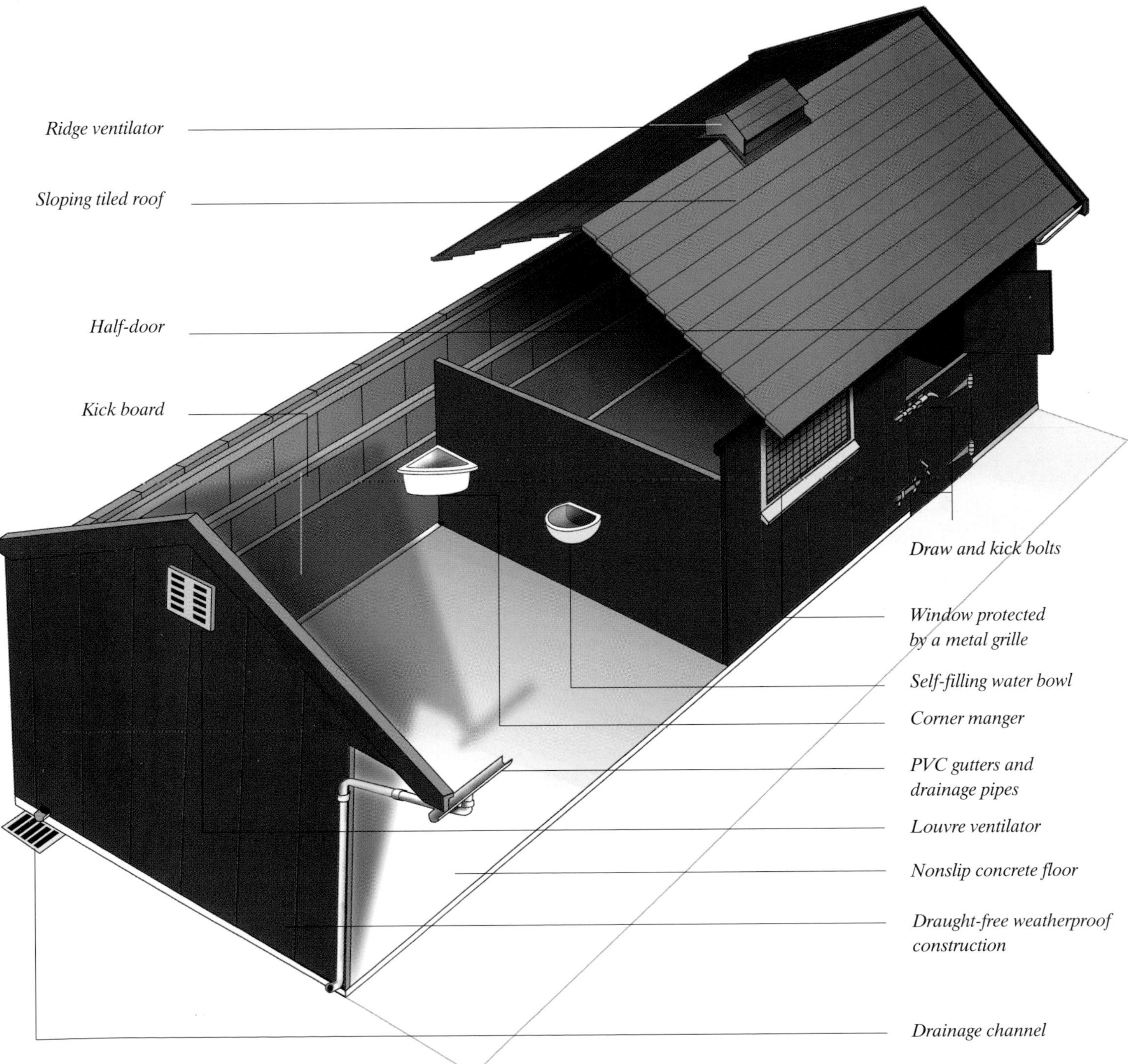

Above *When seeking a livery stable, look for an organized, well-maintained yard.*
Below *A kick-bolt is the ideal lower-door fastening, as it can be opened with the toe of a boot – very handy when your arms are full of tack.*

Ventilation is very important. While the actual temperature in the stable should relate to the ambient temperature, it is protection from draughts and from the elements that keeps horses warm, not central heating. However, in Scandinavia and those parts of the USA and Germany that are prone to sub-zero temperatures, heating systems are often utilized in stables and indoor schools.

Horses are very sensitive to draughts, but they do need a lot of fresh air. In cooler climates or seasons it is easy to maintain the airflow in an outside stable, whereas in barn-type stables, particularly in hotter climates, fans or other supplementary ventilation may be needed to keep fresh air flowing. Airflow is normally enhanced by the high roof clearance required for safety, which should be a minimum of twice the height of the horse's wither.

Every stable should have a window that opens outward and is protected by wooden slats or a metal grille on the inside, so the horse cannot access the glass. Safety (shatter-proof) glass should always be used in stables.

Light should replicate natural daylight as far as possible, with skylights and neon or electric strip lights to enhance this where necessary.

Floors should be nonslip for safety reasons. Concrete floors, for example, should be roughened to facilitate a secure grip and drainage. Although it is expensive, rubber matting is a good investment. In addition to improving grip, it provides a softer base for bedding and is hygienic, as it can be hosed down regularly and disinfected periodically, such as when a new horse moves in or after illness.

The electricity supply must be specially insulated against damp and well secured to prevent horses from getting to any cables or wires. Covered safety switches should be used throughout the yard.

Apart from young stock and mares with foals, for which the communal barn proves an excellent winter management system, horses generally have their own 'rooms' (stables or stalls). Whatever the type of stable – a single unit, an outside yard of individual stables or the indoor 'American barn' style – the horse's actual 'house' is known as a loose box.

Stalls were formerly utilized extensively for working horses, and this remains the case in some countries where horses are used as farm labour. Stalls are still used in the traditional buildings of the Spanish Riding School of Vienna and the Royal Mews; but for horses spending much of their time in the stable, being tethered in a small stall is far from ideal and the larger loose box (see side panel) is preferable.

Fixtures and fittings

Much care needs to go into the selection of fittings. The principle is rather similar to any situation where there are small children around – try to spot any potential hazards and keep them out of the way.

Door catches need to be secure. Numerous accidents can occur in stables when horses get loose. A door catch at both the top and bottom of the stable door is essential, with the top one a specially designed stable safety latch, so as to avoid inquisitive equine mouths getting caught and injured on it. It is also worth noting that a simple rope clip does not provide a good means of extra security on stable doors, as many horses and ponies have injured themselves trying to undo the rope or play with it.

Water troughs and mangers should be situated no lower than the horse's shoulder height, with smooth edges and no protrusions. As a general rule, mangers and water troughs are fitted at the front corners of the stable, away from the door, to ensure

that horses that get excited around feed times don't have a chance, however inadvertently, to catch the retreating bearer of the food with a kicking-out heel.

Food hatches, which enable the food to be delivered from outside the stable into a manger which then swivels round to be secured in place within the stable, are increasingly popular, especially in big indoor yards where they can save a lot of time in the opening and closing of doors.

Water, available as a constant supply, is just as important in the stable as in the field. Water troughs are situated diagonally across from the manger, but if buckets are used, they are best sited near the door, tucked round the corner to make them less susceptible to being knocked over.

When supplying hay, feeding from ground level or from a hay manger is preferable to using hay racks or hay nets, as this helps prevent the ingestion or inhalation of spores and dust. Hay nets, if used, should always be tied with a safety knot and secured by pulling the string to the hay net as high as possible, to avoid a situation where the horse could step on an empty net or get caught up in it.

Bedding

Good bedding is essential for the horse's comfort, as insulation from the cold and for protection as it lies down in the stable. Bedding must also drain well. Choice depends on several factors, but in a busy boarding yard, you should expect to be confined to choosing what the yard in general uses.

Traditional bedding materials, such as straw and wood shavings, are increasingly being replaced by proprietary products, not only because of the emphasis on making stable environments as dust-free as possible, but also because disposal is becoming more difficult. The days when a muck heap was taken away for free by the local farmer are almost over, and disposal of waste is now a cost that needs to be taken into account by stable managers.

Good quality straw – wheat straw being the optimum – makes excellent bedding, as it provides good drainage, is warm and springy, and is aesthetically pleasing for the owner. The drawbacks are that it is not always dust-free and can provide too much of an extra snack for the horse.

Wood shavings are absorbent, less likely to be eaten and easy to manage if droppings are removed regularly. Sawdust is not satisfactory as it gets very damp and also, if ingested with hay, has been known to cause colic. In some countries, peat has a certain following as bedding as it is highly absorbent, but it can be difficult to dispose of.

Shredded paper is entirely dust-free and therefore popular for horses with dust allergies. Proprietary brands of bedding, made of material such as hemp, are also entirely dust-free and absorbent, but can be expensive, although they are effective when managed correctly with the regular removal of droppings. There is also a variety of commercial straw-based products on the market that are guaranteed to be dust-free.

Stable Dimensions

The dimensions of a loose box depend largely on the size of the horse. Stallion and foaling boxes tend to be much larger, but on average, a loose box of 3.7m x 3m (12 x 10ft) is the recommended minimum for a pony, increasing to 3.7m x 4.2m (12 x 14ft) for a large horse. Doorways should be a minimum of 1.1m (3ft 6in) wide and not less than 2.1m (6ft 8in) high, opening outward or sliding. With the traditional outdoor stable door – the half-door – the bottom half should be around 1.4m (4ft 6in) high for horses and correspondingly less for ponies. It is a good idea to have the top edge finished with a smooth metal strip to discourage chewing

In indoor yards, where the partitioning is partly solid and partly grille, the solid area should be at least 1.3m (4ft) high and the total height approximately 2.2m (7ft).

In other words, at least high enough to prevent horses getting to each other over the top or getting caught on the top of the partition in the event of them rearing up.

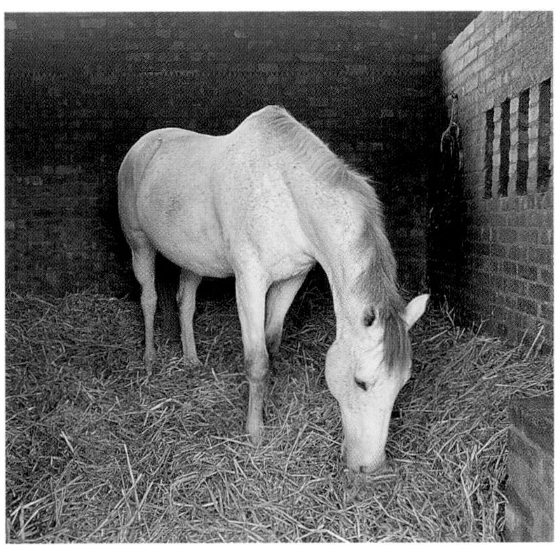

Wood shavings **(left)** *and straw* **(right)** *are widely used forms of bedding.*

Daily mucking out helps to keep the stable environment clean, hygienic and pleasant for the horse.

STABLE MANAGEMENT

Routine makes a yard easy to run and also pleases its occupants. Horses thrive on routine. A typical day in the stables starts with feeding, and revolves around feeding at regular times. Fresh water should be made available before each feed, after which the water buckets are removed and rinsed out.

Mucking out takes place after the first feed of the day. This involves the removal of all droppings and wet patches and the addition of replacement bedding. During mucking out, it is best to tie the horse up securely in the stable, as wheelbarrows, parked however flush in the doorway, have been known to be used as jumps during bids for freedom. Once the horse's rugs have been straightened or removed for the day, and hay distributed, a fresh bucket of water can be put in place.

Feed mangers should be cleaned daily (who wants to eat from a dirty plate?) and the yard swept tidy after mucking out, again before the lunch break and once more at the end of the day.

Tools and equipment should be put away carefully after use, not only for their preservation but also to ensure they do not become safety hazards.

Skipping out (the process of removing droppings and wet bedding) should be carried out whenever possible. This does save time on the once-a-day big muck-out and also saves on the cost of bedding. Certainly stables or stalls should be skipped out before the evening feed and water are provided.

Regular skipping out prolongs the life of bedding and also improves the horse's general stable environment.

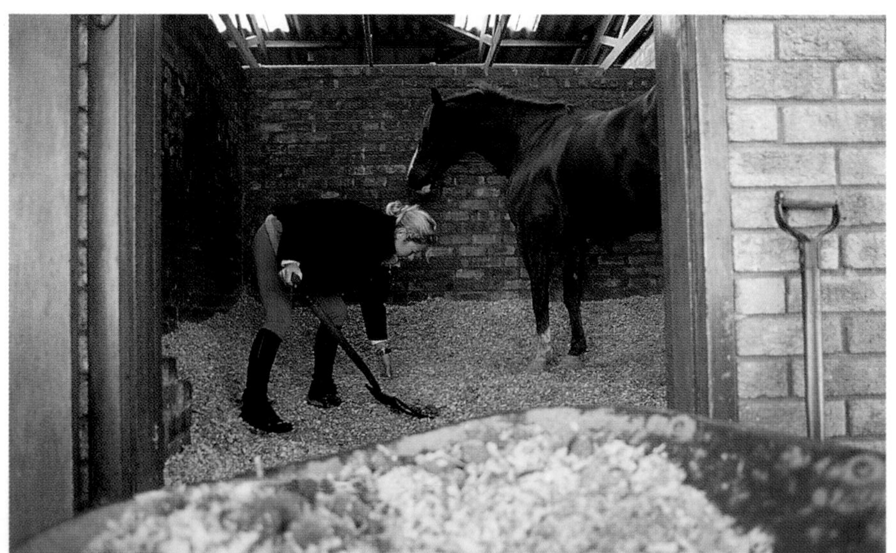

IDEAL DAILY STABLE ROUTINE

7:00

• Fill water bucket • First feed • Muck out and lay day bed
• Brush over horse and pick out feet

9:30

• Skip out • Remove rugs if worn • Saddle up and exercise
• Fill water bucket on return to stable

12:00

• Groom • Put on day rug • Fill water bucket • Second feed
• Refill hay net

16:00

• Pick out feet • Skip out • Shake up bedding • Remove day rug and brush horse • Put on night rug • Refill water bucket
• Third feed

19:30

• Skip out • Lay night bed • Refill hay net and water bucket
• Final feed

Last thing

• If you are able to do so, visit stable to ensure that all is well.

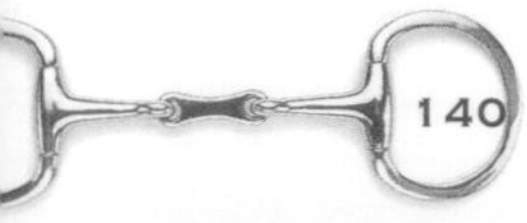

Travelling can be distressing for some horses, but careful handling helps to reduce stress levels for horse and rider.

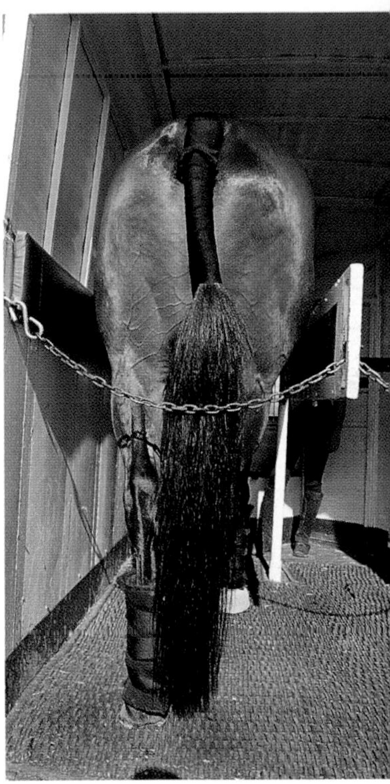

A bandage or tail guard protects the tail against rubbing during transport.

Transport

For most riders, going to a show, veterinary clinic or a new stable, are the prime reasons for transporting horses, but even these can sometimes involve considerable distances, and might require travel by road, air or sea.

When travelling by road, either a purpose-built horse box (also called a van or float) or a trailer towed behind a suitable vehicle are safe conveyances – provided they are driven with care and that the horse's welfare is the driver's prime concern.

For the one-horse owner, keeping a horse box on the road may prove expensive so shared journeys, using reputable transport companies, are often an economical way of getting to your show or event. Whatever mode of transport you choose, it is important to remember that all journeys are demanding even for the happiest equine traveller.

Before any journey, the 'feed one hour before travelling' rule applies. On even medium-length journeys, horses can dehydrate easily, and it is important to offer a 'water break' at least every four hours. Adding electrolytes to the water before travelling can also help to alleviate dehydration.

Equipment: A leather head collar is less likely to rub on a long journey, and in an emergency will break more readily than one made of synthetic material.

Horse's legs are vulnerable and should be protected during transport. Traditional bandages and protective hock and knee boots have given way to purpose-made padded travel boots with Velcro fastenings, which cover the legs from the coronary band to the knee in front and hock behind.

A tail guard, used alone or over a bandage, will protect the tail from rubbing on the side of the trailer.

Rugs depend on weather conditions, but in a well-ventilated container, a light sweat rug will offer protection against draughts.

Loading: Loading horses should be done quietly, efficiently and safely. Handlers should always wear sturdy gloves – rope burns hurt. Partitions should be fastened back beforehand and, in the case of transporters with more than one ramp, alternate exits closed. The horse should be led purposefully towards the ramp, so it has a chance to see where it is going. A helper can encourage the horse up the ramp and be on hand to close the partition once the horse has been manoeuvred into place and safely tied.

Leading a Horse

When leading a horse, the reins should be taken over the horse's head and held in both hands. Gloves should preferably always be worn to protect the hands in case the horse shies or tries to pull away from the handler.

NZ
Atlanta 1996
575
575

CHAPTER EIGHT

COMPETITIVE RIDING

On reaching a reasonable level of riding ability, competitions can provide not just a goal, but also valuable riding experience and an opportunity to develop your riding skills. Even for riders who do not have a competitive nature, successfully taking part in a show class provides a sense of achievement, and it is by no means unknown for an introduction to competitions at club level to lead on to more ambitious pursuits.

There are three categories of equestrian sport within the Olympic movement: show jumping, three-day eventing, and dressage. At World Championship level, endurance riding, vaulting and driving are also included. All these disciplines come under the jurisdiction of the International Equestrian Federation (the FEI – Fédération Equestre Internationale), an organization based in Lausanne, Switzerland, that administers equestrian sports on a worldwide basis.

At national level, the various equine disciplines are usually administered by one or more organizations affiliated to the country's national equestrian federation, which is in turn affiliated to the FEI.

In many countries, riding clubs or schools provide an introduction to the different aspects of the sport and a network for progression. Although rules and tests may vary slightly due to national conditions, each discipline's international rules form the basic game plan against which all other countries set their individual standards.

Previous pages (left to right)
Representing their countries in the three categories of competitive riding are Blyth Tait (New Zealand), three day eventing; Isabell Werth (Germany), dressage; and John Whitaker (Great Britain), show jumping.

SHOW JUMPING

The first show jumping competitions took place during the second half of the 19th century in London, at Ireland's Royal Dublin Society Show (which is still world famous today), in Russia and in Paris. While results in those early days were judged solely on the rider's style, gradually the rules were altered to place more emphasis on jumping ability.

When show jumping was introduced into the Olympic Games in 1912, the rules were very complicated, but after the FEI was founded in 1921, the rules for show jumping competitions were standardized, initiating the modern-day format.

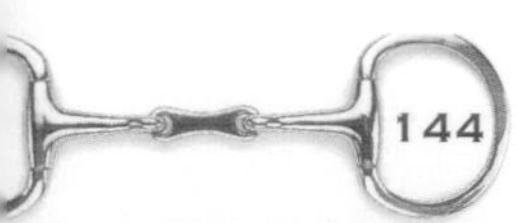

Representing your country in an international competition is the pinnacle of achievement for a talented rider.

Show jumping became the pathfinder for professionalism in equestrian sports, largely due to the advent of sponsorship and television coverage. The sport's profile was further boosted with the introduction of the World Cup in 1979, making show jumping a year-round sport as the traditional outdoor arenas are replaced in winter by an indoor circuit in some of the major cities of the world.

Essentially, show jumping is about riding a set course of unfixed obstacles within a confined area. As the level of competition rises and the fences get higher, the sport becomes as much about training, partnership and the rider's ability to direct the horse on the most economical route as about the scope of the horse's ability to clear the obstacles.

Competitions are about leaving the fences intact. The type of fence and its place in the course design are the main factors that influence show jumping. At entry level, a short course of straightforward fences is there to be jumped fluently and in a good balance and rhythm.

As courses get progressively more difficult, the horse's training and its athletic ability to lengthen and shorten its stride are tested, as the distances between the fences and the combination of fences and obstacles becomes increasingly critical.

Nature's Way

Four faults are incurred for each knock-down, while refusals, taking the wrong course, falling or exceeding the time limit are all penalized.

In classic competitions, all participants who achieve clear rounds in the initial round go through to a jump-off, which is timed. Ultimately, the rider and horse to achieve the fastest clear round wins.

Shows from local to international level may also include speed classes, which are jumped solely against the clock; puissance classes (a knock-out competition with the jumps going higher in each round); Derby classes (which include natural features such as the famous Hickstead Bank); relay classes; and classes where each fence is awarded points for difficulty and the rider has to notch up as many points as possible in the given time.

Countries that have produced successful show jumpers in recent years include Germany, France and the Netherlands, all of which have a history of breeding good show jumpers. The UK has maintained a competitive presence, and the USA is renowned for stylish and effective riders. Brazil, led by Nelson Pessoa and his son Rodrigo, has become a leading nation in show jumping since winning its first team bronze medal at the 1996 Olympic Games in Atlanta, USA.

Qualities of the show jumper

A top show jumping horse needs a good technique with both front and hind legs, suppleness over its head, neck and back (known as the 'topline'), a quality canter and an instinctively careful jump.

Left *Marion Hughes of Ireland riding Flo Jo at Hickstead 1997.*
Above *John Whitaker of the UK rides Milton in the 1992 Barcelona Olympics. Milton was the first horse outside racing to win more than £1 million in prize money. He earned this during the course of his 10-year career as a top show jumper.*

Nelson Pessoa of Brazil, riding Gandini Baloubet du Rouet, takes part in the 1998 World Equestrian Games.

It also needs to be athletic and agile enough to open out and contract its stride to meet variable distances between fences, and turn economically in a jump-off.

While there is no way of determining whether a young horse will one day become a show jumping superstar, the German, Dutch, Irish and French breeding systems are all geared to producing potential stars, as well as all-round quality horses.

EVENTING

Eventing consists of three disciplines (dressage, show jumping and cross country), with the winner being the rider and horse combination with the lowest overall penalties after the three phases.

Eventing, or horse trials as it is also known, originated as a test for military horses. The Olympic Games included a three-day event for the first time in 1912. After observing the 1948 Olympic event at Aldershot in the UK, the Duke of Beaufort offered Badminton Park as a venue for an event that took place the following year – and has done so annually ever since. As well as becoming the most famous and testing three-day event in the world, Badminton has laid the pattern for similar events in other countries.

Apart from the major three-day events, there is an international tour of one-day competitions and a highly competitive ranking formula for top riders.

For many decades the UK, with its tradition of hunting and cross-country riding, dominated eventing. The USA also has a history of success, but Australian, and latterly New Zealand, riders have moved to the forefront of the sport, particularly since New Zealand's Mark Todd won the gold medal at the Los Angeles Olympics in 1984.

DRESSAGE

Dressage is an important phase of eventing, because a supple and obedient horse is more able to carry its rider efficiently and safely across country.

Dressage (see pg 152) is judged on the horse and rider's ability to work in tandem, and is a test of the horse's obedience and willingness to perform at the level required for the category of competition.

Each movement of the set test is marked out of 10, with additional collective marks for general impression. In the test, which must be learned from memory, the judge looks for a confidently fluent, balanced and harmonious performance for top marks.

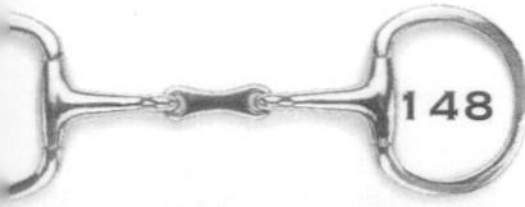

FEI

Founded in 1921 the Fédération Equestre Internationale, the FEI (also known as the International Equestrian Federation), is the governing body of world equestrian sport. The FEI establishes rules and regulations for the conduct of international equestrian events in dressage, show jumping, eventing, driving, vaulting and endurance riding.

Equestrian sport is the only discipline to combine two athletes, rider and horse, the success of which depends on the relationship between them. It is also one of the few sporting arenas in which men and women compete on equal terms at all levels.

A code of conduct, adopted in 1991, includes the following:

- The welfare of the horse is paramount, and its well-being shall be above the demands of riders, owners, trainers, breeders, sponsors, organizers or officials.
- The highest standards of safety, health, sanitation and nutrition shall be observed at all times.
- Emphasis should be placed on education and training in equestrian practices, and all riding and training methods must take account of the horse as a living entity and must not include any technique considered abusive.

There are currently 125 national federations affiliated to the FEI, which is recognized by the International Olympic Committee.

At entry level, the dressage test consists of work in walk, trot and canter incorporating large circles, turns, a few lengthened strides and halts from trot.

At international three-day event level, competitors must show good work in working, medium and extended paces, and a variety of movements on each rein including shoulder-in, half-pass, counter-canter, a single flying change, rein-back and transitions directly from canter to halt. While collection is not asked for in the paces, these movements demand an established degree of balance in order to be carried out correctly and with expression.

SHOW JUMPING

In this phase, the horse and rider tackle a series of coloured, nonfixed obstacles in an arena. Penalties are incurred for knocking down poles, refusals, falls and finishing outside the allocated time.

The height, simplicity or severity of the course depends on the level of the competition. At entry level, the course will be straightforward, with spreads, upright fences and one double combination. Advanced courses include a water jump, treble combination, and a more complex track.

Top and above *Germany's Bettina Overesch, on Watermill Stream, competing in the dressage and show jumping phases of the three-day event at the 1996 Olympic Games in Atlanta, USA.*

CROSS-COUNTRY

This is the most exciting part of eventing, and is the last of the three events to take place in a one-day competition, the second phase in a three-day event. The horse and rider must take on a series of fixed obstacles constructed from natural materials and designed to incorporate natural terrain such as hills, ditches, banks and water crossings.

Obstacles are constructed to predetermined dimensions, depending on the level of competition, but often the natural terrain will add a much more imposing dimension than mere height and width. The course is designed to test the fitness, technique, boldness and all-round partnership of the horse and rider combination.

As the obstacles are fixed, penalties are only incurred for refusals and falls, not for knocking down fences. There is also a time factor, faults being incurred for finishing over the optimum time.

Above *Bettina Overesch and Watermill Stream in the cross-country phase at the 1996 Atlanta Olympic Games.*

Blyth Tait of New Zealand puts Chesterfield through the phases of the three-day event at the 1996 Atlanta Olympic Games.
Top left *Dressage*
Bottom left *Show jumping*
Right *Cross-country.*

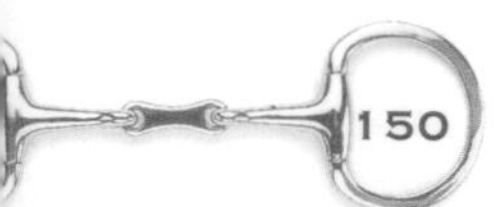

SPEED AND ENDURANCE

At three-day events, there are additional components, making up the speed and endurance phase. The roads and tracks phase is covered at steady trot and canter, with penalties for finishing over the allotted time. Phase A of roads and tracks is followed by Phase B, the steeplechase, a timed circuit over 10–12 obstacles covering approximately 4km (2.5 miles), again to be completed within an optimum time. A further phase of roads and tracks is followed by a compulsory 10-minute halt, during which the horse is examined for fitness, cooled down and prepared for Phase D, the cross-country.

All horses are checked for fitness at the commencement of a three-day competition, and on the final morning, before the show jumping phase.

Qualities of the event horse

A top event horse needs all-round ability and athleticism for jumping and work on the flat plus speed, stamina and a good conformation for soundness. Thoroughbreds are ideal, and those from New Zealand, with their innate toughness from an uncosseted upbringing, are much sought after. Horses with an influence of Irish or warmblood lines are also successful, as a relentless rhythm in gallop can be as effective in making time as sheer swiftness of foot.

Top *Ian Stark of Great Britain on Murphy Himself, at the 1989 Badminton Horse Trials.*
Left *Karen O'Connor of the USA rides Biko at Badminton in 1997.*

DRESSAGE

The word dressage is derived from the French verb *dresser* which, in the context of animals, means to train. From making a horse safe and pleasurable to ride to winning Olympic gold medals, dressage is an element of every type of horsemanship.

Above *Germany's Nicole Uphoff, riding Rembrandt, won two gold medals at the 1988 Seoul Olympic Games, and then repeated the feat four years later at the 1992 Olympic Games in Barcelona.*

The earliest training system for horses dates back as far as the 4th century BC. The philosophy outlined by soldier and horseman Xenophon in his book *On the Art of Horsemanship*, which describes how to train horses using understanding and quiet handling, is as relevant today as it was then.

During the Renaissance the art of classical horsemanship was developed as part of the education of noblemen, and equitation schools proliferated at the royal courts of Europe. Frenchman François Robichon de la Guérinière, who believed in and promoted Xenophon's principle of a kindly approach to dealing with horses, set out in his treatise, *École de la Cavalerie*, the basis of training still used by the Spanish Riding School of Vienna, one of the few establishments in the world dedicated to the preservation of classical and high school riding styles.

Riding as an art continued to develop through the 19th and early 20th centuries via the German, and later Swedish, cavalry schools and the French Cadre Noir. As with the other disciplines, the military influenced the beginnings of dressage as a competition, with only officers being eligible to take part in the first Olympic dressage event in 1912.

An outstanding feature of the development of dressage in recent years has been Germany's supreme domination of the sport, through its system of riding, training and breeding horses. Latterly the Netherlands, another nation with a strong breeding tradition, has made a big impression, but throughout the world, enthusiasm for the sport has grown. The formation in 1985 of the World Cup, an annual winter series of competitions culminating in a final comprising a grand prix test and freestyle to music, has been the most influential development in popularizing the sport for spectators.

COMPETITIVE DRESSAGE

The dressage test comprises a set of prescribed movements and figures. At every level of competition, the test is judged on the way each set movement is performed. Movements are marked out of 10 on a sliding scale from 0 (not performed), 5 (sufficient), to 10 (excellent). There are also collective marks, which are the judge's overall assessment of the quality of the horse's paces, the horse's way of going, and the rider's position and effectiveness. At the basic level, one judge presides; at international level, a jury of five judges individually assesses each test from different points around the arena.

A **basic level test** consists of a simple pattern of large circles and turns in walk, trot and canter. Depending on the nation there may be as many as five preliminary levels of increasing difficulty before reaching **Prix St Georges**, the entry-level international test. Progression through the levels tests the horse and rider's ability to carry out the requirements of more advanced movements correctly, with energy, obedience, confidence, harmony and accuracy.

In a **freestyle** test, the rider can construct his or her own ground pattern but it must include all the required movements for that level.

For the freestyle to music, in addition to the standard marks for technical execution, additional marks are gained for artistic interpretation, choice of music and choreography.

The more thorough the rider's familiarity with the test, the better he or she will be able to present the horse for each movement. Riders have very individual methods of memorizing tests – from rehearsing the pattern on foot to drawing it out on paper.

The actual dressage test is performed in an arena marked out by white boards. The surface was traditionally grass but nowadays at the higher levels of competition, and increasingly at lower ones, a specially prepared synthetic surface is preferred.

The markers for starting and concluding each movement are denoted by letters placed at specific points around the arena (see pg 90). Basic tests at national levels can be performed in an area measuring 40m x 20m, but for international competitions the arena must measure a standard 60m x 20m.

The gaits or paces

In dressage, the quality of the horse's paces – their rhythm and regularity – is of prime importance. Walk is a four-time pace, trot a two-time and canter a three-time pace, but there are many variations within the gaits.

Working paces are employed at trot and canter at the basic levels in tests, and in training at all levels.

Collected paces in walk, trot and canter are the result of training the horse to take more weight back on to the hindquarters, producing an elevated forehand and more cadenced steps. Collection is achieved by degrees, through steady and consistent training over several years.

Medium paces are when the horse moves more forward, lengthening its frame and stride while maintaining balance, rhythm and energy from the hindquarters.

Extended paces display the horse's full capacity for covering as much ground as possible. Extended paces are developed as a consequence of good collection, the gathering power that the horse then uses as a forward thrust for extension.

Transitions between the paces and within the paces, and their development from progressive to direct as the horse becomes more advanced, are a vital tool in both training and test riding.

MOVEMENTS

Lateral work

The horse can be ridden on a single track or laterally (sideways). The key lateral movements are shoulder-in, travers and half-pass (a travers ridden on a diagonal line). In **shoulder-in,** a classic test movement and one of the most important training movements, the horse's forehand is brought inside the track of the outside leg so that its outside shoulder is aligned straight in front of its inside hind leg, which is engaged and carrying the most weight. The horse is bent around the rider's inside leg, away from the direction it is moving into. In **half-pass,** a major part of all advanced tests, the horse is bent slightly around the rider's inside leg and in the direction it is moving into. Its outside legs cross and pass in front of its inside legs, sideways and forwards.

Flying changes

In a single flying change, the horse swaps from one leading leg to the other in canter without breaking pace. In advanced tests, a series of flying changes, known as 'tempi' changes, are performed as four-, three-, two- and one-time changes. In one-time changes, the horse changes lead on every stride.

Below *Top international dressage rider, Anky van Grunsven of the Netherlands, rides Bonfire at the 1998 World Equestrian Games.*

Above left *A full pirouette in canter is one of the grand prix test movements.*
Above right *Susan Blinks of the USA, on Flim Flam, performs a half-pass during a dressage competition at West Palm Beach.*

Pirouettes

A half-pirouette, in walk or canter, is where the horse's forehand moves around its hindquarters. The horse should maintain the rhythm of the pace. Full pirouettes in canter, through 360 degrees, are part of the grand prix test.

Right *The Netherlands' Anky van Grunsven and Bonfire, taking part in the 1994 World Equestrian Games.*

Passage

This is a graceful, measured, highly collected and elevated 'trot' executed with great cadence. It looks as if the horse is trotting in slow motion with great expression and use of its joints.

Piaffe

A highly-collected movement where the horse appears to be marking time on the spot. The weight is on the hind legs and the horse appears to be 'sitting'.

Qualities of a dressage horse

Three good gaits are essential, as well as a good conformation, with strong hindquarters that can be trained to take weight; a well set-on neck that makes the round outline easy to maintain; and a general suppleness and athleticism. The most suitable temperament is one that is 'trainable' rather than merely submissive, as top horses need to exert a presence in the arena. Since Germany's Nicole Uphoff took the dressage scene by storm by winning double gold at the 1988 Seoul Olympics with her Westphalian horse Rembrandt, the favoured dressage type underwent a change from the big, strong, powerhouse horse to a lighter, more elegant type, often with more Thoroughbred influence.

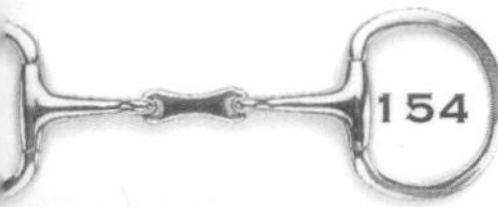

ENDURANCE RIDING

In endurance riding, the horse and rider must cover a predetermined distance either against the clock or at a set speed. Distances range from around 32km (20 miles) at entry level to 160km (100 miles) at championship level, with riders encountering a variety of conditions and terrain over the route.

The well-being of the horse is paramount, and endurance riding is as much about horse management as the rider's judgement in achieving the distance in the given time. The horse's general level of fitness, the condition of its feet and legs, its pulse rate and hydration levels are assessed by veterinary officials at regular checkpoints, or 'vet gates'.

Endurance riding is increasing in popularity, as it is accessible to amateur riders of all ages and levels of competence who enjoy riding in the countryside but might not necessarily want to jump. Beginners can participate over the shorter distances on any sound riding horse.

At the higher levels, where endurance competitions can involve covering over 80km (50 miles) per day of race riding, the type of horse selected becomes more important.

A lean, forward-going horse with good stamina is essential, which is why Arabs and Arab crosses are very popular. From the rider's point of view they are also generally very comfortable to ride. However, it can take three years or more to train a horse to compete in endurance riding at championship level.

At any ride over entry level distance, a good back-up crew (often family or friends who provide indispensable support and encouragement) is vital. They follow and assist riders and get to work cooling and hydrating the horse before each vet check.

Endurance riding is relatively new as an international sport, but has been boosted by the involvement of riders and sponsors from the United Arab Emirates, which has invested heavily in the sport and hosted the first 100-mile ride through the Arabian desert outside Dubai in December 1998.

Below left *A horse is cooled off and hydrated before a compulsory vet check.*
Below *Rick Burnside competing in the 1990 Endurance Championships in Stockholm.*

COMMON AILMENTS

Abscess: Build-up of infection under the skin causing a painful lump. Treat with hot compresses to encourage drainage. Long-standing abscesses may be lanced by the vet. When this happens or an abscess bursts, protect the surrounding skin by applying a barrier cream. Wash the area with saline solution to flush out any remaining infection, then apply antibiotic cream or the vet's prescription.

Anaemia: If the horse is dull, listless and lethargic and the mucous membranes around the eyes and mouth look pale, a blood test may establish anaemia.

Arthritis: The inflammation of joints by wear and tear, predominantly found in older horses. Often manageable under veterinary direction, it is frequently treated with herbs and alternative remedies.

Arthrosis: Common in older horses, this is a condition which results in abnormal bone growth on the edges of joints, such as ringbone on the pedal, pastern or fetlock joint, and spavin on the lower hock joint. Specialist veterinary treatment helps, as does special shoeing, but the condition will result in varying degrees of lameness.

Capped Hocks: Swellings around the point of hock caused by abrasion. They are usually prevented by the provision of good bedding.

Chronic Obstructive Pulmonary Disease (COPD): This occurs when the horse's airways become obstructed by thick mucous and breathing is impaired. It is caused by a reaction or allergy to the fungal spores found in hay and straw. The horse will need to be managed in as dust-free an environment as possible on a permanent basis. Veterinary treatment may include antihistamines and/or the use of bronchodilators to clear the airways.

Corns: Pressure sores or bruises on the sole of the foot causing pain and lameness. Often caused by ill-fitting shoes or waiting too long to replace shoes. They are difficult to spot. On removing the shoe, the vet will cut away the affected horn. Poulticing can draw out latent infection and the horse may require special pressure-relieving shoes.

Cough: Can be a symptom of an allergy or virus and thus will be accompanied by other symptoms. Will need expert diagnosis to find the cause.

Cracked Heels: Occur in wet and muddy conditions, when the back of the pastern becomes cracked and inflamed with thickening of the skin. It can be prevented by ensuring the heels are kept as dry as possible in such conditions. Treat with applications of antibacterial ointment.

Degenerative Joint Disease (DJD): This is an arthritic condition caused by stress on the joints.

Dehydration: Following diarrhoea, particularly in hot weather or during intense competition, the horse may require additional electrolytes to replace lost fluids, salts and minerals. An indication of dehydration is if the skin does not return flexibly when it is pinched. In extreme cases, dehydration can lead to azoturia or 'tying up'.

Epidemic Influenza Virus: Symptoms include a high temperature, nasal discharge, cough and swollen glands under the jaw. It is highly infectious, but can be prevented by regular vaccination.

Fungal Infections: Ringworm and other fungal infections, visible as bald, crusty patches on the skin, tend to spread through yards. In the case of an outbreak, all tack and equipment must be treated to prevent re-infection. Horses with fungal conditions should not travel. Treat with antibiotics or anti-fungal wash.

Galls: Swollen, sensitive patches caused by ill-fitting tack, so the cause needs to be identified and removed. Once galls have healed, hair loss may be replaced by white hairs.

Lameness: Caused by pain in the horse's body causing it to move unevenly, most noticeably at the trot. The degree of lameness usually directly corresponds with the amount of pain, and therefore the seriousness of the condition. Some causes of lameness, such as injury, will be easily apparent, others will need to be diagnosed by a vet as it is easy for the layman, however experienced, to be misled. If a clinical examination does not locate the cause, a veterinary surgeon may use other methods, including nerve blocks, X-rays, ultrasound and bone scanning.

Lice: Small skin parasites which irritate the skin, causing raw patches. Common in under-conditioned animals. As well as treating the horse with anti-lice shampoo, all tack and equipment needs to be treated to prevent re-infection.

Lymphangitis: An inflammation of the lymphatic vessels. Known as 'Monday morning disease' as it commonly occurs when animals are left in the stable on full feed rations, and not exercised. Recognizable by swollen, puffy legs and treated by gentle walking to improve circulation, cold hosing to reduce swelling, and reduction of feed the night before and during rest days as a preventative measure.

Mud Fever: A skin infection affecting the lower legs and caused by the bacterium *Dermatophilus.* Tends to occur in wet, muddy areas, hence the name. Using a barrier cream during exercise or when the horse is turned out can help. Treatment involves the removal of scabs and swabbing with antibacterial wash, after which the area must be gently but thoroughly dried. When found over the back, the condition is known as rain scald.

Periodic Opthalmia: Also known as 'moon blindness'. This is a disease of the eye, which can occur suddenly and tends to recur. Little is known about the disease, which causes the cornea to become white and milky, the pupil to constrict and the eye area to become inflamed. It can eventually lead to blindness in the affected eye, but though there is no definitive treatment, prompt veterinary action can prevent permanent damage.

Navicular Disease: A chronic condition, which appears as gradual lameness in one or both front feet. Corrective shoeing and prescription drugs to stimulate circulation can alleviate the condition.

Nettle Rash (Urticaria): This occurs as patches of raised swellings which tend to suddenly appear, then disappear just as quickly. It can occur in connection with other illnesses or infections, or as an allergy to drugs, a particular feed or nettles. Usually harmless, but if it becomes excessively irritating the vet can prescribe a painkiller.

Overreach: A bruise or wound caused by the hind foot striking the heel of a front foot. Can be prevented by use of overreach boots during exercise, especially fast work and jumping. Treat by cleaning the area thoroughly, use a poultice for a short period if the area is very dirty, and apply antibiotic dressing. The vet should be called if the wound is large or deep or if the swelling is excessive, as this may indicate deeper damage.

Pus-in-the-foot: A common condition arising usually from a puncture to the sole of the foot, which causes an abscess within the foot. The horse will be acutely lame and the foot will feel hot. The vet will cut away the horn in the area of the abscess to drain the infection. A poultice must be applied two or three times a day until all infection is drawn out, and the foot must be kept bandaged. The hole can then be plugged with cotton wool soaked in antibiotic spray. The application of a sugar and iodine paste over the area will help to harden the horn.

Quittor: An infection located at the coronary band (the cartilage on the side of the foot). It is caused by injury or by a puncture, and is signified by swelling, inflammation and pain. The vet will treat it with antibiotics.

Sandcrack: A vertical crack in the hoof caused by injury or poorly cared for feet. Cracks require special care from the farrier, who may insert clips or fill the crack with synthetic paste until it has grown out.

Sarcoids: Horny, tumour-like warts on the surface of the skin which, if they get very large, may rub or become infected. In this case they should be removed surgically. Sarcoid warts can recur.

Seedy Toe (Separations): When the hoof wall separates from the sole at the toe. If the sensitive tissue becomes inflamed, lameness will ensue. The farrier or vet will cut away dead horn and dress the foot.

Splints (Periostitis): Bony formations which arise between the splint bone and cannon bone, usually in growing horses, or through stress. While forming, they can cause short-term lameness. Cold packs can alleviate any inflammation. Veterinary treatment may consist of cortisone injections.

Strangles (Equine Distemper): A highly contagious glandular inflammation, occurring particularly in foals and weakened animals. It is accompanied by high fever, breathing difficulties and smelly nasal discharge. Strangles is caused by the *Streptococcus equi* bacterium, which affects only horses and donkeys. Treatment must involve isolation, strict hygiene (discharges and pus which may be released from swollen glands around the jaw are highly infectious), hot fomentations to encourage discharge, and in some cases antibiotic treatment.

Sweet Itch: A skin irritation caused by midge bites, which are then rubbed raw by the affected and irritated horse. Usually occurs along the line of the mane and at the base of the tail. Susceptible horses should be stabled morning and evening when the midges are most abundant. Fly repellent should be used and special sweet itch lotion will help to soothe sore areas and repel further attack.

Tetanus: Every horse should be regularly vaccinated against this infection of the nervous system, which is caused by bacteria entering a wound. At the first signs of tetanus – stiffness, convulsions, muscle spasms and refusal to eat or drink – veterinary advice should be sought urgently.

Thrush: An infection of the horn of the hoof, it is commonly found in horses kept on damp bedding or in muddy conditions. Recognizable by the foul smell emanating from the affected foot. The foot needs to be dried out, the affected horn cut away and anti-thrush dressing applied.

Windgalls: These are painless, soft swellings usually found at the back of the leg, just above the fetlock joint. They are unsightly but harmless. Stable bandages and support bandages while exercising can help prevent the tendency to windgalls. A soft swelling located just above the hock joint is known as a Thoroughpin.

Worms: There are various forms of infestation to which a horse may be susceptible, depending on the season, the age of the horse and, to some extent, the area. Prevention measures include good paddock management and regular dosing with anti-parasite drugs. Worm infestation can be serious, even fatal in some cases, so control is essential.

INDEX

FEI NATIONAL FEDERATIONS

The following national equestrian federations are members of the FEI. Contact them for details of riding schools and instructors in your area. All information was correct at the time of going to print.

Australia
Equestrian Federation of Australia
Level 2, 196 Greenhill Rd, Eastwood
SA 5063
Tel: +61 88 357-0077 Fax: +61 88 357-0091

Austria
Bundesfachverband für Reiten und Fahren
in Österreich
Geiselbergstrasse 26-32/512
Wein 1110
Tel: + 43 1 749-9261 Fax: + 43 1 749-9261

Belgium
Féd. Royale Belge des Sports Equestres
Avenue Houba de Strooper 156
Bruxelles 1020
Tel: + 32 2 478-5056 Fax: + 32 2 478-1126

Denmark
Dansk Ride Forbund
Hestesportens HusTraverbanevej 10
Charlottenlund
Tel: + 45 39 962070 Fax: + 45 39 962075

France
Fédération Française d'Equitation
9 Boulevard MacDonald
75019 Paris
Tel: + 33 1 53 26 15 15 Fax: + 33 1 53 26 15 00

Germany
Deutsche Reiterliche Vereinigung
Freiherr-von-Langen-Str. 13
48231 Warendorf
Tel: + 49 2581 63620 Fax: + 49 2581 62144

Great Britain
British Equestrian Federation
National Agricultural Centre
Stoneleigh Park, Kenilworth
Warwickshire Warcs CV8 2RH
Tel: + 44 1203 698871 Fax: + 44 1203 698871

Ireland
Equestrian Federation of Ireland
Ashton House
Castleknock
Dublin 1515
Tel: + 353 1 838-7611 Fax: + 353 1 838-2051

Italy
Italian Equestrian Federation
Viale Tiziano 74
Rome 00196
Tel: + 39 6 32 33 745 Fax: + 39 6 32 33 772

Luxemburg
Féd. Luxembourgeoise des Sports Equestres
14, Avenue de la Gare
Luxembourg 1610
Tel: + 352 484-999 Fax: + 352 485-039

Monaco
Féd.Equestre de la Principaute de Monaco
Villa Gardenia, 3 Avenue Saint Michel
Monte Carlo 98000
Tel: + 377 93 50 80 54 Fax: + 377 93 50 80 56

Netherlands
Stichting Nederlandse Hippische Sportbond
Amsterdamsestraatweg 57
3744 Ma Baarn
Tel: + 31 35 548-3600 Fax: + 31 35 541-1563

New Zealand
New Zealand Equestrian Federation
PO Box 6146, Te Aro
Wellington
Tel: + 64 4 801-6449 Fax: + 64 4 801-7701

Norway
Norges Rytterforbund
Servicebox 1U.S.
Sognsveien 75
Oslo
Tel: + 47 21 02 96 50 Fax: + 47 21 02 96 51

Portugal
Federação Equestre Portuguesa
Avenida Manuel da Maia No. 26
4eme Droite
Lisbon
Tel: + 351 1 847-8784 Fax: + 351 1 847-4582

South Africa
SA National Equestrian Federation
PO Box 30875, Kyalami 1684
Gauteng
Tel: + 27 11 468-3236 Fax: + 27 11 468-3238

Spain
Real Federaçion Hipica Espanola
Plaza Marques de Salamanca, No. 2
28006 Madrid
Tel: + 34 91 436-4200 Fax: + 34 91 575-0770

Sweden
Svenska Ridsportförbundet
Sandhamnsgatan 39
PO Box 27857, Stockholm 11593
Tel: + 46 8 56705600 Fax: + 46 8 56705670

Switzerland
Fédération Suisse des Sports Equestres
Papiermühlestrasse 40H
Case Postale 726
Berne 22
Tel: + 41 31 335-4342 Fax: + 41 31 335-4358

United States of America
American Horse Shows Association Inc.
220 East 42nd Street, Room 409
New York NY 10017
Tel: +1 212 972-2472 Fax: +1 212 867-5561

Fédération Equestre Internationale (FEI)
PO Box 157, Lausanne, Switzerland
Av. Mon Repos 24, 1000 Lausanne 5, Switzerland
Tel: + 41 21 310-4747 Fax: + 41 21 310-4760
http://www.horsesport.org

PUBLISHER'S ACKNOWLEDGEMENTS

The publisher would like to thank Muriel Faienza, communications manager, FEI, Lausanne, Switzerland, and Nichola Gregory, press officer of the British Horse Society, for background details and contact addresses; Christine Smy, Spillers Horse Feeds (UK), and Dr David Mullins, Mooi River Veterinary Clinic, KwaZulu-Natal, South Africa, for information on feeding; Yvonne McFarlane, New Holland Publishers Ltd (London), and Jennifer Lane, New Holland Publishers Ltd (Sydney). In Cape Town, the following people provided assistance, advice or equipment for photography: Riaan Verster; Lynette Mouton and Megan de Schally of Waterloo Equestrian Centre; Samantha Harris of the Hout Bay Riding Centre; Allison van der Bergh and Hildegard Schabort of the Milnerton Riding School; Gail Humphreys from Halliford Arabian Stud Farm; Eve Gorille and Tanya Simenhoff of The Tack Shack in Durbanville; and Johan Ehlers of Agri-Expo.

PHOTOGRAPHIC CREDITS

All photographs by **Struik Image Library/Kelly Walsh,** except for the photographers and/or agents listed below.
Arnd Bronkhorst: pp 12–13, 16–17, 18, 20 (centre), 23 (right), 45, 64 (right), 92–93, 100, 119, 141, 145.
Clix: pp 104, 105.
Kit Houghton: pp 56 (bottom right), 57 (top left), 61 (bottom right), 65 (left and right), 76 (bottom left and right), 80, 84 (bottom), 97 (left), 98, 101, 120, 130, 142–143 (centre), back flap.
Bob Langrish: pp 19, 24–25, 26, 49 (top and bottom right), 54 (bottom right and left), 55 (top left and bottom right), 57 (top right, bottom left and far right), 70, 76 (top), 81, 83 (left and right), 84 (top), 85 (top and bottom), 86 (top and bottom), 91 (top), 96, 99, 100, 113 (right), 114 (top left), 128–129, 132, 134, 136 (top right), 138 (top left), 142–143 (left and right), 146, 147, 148, 149 (top and bottom), 150, 151 (top and bottom), 152, 153, 154 (top left and right), 155.
Ian Michler: p 103.
Sport Library/Margot Seares: p 102.